STUDIES IN LITERARY CRITICISM

MOHIT K. RAY

ATLANTIC
PUBLISHERS & DISTRIBUTORS (P) LTD

Published by

ATLANTIC

PUBLISHERS & DISTRIBUTORS (P) LTD

7/22, Ansari Road, Darya Ganj, New Delhi-110002
Phones : +91-11-40775252, 23273880, 23275880, 23280451
Fax : +91-11-23285873
Web : www.atlanticbooks.com
E-mail : orders@atlanticbooks.com

Branch Office
5, Nallathambi Street, Wallajah Road, Chennai-600002
Phones : +91-44-64611085
E-mail : chennai@atlanticbooks.com

Printed in India at Nice Printing Press, A-33/3A, Site-IV, Industrial Area, Sahibabad, Ghaziabad, U.P.

In Memory of

Professor Subodh Chandra Sengupta

—A Teachers' Teacher

Preface

My esteemed teacher Professor Subodh Chandra Sengupta happened to have read some of my articles; he liked them and advised me to bring out a volume of my critical essays for the benefit of all concerned. Affection makes one a bad judge of worth and, I felt, perhaps he had overestimated the value of my articles. However, when I met him for the last time before his death in 1998 I promised him, on his insistence, to publish a selection of my articles. And this book, for whatever it is worth, is a fulfilment of the promise as a homage to the memory of my teacher.

It was my great fortune and rare privilege to study Literary Criticism at the feet of Professor Taraknath Sen of Presidency College, Calcutta, an outstanding scholar of legendary fame. I gratefully acknowledge his influence on me.

I should also mention in this connection that my teacher professor R.K. Dasgupta, the greatest scholar living in this part of the country at present had also encouraged me — verbally and in writing — to bring out a selection of my papers. It was Professor Dasgupta who opened up before me the ever-widening horizon of Comparative Literature, encouraged me to send some of my papers to international conferences and thus prepared the way for my international recognition. He has been and continues to be a sage-like preceptor for me and I make obeisance to him in profound gratitude.

I am also deeply indebted to my teacher Professor Ramaranjan Mukhopadhyaya who initiated me to Aesthetics in 1955 and later introduced me to the fascinating world of Sanskrit poetics. I am still under the spell he cast on me more than four decades ago.

Some unavoidable overlappings notwithstanding, the essays, diverse though they are, may be broadly divided into four categories : essays on critical issues; essays on individual authors; essays in Comparative Literature; and essays on Language. The essays originated as papers for various seminars and conferences and were published in different books and journals over a long period of time. I have not retouched them, because any attempt to edit them would lead to drastic revision and reformating. However, the only rationale of reprinting them is that, by and large, I still subscribe to the views expressed in them.

I had occasion to discuss these essays with my junior colleague Dr R. Kundu, whom I hold in affection. She has assiduously gone through the entire manuscript and has done the indexing; I am indebted to her in more ways than one. I am also grateful to my wife and children for giving me ample freedom and leisure necessary for any scholarly pursuit.

In writing the essays included in this volume I received assistance, inspiration and encouragement from various persons and it is not possible to mention all of them, but I am grateful to all of them for their sincere solicitations.

I am also grateful to Dr K.R. Gupta, Managing Director, Atlantic Publishers and Distributors for taking interest in the book and for seeing it through the press. And, finally, I alone am responsible for the various lacunae that may come to one's notice while reading the book.

MOHIT K. RAY

Acknowledgments

Acknowledgments are due to the following books and journals :

Criticism and Research, Banaras : Banaras Hindu University.

Journal of Research, Santiniketan : Visva-Bharati.

Literary Theory and Criticism (Eds. A.P. Dani and V.M. Madge), Delhi : Pencraft International, 1998.

Literature and Criticism, Berhampore : Berhampore University.

The Critical Endeavour, Cuttack : Researchers' Association.

Journal of the Department of English, Burdwan : Burdwan University.

Revaluations, Bhubaneswar.

Journal 96, Midnapore : Vidyasagar University.

Comparative Poetics (Ed. Claudio Guillen of Harvard University), New York : Garland Publishing Inc., 1985.

Journal of the Department of English, Raja Rammohunpur : North Bengal University.

Meerut Journal of Comparative Literature.

Historical and Cultural Contexts of Linguistic and Literary Phenomenon, Guelph : University of Guelph (Canada), 1989.

Bankimchandra : Essays in Perspective, New Delhi : Sahitya Akademi, 1994.

Forces of Vision, Tokyo : Tokyo University Press, 1994.

Visva-Bharati Quarterly, Santiniketan : Visva-Bharati.

Language Forum, Delhi.

Journal of Comparative Literature, Jadavpur University.

Indian Journal of Applied Linguistics, Delhi.

Interlitteraria 3, Tartu : University of Tartu, Estonia.

Indian Journal of Canadian Studies, Delhi.

American Literature, New Delhi : Creative Books, 1999.

Contents

1

Objectivity in Literary Criticism*

The present age may be seriously regarded as the age of criticism.[1] The huge knowledge-explosion[2] that took place particularly in the first three decades of the present century and the consequent opening up of new horizons in various departments of knowledge led to the development of a number of critical theories. Marxist criticism, psychoanalytic criticism, organistic formalism, archetypal criticism, genre criticism, for example, are some of the major areas explored in depth in recent times. None of these theories, however is absolutely original. We had antecedents of them, though often in embryonic form, in the writings of earlier times. Even Marxist criticism can be traced, in some respect, to the realistic criticism of the nineteenth country.[3] Moreover, the directions along which these critical theories have moved are not sharply distinctive; there are inevitable overlappings and cross-influences. Northrop Frye, for example, is both a genre critic and an archetypal critic.

New criticism or the new organistic and symbolistic formalism is, in many respects, the most important development of our time. The term 'New Criticism' was first coined and given wide currency to by John Crowe Ransom with the publication of his book, *The New Criticism* in 1941. By 1941 Eliot, Richards and Empson were considered as major influences on the modern critical sensibility. Their impact was so great that Ransom 'canonized'[4] their achievements. About Richards, Ransom wrote in the very opening section of the book :

> Discussion of the new criticism must start with Mr. Richards. The new criticism very nearly began with him.

---

* FILLM (International Federation for Modern Languages and Literatures), Budapest, Hungary, 1984.

And Eliot had already tried "to divert the attention from the poet to the poem"[5] and had recommended that "honest criticism and sensitive appreciation are directed not upon the poet but upon the poetry."[6] Eliot and Richards provided the perspective for reorienting literary criticism toward a new object, new methodological form and new epistemological structure.[7]

Various lists of New Critics do not quite tally with one another and New Critics, though belonging to the same powerful intellectual movement, are not unanimous in their beliefs and practices. William Elton has divided the New Critics into two broads groups. Eliot, Ransom, Leavis, Tate and Blackmur, for example, belong to one group, while Richards, Winters, Burke and Empson, among others, are placed in another group.[8] However, as indicated by Ransom, what binds the New Critics together, is their serious concern for literary criticism, their conviction that literary criticism should be *literary* and their imitation of science in the critical approach.[9] The immediate occasion for this opinion was the dissatisfaction with the philosophical, historical, biographical and impressionistic criticisms — in fact all kinds of criticism that diverted the attention away from the literary work, the poem itself; for example, Ransom rejected the criticism of his predecessors as 'shapeless miscellany' and expected that New Criticism as a kind of collaborative effort would be "as definitive as the new physics or the new logic."[10]

The novelty of the new position is most clearly manifest in an ambivalent attitude to science. While criticism was put on scientific lines, scientism was rejected in their defence of literature as a unique mode of cognition, different from and superior to science. Imitation of science was seen in the attempt to look upon the poem as an object, isolate it for analysis and evaluation.

Tate's theory as enunciated in "Tension in Poetry" (1938) is close to Ransom's in broad outline and the basic assumptions. René Wellek and Austin Warren also in their bid to make criticism objective devoted about one-third of their book, *Theory of Literature* (1949) to the criticism of the extrinsic approaches. In the second chapter of the book we are told that a literary work is a "highly complex organization of stratified character with multiple meanings and relationship." Furthermore, we are told in the twelfth chapter that a literary work "appears as an object of knowledge *sui generis* which has a special ontological status." René Wellek and Austin Warren insisted that there is a hard core to all readings and claimed that our best access to the common centre is through close study of the work's formal structure. Blackmur also believed in close reading as the dominant mode of literary analysis and his essays collected in *The Double Agent* (1935) and *The Expense of Greatness* (1940) became models of New Criticism.

II

The New Critics in their bid to put criticism on scientific lines insisted on looking at a poem as an organic object. Ransom wrote :

> A beautiful poem is an objective discourse what we approve, containing objective detail what we like.[11]

A literary work, it was claimed, was something external, observable by others. And as in science the faulty observation of an individual observer can be corrected subsequently by others, so the defective sensibility of a particular critic could be corrected over a period, by other critics. Sensibility, in the context of criticism, was similar to sense organs in relation to scientific experimentations. At the back of all these contentions worked the idea that literary criticism must be literary and not something else. The approach was monistic. But this monistic approach was as much at variance with the nature of literature as it was with the nature of people. In the first place a literary work is not purely literary. A literary work contains ideas and no criticism can completely ignore them. The greatness of *The Divine Comedy* is as much due to its aesthetic richness as to the philosophy enunciated in it. Secondly, since a man is a man, and not a machine, he can never attain mechanical objectivity in relation to a literary work as his judgment on it has to depend largely on his reaction to it. It is the human predicament that makes complete objectivity in literary criticism well-nigh impossible. An examination of the critics in action will reveal how they struggle in vain to attain objectivity and how their personal likes and dislikes — their personalities, in fact — interfere with their critical activity. They try to "see the object as in itself it really is," but soon reach out to other areas. Blackmur uses biography in his "The Later Poetry of W.B. Yeats." Allen Tate relates biography to Emily Dickinson's poetry in "Emily Dickinson." The old South was for Tate the model for traditional Christian Society and this allegiance governs his criticism.[12] Ransom himself, in spite of his insistence on being objective, fails to be scientific in a number of ways. Hotopf has shown how "Ransom quite fails to realize that Richards favoured a psychological theory with regard to the scientific as well as the emotive use of words.[13] Hotopf also points out how Ransom and Tate use the word 'abstract' in two different senses. The essay "Tension in Poetry" reveals that Tate and Ransom are, without being aware of it, using the word 'abstract' in at least two different senses in order to win their arguments. According to one, it is opposed to concrete, referring to universals rather than particulars, and, as such an easy though surely superficial means of contrasting different kinds of poetry. According to the others, it refers to the abstracting, *from* what is presented of that alone which is relevant *to* our practical purposes.[14]

If criticism is to be objective each term must have scientific precision about its denotation and connotation. Tate also expressed his annoyance about Ransom's critical pronouncements. He felt that "after the elaborate essays in Kantian philosophical aesthetics, the simple structure-texture formula is a sad anticlimax — as sad as the late Yvor Winters formula".[15] Fekete analyses the more serious lapse of Ransom that arises out of his insistence on scientific objectivism. Fekete remarks:

> In this fashion, the work of art is insulated and fetishized, and the problem of historical relation to the world is reduced to the problem of cognition of preconstituted objectivity....
>
> In consequence, the embryonic New Critical scientific paradigm remains an alienated scientific paradigm that deepens the reification of subjectivity.[16]

III

It is not that the inherent flaws of critical monism were detected only recently. A careful scrutiny of the critical statements of major critics reveals a dim awareness of the practical problems involved. Blackmur wrote :

> Poetry is life at the remove of form and meaning, not life lived but life framed and identified. So the criticism of poetry is bound to be occupied at once with the terms and modes by which the remove was made and with the relation between — in the ambiguous stock phrase — content and form; which is to say with the establishment and *appreciation of human or moral value.*[17]

Plurality of values recognized at the very outset of his critical career accounts for Blackmur's growing preoccupation with moral judgment and not just close reading or text-based analysis. Ransom's recognition of his inability to see how "concrete and universal could form a single unit"[18] also points to the problems involved in plurality of values embedded in a literary work. The Chicago critics raised their voice against the endeavour of the New Critics to reduce literary criticism to a science. Crane's intention, however, was not to denigrate New Criticism, but to enlarge it by placing it in the larger perspective of the humanities. Crane strongly recommended that we should have as many different critical methods as there are "distinguishable major aspects in the construction, appreciation and use of literary works.[19] Yvor Winters whom we can least do without is an avowed moral critic. He writes :

> We regard as greatest those works which deal with experiences which affect human life most profoundly.[20]

Harry Levin wrote in 1957 that "literature appeals to so many values, aesthetic and otherwise, that it requires a pluralistic approach.[21] He contended that

> literature can never be self-contained; its expressiveness springs from its innate capacity for leaving the page, entering our mind, and mingling with other matters: its verbal constructs are esthetic objects not in themselves, but by virtue of sounds and associations, metaphors and conventions. That is why a text cannot be meaningfully uprooted from its context.[22]

The plurality of values leads to the human predicament, the interference of the personality of the critic. One of the earliest and best expositions of the problem was made by Eliot as early as in 1930. Eliot wrote:

> To suppose that anyone likes only the *best* poetry, and that he likes all the best poetry equally, and that he likes all the second-best poetry in a second-best liking, and so on until he detests all of the worst poetry equally is to suppose a monster. I do not suppose that there ever has been, or ever will be, a critic of any art, *whose appreciation was a separate faculty, quite judicious and wholly isolated from his other interests and his private passions* : if there was, is or will be, he was, is or will be a bore with nothing at all to say.[23]

Eliot re-affirmed in 1956 that

> the literary critic is not merely a technical expert who has learned the rules to be observed by the writers he criticizes; *the critic must be the whole man, a man with convictions and principles*, and of knowledge and experience of life.[24]

Harry Levin came almost to the same conclusion in 1967 when he wrote :

> Value cannot be an innate property; it is a rating placed upon a work by observers. Hence it must express *their* scheme of values, while it reflects some feature of the work which has

> elicited their interest. Works exist not in the timeless vacuum of a House Beautiful or a Temple of Fame, but in a continual flux of evolution and revaluation.[25]

The last sentence in the excerpt just quoted is profoundly significant. Since every new work of art alters the tradition, criticism must constantly define its frontiers and correct itself. It can never move towards a hypothetical ideal mainly for two reasons. First, the values embodied in a literary work keep on changing although a literary work is produced at a particular point of space and time. Secondly, and more importantly, the personality of one critic will always differ from that of another critic by virtue of his experience, knowledge, and beliefs, and practically speaking, one can never completely get rid of one's personality.

To attempt objectivity in literary criticism is like moving along an asymptote, the mathematical curve that ever approaches but never reaches. To say that objectivity is unattainable is not to suggest that it is not desirable. It is, in fact, a highly desirable ideal but it can never be completely realized in practice.

REFERENCES

1. René Wellek, *Concepts of Criticism* (1963), p. 334.
2. See Cleanth Brooks, "Foreword" in R.W. Stallmen, ed., *Critiques and Essays in Criticism* (1920).
3. See René Wellek, "The Main Trends of Twentieth Century Criticism" in *Concepts of Criticism.*
4. See Daniel Holfman, ed. *Harvard Guide to Contemporary American Writing* (1979), p. 53.
5. "Tradition and the Individual Talent" (1920).
6. *Ibid.*
7. Ransom hailed Eliot as the 'intensive' critic in his concentration on the test itself as opposed to the 'extensive' critics who constantly moved away from the text. See "T.S. Eliot on Criticism" in the *Saturday Review of Literature* X, 24 March 1934.
8. See William Elton : *A Glossary Of New Criticism*, Chicago, 1949.
9. *The World's Body*, New York, 1938, pp. 329 and 347.
10. "Ubiquitous Moralists". *The Kenyon Review* iii. Winter, 1941.
11. *The New Criticism*, New York, 1941, p. 54.
12. In this connection George Core comments in "A Metaphysical Athlete : Allen Tate as a Critic" in *The Southern Literary Journal*, Autumn, 1969. "In seeking to define the strange brilliance of the Southern renascence Tate is at once probing his own aesthetic conscience with the intense historical, aesthetic, and moral judgement which is typical of him."

13. W.H.N. Hotoph : *Language Thought and Comprehension*, London, 1965, p. 182.
14. *Ibid.*, pp. 180-181.
15. See *Memoirs and Opinions* 1926-1974, Chicago, 1975.
16. John Fekete : *The Critical Twilight*, London, 1977, pp. 101-102.
17. See "A Critic's Job of Work" in *The Double Agent : Essays in Craft and Elucidation*, New York, 1935. My emphasis.
18. "Criticism as Pure Speculation" in *The Intent of the Critic* edited by Donald A. Stauffer, Princeton, 1941.
19. *The Languages of Criticism and the Structure of Poetry*, 1953.
20. *The Function of Criticism*, Denver, Swallow, 1967, p. 27.
21. "Criticism in Crisis" in *Contexts of Criticism*, Cambridge, 1957, p. 257.
22. *Ibid.*, p. 264.
23. "Poetry and Propaganda" (1930). My emphasis.
24. "The Frontier of Criticism" (1965) included in *On Poetry and Poets*, London, 1957, p. 116. My emphasis.
25. *Why Literary Criticism Is Not an Exact Science*, Cambridge, Massachusetts, 1967, p. 21. My emphasis.

2

In Defence of Pluralistic Criticism*

Advocates for the autonomy for poetry claim that a work of art is an aesthetic object and that our experience of it is an aesthetic experience. This leads to the further claim that aesthetic criteria alone are sufficient for evaluating a work of art, because it is possible to discern in the object the particular qualities and characteristics which occasion that experience. These qualities are generally related to harmony, intensity, depth, structural tension etc. It is evident that a literary theory which emphasises the uniqueness of the literary object and analyses it in terms of the inner consistency of parts is confined to the area of aesthetic analysis and judgment.

The view of the work as a self-contained, autonomous, organic object having no extra-territorial loyalty seems to be the best view of the nature of object according to our aesthetic experience of it. The New Criticism was primarily concerned with the development and practice of this method. Sometimes the term 'formalism' was used to describe such criticism, and frequently, 'formalism' and 'aesthetic' are interchangeable terms in their critical discussions. The New Critics' approach to the problem of criticism, as guided by their view of literature, was reducibly monistic. But at the same time, their speculations about the nature of literature gradually revealed a built-in dilemma. It was found that a literary work, a poem, for example, was both an organic object having a unique structure and a cognitive discourse. How is the critic to judge and evaluate an organic object which does not seek our assent but only our contemplation while at the same time, as a cognitive discourse it appears to say something about human experience? In very broad

* National Seminar on Linguistics and Literary Criticism, Burdwan, 1977.

terms, the problem is this : the view of the work as an organic object, an autonomous unit whose meanings are immanent and intransitive rather than immediately referential as is the language of science is the best view of the nature of the object according to our aesthetic experience of it, but at the same time, the organic object is referential and does seem to reveal something of the external world. So a literary object is at once non-referential in terms of its inviolable context and referential in terms of the outside world from which it can never be completely alienated. In other words, the problem is one of reconciling a theory of the work as an aesthetic object and a theory of poetry as knowledge. Pushed to its logical conclusion, the problem is one of reconciling, aesthetic value-criteria and non-aesthetic value-criteria in a total literary judgment.

In addition to the aesthetic, the other values usually claimed for literature are cognitive and moral. It is necessary to discuss them in some detail. The claim that literature has cognitive value can be divided into three major groups according to the cognitive theories involved. The predication theory is based on the claim that literature is a verbal discourse in which statements are either made or implied. Let us take a few examples :

(i) The isles of Greece, the isles of Greece!
Where burning Sappho loved and sung,
Where grew the arts of war and peace,
Where Delos rose and Phoebus sprung!
Eternal summer gilds them yet,
But all, except their sun is set.[1]

(ii) Amen stuck in my throat.[2]

(iii) I fall upon the thorns of life! I bleed![3]

(iv) ...it is a tale
Told by an idiot, full of sound and fury
Signifying nothing.[4]

The first illustration refers to a supposedly existing past situation. It is possible to ascertain the historical validity of the statement. It is possible, theoretically, to examine the validity of the second report also. The historical validity of the third report can be examined in the light of the available biographical data of Shelley, although the finding can never be conclusive, because it is a figurative statement. The fourth statement, however, does not refer to any really existing thing, and there is no way to determine whether the statement is historically true or even true within the framework of the drama itself. But we must hasten to add that truth or falsity of reports in these cases have little bearing on the literary value of the lines quoted above. In literature, sometimes we have implicit reports verifiable on the basis of the various situations, dialogues, events, etc. which support that statement. Take *A Tale of Two Cities* for example. Besides the general historical atmosphere of the novel a character like Jerry Cruncher, for example, would point to certain social phenomena which are historically verifiable. In fact, any literature that draws its material from history is sure to contain many implicit reports. This does not mean, however, that implicit reports are available only in historical novels or romances. Even a poem like "Ode to a Nightingale" contains implicit reports verifiable biographically. The fourth statement quoted above is usually called a 'thesis.' We must remember in this connection that a thesis of one work would invariably differ from the thesis of another work, so that there is possibility of infinite range and variety of theses of different literary works. The thesis or philosophy or idea may be more or less coherent as the case of *The Divine Comedy* or *The Faerie Queene* or *The Pilgrim's Progress*. It may be more or less complex as in the case of "The Waste Land" of "Sailing to Byzantium." It may be trite as in the case of "Elegy Written in a Country Church Yard" or "In Memoriam." How is the critic to consider the thesis? Is it to be judged true or false? If so, what is the relation of the truth value of its thesis to the work as a whole? Take the case of "Alastor" or "Ode on a Grecian Urn." Is the poetic value independent of the value of thesis? The critics are sharply divided on this issue. The New Critics with their monistic view of literature would contend that the cognitive value does not in any way affect the literary value. But critics like Sidney, Arnold, and Babbitt on the other hand would advocate that the cognitive value and the literary value are inextricably interlinked. This might be true, in fact, about all moral critics, because moral value of literature is a function of the cognitive value. Some critics like Eliot would hold that cognitive value and literary value are separable but a work cannot be great unless its thesis or philosophy is profoundly true.

The revelation theory of knowledge claims that a work of art through the concrete particular reveals the universal. An exponent of the revelation theory may claim, for example, that through the particular depiction of Othello's jealousy Shakespeare has revealed a universal passion. The idea is very close to the theory of imitation as it is generally understood. Butcher explains :

> 'Imitation' is the expression of the concrete thing under an image which answers to its true idea. To seize the universal, and to reproduce it in simple and sensuous form is not to reflect a reality already familiar through sense perception; rather it is a rivalry of nature, a completion of her unfulfilled purposes, a correction of her failures.[5]

And when Denis de Rougemont[6] defines a work of art as "an object of which *raison d'etre* necessary and sufficient is to signify organically and by means of its own structure," his claim is revelatory.

Another major claim for the cognitive value of literature is based on the intuition theory. The intuition theory of literary cognition is derived mostly from the aesthetics of Croce. The intuitionist asserts that there is a kind of knowledge of non-conceptual form which is immediately intuited by a special faculty usually called the imagination. The peculiarity of the intuitive knowledge is that it is not generalised or abstracted, but a knowledge of the particular thing or situation in all its concrete individuality. Unlike scientific knowledge it cannot be communicated in the form of a logical proposition. It is this insistence on the intuitive aspect of poetry that leads Croce to talk about the impossibility of ever rendering in logical terms the full effect of poetry. Croce writes :

> The critic does not offer as his completed judgment either intuitive remakings or logical equivalents of poetry but does something very different : he gives a characterisation of it. This characterisation is properly based on the content of poetry, the sentiment that the poem has amplified by transference to the poetic atmosphere. The object of this investigation...is human reality in its completeness, in all its infinite subdivisions.[7]

While discussing the nature of literature Jacque Maritain also writes :

> The fine arts aim at producing, by the object they make, joy or delight in the mind through the intuition of the senses. Such joy is not the simple act of knowing, the joy of possessing knowledge or having truth. Such joy, therefore, presupposes knowledge, and the more knowledge there is, the more things given to the mind, the greater will be the possibility of joy. For this reason art, as ordered to beauty never stops — at all events when its object permits it — as shapes or colours or sounds or words, considered in themselves as *things* — (they must be so considered to begin with, that is the first condition) but considers them *also* as making known something other than themselves,

> that is to say as *symbols*. And the thing symbolized can be in turn a symbol, and the more charged with symbolism the work of art (but spontaneous symbolism *intuitively* apprehended not heiroglyphic symbolism), the more immense, the richer and higher will be the possibility of joy or beauty.[8]

Similarly, when Ralph Ross[9] argues that "art yields knowledge of particulars, of the quality of experiences, and of the meanings of life," he is, I believe, lodging an intuitional claim for art.

In addition to the cognitive values of literature moral value is frequently claimed by those who object to purely aesthetic criticism. The claim that literature has moral value has many facets for each of which we have advocated. It may mean, for example, that the process of making a work of art is a moral act. It may also mean that the experience of reading a poem or any work of literature for that matter, has, can have, or should have an effect on human acts. It is possible that the process of making a work of art is a moral act, and incidentally, there is no opinion to the contrary. All discussions regarding moral judgments of literature invariably centre round the second proposition. It is well nigh impossible to demonstrate experimentally the actual effect of literary study on human acts, although we sometimes hear of cases where the study of a particular work of literature shaped the course of a reader's life. The central thesis of Sidney's *Apology for Poetry* can be seen to be this. The writer through his portraits of Achilles, Cyrus, Aeneas, Turnus, Tydeus and Rinaldo "doth not only teach and move to a truth, but teacheth and moveth to the most high and excellent truth."[10] The claim that literature has moral value does not, I think, mean that an effect on human act is necessary; but only that a work of art can have capacity to affect human acts.[11] The very idea of the two-fold aim of literature — to delight and to instruct — presupposes this capacity.

Some of the moral effects of literature are indirect and flow from its aesthetic functions. In other words, it may be argued that an aesthetic experience cannot be absolutely free from moral ramifications. When Beardsley,[12] for example, pleads that "the aesthetic experience resolves tensions and quiets destructive impulses," he is actually describing an indirect moral effect. It is possible to argue further that a greater aesthetic value would necessarily imply a greater capacity for occasioning such indirect moral effects, although the converse of the proposition may not be always true.

The critical dilemma in question is not concerned with such moral effects, because they are part of the aesthetic experience itself, and any evaluation of the aesthetic experience would automatically include an evaluation of these indirect moral effects. There is no real critical problem here because the aesthetic value and moral value do not conflict. The problem arises when moral effects flow not directly from the aesthetic experience, but from the cognitive aspect of literature, because the criteria for aesthetic value and the criteria for cognitive value are not exactly the same. As long as we subscribe to the view that poetry is knowledge we have to admit that it illuminates life and thus aids the reader in sitting in judgment over life. Morality in literature is, at bottom, criticism of life. A great work of art has to be morally right. *The Divine Comedy* is a case in point. The greatness of the work is as much due to its aesthetic richness as to the philosophy enunciated in it. And to take an extreme case, can there be an aesthetically valuable pornography? If not, it would logically follow that aesthetic criteria alone are not sufficient for the evaluation of a work of literature.

The key-issue then is the contention that a purely formal or aesthetic analysis and evaluation is not adequate for a total evaluation of literary work. But such a question inevitably leads to the ontological problem in literary theory : What is the nature of literature? The aesthetic problem is involved in the task of defining or describing the nature and function of the literary work as an aesthetic object. The cognitive problem is the task of defining or describing the nature and function of the work as knowledge so that the distinction between Spenser's *Faerie Queene* and Orwell's *1984* is preserved. By moral problem I understand the task of demonstrating why or how the work has an effect on human action. All these various problems are facets of the ontological problem, because questions of nature and function of literature are involved in each.

In view of the above it is suggested that aesthetic criteria alone are not sufficient for evaluating a literary work and that the critic must employ two-fold criteria — aesthetic and cognitive-moral — while evaluating a work of literature. A poem, for example, has to be judged aesthetically first and once it is found aesthetically satisfactory the critic should employ cognitive-moral criteria to examine it further. In other words, the critic must apply principles of pluralistic criticism.

The point of view I am struggling to attack is the theory that poetry is autonomous and has no extra-territorial loyalty. My contention, on the other hand, is that as long as poetry continues to be a cognitive discourse it cannot disown loyalty to life; it can never remain completely immanent and intransitory.

REFERENCES

1. Byron, *Don Juan*, Canto, iii.
2. *Macbeth* Act II. Sc. ii.
3. Shelly, "Ode to the West Wind."
4. *Macbeth* Act V. Sc. v.
5. H. Butcher : Aristotle's *Theory of Poetry and Fine Art*, Dover Publication, 1951, p. 154.
6. Denis de Rougemont : "Religion and the Mission of the Artist" in *Spiritual Problems in Contemporary Literature* ed. Stanley R. Hopper, New York, 1952, p. 176.
7. Guy Wilson Allen & Aarry Hayden Clark, *Literary Criticism Pope to Croce,* Deroit, Waine State University Press, 1962, p. 637.
8. Jacque Maritain : "Imitation in Art" in *A Modern Book of Aesthetics*, Holt, Rinehart and Winston, Inc., 1973, p. 31.
9. Ralph Ross : "Art as Knowledge" in *The Sewanee Review*, LXIX, October 1961.
10. Sir Philip Sidney : *An Apology for Poetry*, Cambridge, 1951, p. 37.
11. Incidentally it may be mentioned here that a few years ago when a course of humanities, flanked on the one side by history and on the other by philosophy, was introduced in technical institutions first in America and later here in India the pronounced intention was to humanise the engineers who it was feared, would otherwise turn into mere machines. It was assumed that a humanistic education would have the desirable effect on the students in making them good units in the society.
12. Monroe C. Beardsley : *Aesthetics*, New York, Harcourt Brace, 1958, p. 575.

3

Genealogy of Postmodernism*

Literary criticism can never be an exact science. Any attempt at a precise definition is bound to speak as much of the time when it is made as of the thing defined. Yet, it is always possible to identify certain distinctive features when a phenomenon assumes the nature of a movement, and attempt a provisional description of the movement. However, before we proceed further it is necessary to bear in mind the semantic differences between the words like 'contemporary' and 'modern.' The word, 'contemporary' is timebased. Anything that happens in our time is contemporary. It is a historic fact. We must however, admit that the word is quite flexible in the sense that by saying 'contemporary poetry' we can mean the poetry of the 90s or the poetry since the 70s, 60s or even since the beginning of the century. We have to define the limits of the contemporary when we discuss something as 'contemporary.' But everything that is contemporary is not necessarily modern. Modernity is a matter of sensibility. To be modern is to be aware of the contemporary scenario as changed by the growth of knowledge; a sensitive perception of the world in the present state of knowledge. The perennial stuff of literature as reality is an ongoing process; it keeps on changing with the development of knowledge. We are aware of the huge knowledge explosion during *fin de siècle* and the beginning of the century. In 1895 Lumiere brothers invented cinematography and Rontgen discovered X-rays and Marconi invented wireless telegraphy; in 1897 Thomson discovered the electron; in 1898 the Curries discovered radium; in 1910 the first wireless communication was established between Europe and America; in 1905

* Originally delivered as "From Modernism to Postmodernism", Anandeswar Sarma Memorial Lecture, Guwahati, 1994.

the first motion picture theatre was opened in Pittsburgh, and so on, just to mention a few epochmaking events.

Let us look at the turn of the century philosophers : Bergson, James, Bradley, Nietzsche and Hulme. They are all concerned with the epistemological issue : the opposition between conceptual abstractions and immediate experience. Their subtle differences notwithstanding, all agreed that intellectual formulations are simply practical instruments for arranging the sensory flux in a convenient manner. The spectrum of this idea ranges from Bergson at one end to Nietzsche on the other. Such theories attacked the 19th century positivistic certainties that objective truth either existed at all or could be ascertained through the application of reason and science. Bergson opposed the utilitarian falsifications of reality that we produce through the exercise of our analytical intellect. He called for the development of 'intuition' to restore us to the perception of reality. Nietzsche, on the contrary, regards the experiential flux as a valueneutral meaningless 'chaos of sensations,' by no means an identifiable objective reality at all, but rather mere manifestations of the 'will to power' by which life perpetually creates new forms that lack underlying unity with no first cause and no final goal. His response calls for the bold affirmation of life, the proud assertion of our power to lay down new values, new interpretations, new forms that create and sustain a self-authenticating existence. Bergson identifies art with the recovery of immediate experience, Nietzsche identifies it with the creation of new abstractions that impose shape and significance of experience. For William James art is at once invention and discovery. The roots of literary modernism must be traced to the ideas of these philosophers.

Then there are others : Darwin, Marx and Freud, for example. The modern writers or the writers who wanted to be modern had to come to terms with a view of human beings emerging from the ideas of these philosophers. The human being popularly conceived as a fallen angel, became after *The Origin of the Species* (1859) a cultured ape. In the popular conception of history, before Marx, the individual effort could play a crucial part. After *Das Kapital* (1867), it had to contend with the possibility that a great deal of it had been responding instead to economic imperatives. If the popular conception of human action, before Freud, had been based upon a possibility of self-knowledge, of presence of mind, *The Interpretation of Dreams* (1990), *The Psychopathology of Everyday Life* (1901) and other works established the disturbing possibility that one could never really know more than the ostensible reasons for such an action. If the popular conception of morality before Nietzsche was of something in essence indisputable, anchored by a concept of a good outside the human machine, and so not subject to the vagaries of mortality, it became, after *Thus Spake Zarathrusta* (1883-85) but a necessary and effective human fiction subject to human readjustment, leading to existential anguish. Briefly, from about the middle of the 19th century the foundations of an earlier understanding of the nature and place of humanity were so shaken that by the end of the century a great many artists and writers throughout the Western world had developed a kind of future shock, a sense that the old view of the world and meaning of human existence had been taken away from them and that a replacement had not yet arrived, or that sometimes a bewildering array of possible replacements were contending for sovereignty. The broadest view of modernism is that unconsciously as well as consciously, technically as well as thematically, it encompasses not only comprehensions and accommodations, but also the initial apprehensions of this change. The modern sensibility is evinced in a disdainful disregard for authority, a feeling of urgency to break new ground, flirtation with anarchy, temptation to test out chaos and the demonic. It is further evident in a desire to remove all standards, to alter the very nature of language, reorganize our perceptions, and finally stress on the principle of change as an end in itself. The four major preoccupations of modern writers according to Bradbury and McFarlane are : preoccupation with the complexities of form, preoccupation with the representation of inward states of consciousness, with a sense of the nihilistic disorder behind the ordered surface of life and reality and with the freeing of the narrative art from the dominations of an onerous plot.

It is difficult to find a clear date for the beginning of the movement or movements known as modernism. The movements had been coming in waves along the London-Paris-New York axis for a long time in the 19th century. But we must have a tentative date in terms of a literary history. For Frank Kermode the nineties are the forerunners of modernism : Richard Ellmann would prefer 1900. D.H. Lawrence claimed in *Kangaroo* (1923) that "It was in 1915 that the old world ended." Virginia Woolf insisted in "Mr. Bennet and Mrs. Brown" (1924) that "On or about December 1910 human nature changed.... All human relations shifted... those between masters and servants, husbands and wives, parents and children. And when human relations change there is at the same time a change in religion, conduct, politics, and literature." The death of Edward VII and the first post-impressionist exhibitions were crucial for Woolf. Harry Levin, however, would like to fix it at 1922, the year of a rich literary harvest : *Ulysses, The Waste Land, Duino Elegei Sonnets to*

Orpheus, Brecht's first play *Baal*, Lawrence's *Aaron's Rod*, Virginia Woolf's Jacob's *Room*, Proust's *Sodom and Gomorrah* and O'Neill's *Anna Christies*.

To confine modernism, or any literary movement for that matter, to a strict period has its dangers. Subjected to the kind of careful reading that Nietzsche recommends in the Preface to *Daybreak* ('slowly, deeply, looking cautiously before and after, with reservations, with doors open, with delicate eyes and fingers' 1881) almost any text will be found to qualify itself, to divulge antecedents, to share as much of the past as it does of its own movement, and to seem to support the assertion of Paul de Man and many others that much of what at first seems to distinguish a work of one period from a work of another can in fact be found in both, and that the apparent demarcations of literary history may owe less to radical destruction than to failure of close reading. A close reading would possibly reveal that within the rubric of the movement of modernism there are distinct ups and downs. If the 1920s were dominated by radical modernism, the 1930s clearly registered a shift in emphasis. Auden, Ishwerwood, Spender, for example, criticized their immediate predecessors for their elitist assumptions and their failure to communicate to a wide audience. With the poets of the 30s realism came back. In the 1940s, again, the emphasis shifted in favour of rendering the refinements of individual sensibility rather than collective experience. Eliot returned with vengeance, as it were, with his poetic drama. In the 1950s, the Movement poets, were suspicious of, if not actually hostile to, experimentations. The literary history is never a straight, linear movement; it progresses through a continuous dialogue between the present and the past. What, however, brings all the writers under the canopy of modernism is their serious concern for literature and their religious devotion to the vocation of an artist. De Man indeed chooses to speak not so much of modernism itself as of a modernity that denotes not the one isolable historical period but a series of "incandescent" movements of a desire "to wipe out whatever came earlier in the hope of reaching at last a point that could be called a true present, a point of origin that marks a new departure" (*Blindness and Insight*). Terry Eagleton seems to elaborate the particular quality of such points when he writes of "a sense of one's particular historical conjuncture as being somehow peculiarly pregnant with crisis and change.... A portentious, confused yet curiously heightened self-consciousness of one's own historical moment, at once self-doubting and self-congratulatory, anxious and trimphantistic together.... At one and the same time an arresting and denial of history in the violent shock of the immediate present from which vantage point all precious developments may be complacently consigned to the aschan of tradition" (*Against the Grain : Selected Essays, 1986*), Modernism accordingly might be seen not as the only but as the most recent and most salient of such moments and modernity as a term applicable to several periods of literary history as useful in describing certain Jacobean writers, Donne, Browning and Hopkins, for example. Quinones in his *Mapping Literary Modernism* has tried to map out four phases of literary modernism in terms of Time.

The first phase is the rebellion itself against a linear, mechanical time-world deriving from the Renaissance, a time-world that in its late-Industrial incarnation empties time itself of all innovative freshness of meaning for its human inhabitants by trapping them in soulless repetitiveness of the production line. Time becomes a commodity. On the experimental level the mechanistic time-world for the modernist author comes to include all the concrete pressures in life toward social conformity, and among them, most intimately, the bond of family represented primarily by the mother. The real problem is to achieve freedom from the mother. Mann, Joyce and Lawrence are examples. Lawrence's major novels, for example end with a striking rejection and defeat of the codes of marriage and continuity, codes of the mother. The second phase of modernism is marked by the development of the complex central consciousness, a new character type that is inward and passive and yet paradoxically, by retreating from willed entanglements with the historical continuum, provides a window outward onto the complex happenings and shiftings of society and shows a remarkable freedom and variety. Major examples are : Proust's Marcel, Mann's Hans Castorp, Joyce's Bloom. In the third phase of modernism new meanings are discovered through the appeal of the mythic by which the self is enhanced and even vindicated by its identification with a larger coherence. The fourth and final phase of modernism deals with the return of the sense of historical reality.

Many of the central works of modernism — *The Waste Land, The Cantos, Ulysses* — which endeavour to waken from a "nightmare of history," the past, and particularly the literary past, have a high and complex profile within them. Far from ignoring or defying tradition, they attempt to redefine it, to see beyond the formal imperatives of the immediate past and to re-select from the vast body, domestic or otherwise, of the literature which preceded them. Finding their impulse in a creativity highly conscious of its own departure, they must also, as a consequence, constantly remind us the very things which they seek to jettison or modify. Whether we see such a phenomenon as definitive of modernism itself or simply as marking an essential or climactic stage in its development, it would seem that the identity of modernism is better seen as inhereing in the nature, range and profile of its dialogue with history than in a clear severance from it.

In fact, in the years before the War many works of literature seem to have been governed by a sense of loss, of personal and cultural displacement. The pursuit of knowledge overreaching itself and resulting in a radical discomfort, an alienation of the human free from its former image itself, is clearly registered in works as diverse as Conrad's *Heart of Darkness* (1902), Wilde's *The Picture of Dorian Gray* (1890), Moore's *Esther Wasters* (1894), Wells's *Tono Bungay* (1909), Ford Madox Ford's *The Good Soldier* (1915) and Golding's *Lord of the Flies* (1954) at the end of each of which the central characters having explored beneath the surface of their prior knowledge and experience, find themselves isolated, somehow deprived by their own efforts of the very world they had sought to know or save. In high Modernism, in Eliot and Pound, experience and investigation are seen not as agencies of alienation, but, for those who can withstand the initial disorientation, as the most likely means of restitution or accommodation. *The Waste Land, Ulysses* and the *Cantos* in particular are dominated not by a myth of unwitting destruction, but by one of quest. The protagonist, hitherto alienated by investigation, now becomes its agent. Punished for irreverence he or she now learns or re-learns, through arduous experience, lessons which had somehow been disastrously forgotten.

This is why the texts of Joyce, Pound and Eliot are marked by an increasing self-consciousness. The texts break up or dislocate conventional narrative or presentational procedures, sometimes even the sentence and the word, and in so doing not only draw attention to and undermine conventional notions of what a novel or a poem or a drama should be, but attempt to circumvent the intrusion of established discourse upon their presentations, whether or not these are seen by their writers to be presentations of the "real." So each of the chapters of *Ulysses*, for example, employs a different narrative mode and invites the reader to compare the ways in which the material therein is reflected. So the narrative strategy of Eliot in *The Waste Land* endeavours to avoid the connective tissue of conventional discourse and invites the reader to arrange and explain its imagistic fragments in accordance with his or her understanding or ability.

It is perhaps inevitable that the widespread detection and analysis of the systems underlying or even comprising human being should come down to language itself as a system in Ferdnand de Saussure's *Course in General Linguistics* (1916), a theory which would underpin and consolidate this very perception. Saussure's insistence that an element can be explained by its place in a network of relations rather than in a chain of cause and effect partly justified the growing desire to abandon literary history, and autobiographical criticism, and to study literature as "*un-système qui ne connaît que son ordre propre*" — a system with its own order. Since the material of literature is language the structuralists, drawing on the insight of Saussure, insisted that literature should be analysed as a self-contained, relational system, with its own rules, a system that does not depend on outside reality for validity. Once the outside reality is derecognized as the authority for literature, the author and the reader are also rejected. If Saussure provided the methodological assumptions of the structuralists Claude Levi-Strauss brought it to the forefront of intellectual activity with the publication of *Structural Anthropology* in 1963.

II

To come to postmodernism is to enter the great Serbonian bog where whole armies have sunk. In the first place the word is semantically anomalous. The prefix "post" means after. Then, how can something which is a contemporary phenomenon come *after* the present? To say "I am postmodern" would sound like saying "I am dead." But the confusion begins to clear up when we focus our attention on the suffix ISM in postmodernism. Then it seems to refer not so much to a historical time as to a specific movement in culture and criticism. The ISM then would imply that postmodernism is not just a chronological division but an organized system of poetics and aesthetics. Even when the semantic problems are somehow solved the ideational problems remain, because there are different versions of postmodernism. Used first by Toynbee the word was originally used extensively in architecture. But soon it migrated to other areas so as to designate an aesthetic style, a cultural situation, a critical practice and an economic condition. And the problem is further complicated by the fact that the word means different things to different people. For John Barth it is the literature of replenishment, for Charles Newman it is the literature of an inflationary economy, for Jean Francois Lyotard it is general condition of knowledge in the contemporary informational regime; for Ihab Hassan it is a stage in the road to spiritual unification of human kind. Harry Levin, Leslie Fiedler, Irving Howe, Terry Eagleton, Douwe Fokkema, Fredric Jameson and others have also used the term in their own ways. The diversity makes one feel that there is not one postmodernism but many, as Lovejoy had remarked about romanticism. But, I believe that it is possible to identify a singular feature — the hallmark of postmodernism — which would suggest a unity in diversity, and bring not only different versions of postmodernism but also postmodernism and poststructuralism into a harmonious whole, or as manifestations of the same basic principle.

But before that let us have a close look at poststructuralism, because poststructuralism and postmodernism are partners in the same paradigm. Together they exercise a joint critique of modernist ideas of order and unity. Both share a profound ontological uncertainty.

Historically poststructuralism had its origin in October 1966 during the symposium on "The Language of Criticism and Sciences of Man" held in John Hopkins Humanities Center where the objective was to "bring into an active and not uncritical contact leading proponents of structural studies in a wide variety of disciplines." Lucien Goldmann, Todorov, Barthes, Lacan and Derrida, among others, were present. It is here that Derrida presented his now famous "Structure, Sign and Play in the Discourse of the Human Sciences" in which he attacked the traditionalist position in general and the Levi-Strauss version of structuralism in particular. He shows how the structuralist texts like Levi-Strauss's can be made to embarrass their own logic. Derrida contends that the "structurality of structure has always been neutralized or reduced, and this by giving it a center or referring it to a point of presence, a fixed origin." Derrida coins a word "differance" out of two words : "difference" and "deference." The structure of the sign is conditioned by differing and by deferring. "Differance" denotes two actions : differing and deferring. Differing is the one not being the others; it is spatial. Deferring is something delayed or postponed: it is temporal. In other words, the structure of the sign is "differance" which means that a sign is something which is different from another sign, and something that is not fully contained in the sign. Therefore the half of the sign is what it is not and the half of it is what is not there. A sign has no fixed meaning; all that it can do is to send us in search of meaning. The sign, therefore, is a trace and a literary work is a structure of traces.

By "decentering" Derrida means that outside discourse there is no fixed point from which one can establish metaphysical boundaries for legitimate signifiers. The critic's desire to find a centre is a kind of wish-fulfilment and such centering should be summarily dismissed as the useless legacy of the old metaphysics. The idea of decentering has opened up what was supposed to be a closed system of empirical data and the result is free play and indeterminacy. There is such an indeterminacy in any fictional art work that neither consistency nor certainty is possible. The text must be read as slippery, deceptive, unknowable, and most importantly, an unstable narrative. Language lets us down just when we think it meaningful. The meaning is indeterminate. The text is not a closed system but an open one into which we can have access through many different entrances none of which can be claimed as the main one. Each single text, again, is a network that recalls many other texts and opens up the horizon of intertextuality. A text is no longer seen as a veil hiding a meaning, but a web without a centering spider, free play without closure. Once the physical condition of a book is separated from the chain of communication associated with verbal discourse, the book became a simple code that can be interpreted as one interprets hieroglyphics. For Stanley Fish a text is a kind of empty container waiting to be filled with meaning. The reader is the co-author and the text or, more precisely a subtext, emerges out of the vital interaction between the text and the reader. In S/Z Roland Barthes uses Balzac's *Sarrasine* as the object of a speculative game and the main interest of Barthes's book lies in his exploration of the other possible stories that can be constructed on the basis of the possible different literal meanings of *Sarrasine*. In the process a traditional fiction is remotivated for the avantgarde. Derrida, Paul de Man, Roland Barthes, J. Hillis Miller and Geoffrey Hartman have managed to create a genuine controversy that involves the traditional historicists, the Chicago neo-Aristotelians, the myth critics and the New Critics. The traditionalists held that the historical and critical methods can produce positive knowledge of texts and their environments, provided we accept three basic premises : (i) that written text says something determinate, (ii) that the determinacy is grounded on authorial intention and (iii) that the properly equipped historian can produce a reading that would be accepted by others as objective. The deconstructionists, on the other hand, argue that positive knowledge is not available because there is no stable ontological ground for it.

Mention should also be made of Jacques Lacan's theory of the role of the mirror stage in a child's development, because of its numerous linguistic and philosophical implications. A child's first experience of seeing himself reflected in the mirror is a momentous experience. It makes him aware of his individual status and enables him to link himself up with the generic man, with other men. Lacan believes that this experience goes a long way in shaping the child's ego, and suggests that it is possibly as distorted as the reflection in the mirror. Applying this idea to literary criticism Lacan contends that there is a text lying just outside the individual's discursive power. The text is that unconsciousness which must be unravelled through language. But what will be discovered are predetermined : childhood memories and obsessive patterns. Michel Foucault looks at a text from another angle and in his writings he has exposed the power of discourse and the discourse of power in his attempt to discover politics of knowledge. Foucault also holds that a selfish interest precedes all power and knowledge and everything is moulded and reshaped to satisfy one's desire and ideals.

The advent of semiotics in the last twenty years really looks like the ultimate in postmodernism. Its isolation of the text, its stress on the self-referral, its insistence on scientific models, its use of synchronism and diachronism, its divorce from the signifier, its reliance on the signified, its concern with objects and not the thought behind them have led to a kind of intellectual anarchy. Semiotics has replaced traditional linkage between the author and the book with what Barthes has called a "set of institutional conventions within which the activity of writing can take place."

The deconstructionists, in general, have challenged the stability of a work so vigorously that criticism has lost its proper subject and is plagued by an anarchy of interpretation. There is no reading but only misreading; there is no understanding, but only misunderstanding. There is no text but only subtexts. This denial of any authority of the text has led the critics to fantasize, to write fiction instead of criticism and to spin webs of personal and private associations. For the deconstructionists the work is only a site, a crossroad of communicative highways linked by external and extra-textual circumstances. The object, however valuable in itself is just inadequate for them, and in this arena of open ended intertextuality we are bound to be caught in a tangled skein. The result is a new situation marked by semiotic volatility and necessary complicity. Thus in postmodernism, modernism's commitment to the autonomy of art has given way to an elaborate intellectual game of remotivation. The most important postmodern feature is indeterminacy. Nothing is certain : we cannot be certain about anything. Heisenberg's principle of uncertainty, Bloom's "anxiety of influence," Man's allegorical reading, Barthes's analysis of *Sarrasine* are functions of the doctrine of indeterminacy. This indeterminacy is also partly due to our sense of fragmentation. The seamless totality of the classical and the Christian worlds are lost to us. With the death of God the world is fragmented; the society is fragmented;

the family is fragmented, and the process of fragmentation is an ongoing process. In postmodernism this is reflected in the breaking of forms, use of montage and collage and mixing of genres in an unexpected manner. Since postmodern culture is essentially mass culture all canons are discredited. The traditional values are flouted; culture is decanonized. The classical example is Duchamp's presentation of Mona Lisa with a goatee. Art is trivialized and carnivalized. This carnivalization only reflects the comic and/or absurdist ethos of postmodernism. Benjamin believes that all this actually started in the mid-nineteenth century Paris when the first shopping centers were introduced in the Paris arcades. Drawing on industrial revolution France anticipated and promoted what may be called consumerism. While the reactionary movement arising out of the nervous hostility to the democratization of taste led to modernism, the slower but stronger movement spawned mass culture and eventually led to postmodernism. Modernism gave way to the energies of mass culture and a demand for an aesthetics of Kitsch. Postmodernism insisted on the pleasure of the moment, *monokronos hedonis*, and looked for things easy to like. The pleasure principle of postmodernism has inevitably led to an endless mixing of genres and media and modes of aesthetic thinking and conceptual art : film and literature, avantgarde and mass culture, the tragic and the comic, the sublime and the ludicrous, interior monologue and magic realism. All kinds of stuff are lumped together into a form which reflects the instinct of *via nuova*, trying to forge a new aesthetics that would correspond to the postmodern situation.

David Lodge has identified five narrative strategies generally used in postmodern fiction : Contradiction, Permutation, Discontinuity, Randomness, and the Short Circuit.

The first sentence in the opening paragraph of Alain Robbe-Grillet's *In the Labyrinth* announces that it is raining and the second sentence contradicts the statement and says that the sun is shining. The purpose of the strategy is to disrupt the link between language and reality. A typical example of permutation is provided by the passage in Beckett's *Molloy* where the hero struggles with the problem of distributing and circulating his sucking stones in his four pockets in such a way that he will always suck them in the same sequence. Permutation often leads to discontinuity of text and, also introduces randomness. The loose-leaf novel of B.S. Johnson or Saul Saporta is a typical example of randomness, which the readers can shuffle into different orders. Excess is the device of presenting the reader with more data than he can synthesize and thus resist interpretation. Short circuit takes place when the real, historical author appears on the same plane as his fictitious characters.

We can sum up the postmodern situation with the lines Donne had written in "The Anniversary of the World" (1611) :

The new philosophy calls all in doubt....
'Tis all in pieces, all coherence gone,
All just supply and all relation...
For every man alone thinks he hath got
To be a phoenix, and that then can be
None of the kind, of which he is, but he.

III

It is now time we considered some of the basic differences between modernism and postmodernism. Modernism cultivated austerity; postmodernism is interested in pleasure. Modernism tried to capture reality through individual consciousness which was equivalent of life itself. Virginia Woolf saw life as a "semitransparent envelope," "a luminous halo." Eliot's objective correlative, Joyce's epiphany and the imagist doctrine offer glimpses of reality. Modernism believed that there is a centre and, in the words of Henry James "a pattern in the carpet." Myth and musical form were often used to give a structured unity to a chaotic material. For postmodernism "realism" is just an incoherent and deluding notion. Against the modernist's struggle for wholeness and unity postmodernism posits a radical indeterminacy. For postmodernism the pattern, or the centre is only a wishful thinking; an imposition. The idea of a meaningful pattern is a comforting fiction at the best. No amount of research can, for example, establish the identity of the man with the heavy coat and hat and stick encountered by Moran in Beckett's *Molloy*. It is impossible to comprehend the plot of John Fowles' *The Magus* or Thomas Pynchon's *The Crying of Lot 49*. These novels are more concerned with ontological rather than epistemological issues. One way to understand the contrastive features of modernism and postmodernism is with the help of a table.

Modernism	*Postmodernism*
Form	Antiform/disjunctive/open
Purpose	Play
Design	Chance
Art Object	Process
Distance	Participation
Creation/Synthesis	Deconstruction/Antithesis
Presence	Absence
Determinacy	Indeterminacy

IV

Although it may appear that postmodernism has completely broken away from modernism in a radical way, it is however, possible, at least in case of postmodernism in criticism, to trace some of its basic ideas to earlier periods of literary history. Sterne's *Tristram Shandy* written in the 1760s can be seen as a postmodern novel the substance of which consists in defining its own structure. In this century Andre Gide's *Les Faux Monnayeurs* (1927) provides another example of self-reflexive novel. Again, if unknowability is one of the major aspects of postmodernism, it is abundantly evident in Camus's *The Fall* and *The Outsider*. In Camus, there is no centre, no fixedness outside the discourse itself, and even that is vague, uncertain, indeterminate. When the deconstructionists stress the fact that language always betrays us at the moment when we most seek certainty or stability from it, they are only calling attention to an aspect of communication that has been a major concern of Kandinsky in his earliest phase, of Pound in *The Cantos*, of Eliot in *The Waste Land* and Rilke in *Duino Elegies*, just to name a few. If Derrida insists that there can be no real division between fiction and nonfiction, that is exactly what Rimbaud in his letters to Demeny (1871) and in his poem "Le bateau ivré" (The Drunken Boat) was trying to suggest. The idea of redirection effected by the notion of reader as co-author can be traced to Baudelaire (*Hypocrite lecteur : monsemblable, mon frère*) and Kafka. Kafka's *The Castle* forces a constant realignment of text and reader through irony, tone and decentering. Even Baudelaire's voyage-images are multi-levelled in their evocative power : the voyage is a kind of linkage between the artist and the reader. Lacan's mirror-image theory reminds one of Mallarmé. In *Herodiade* and many other poems, notably in "*Un Dentelle s'abolit*" the mirror is the window with which the lace curtain interacts, and this interaction produces an unconscious language leading to creativity, as the mirror works with the reflections of meaning which lie in the unconscious. Mallarmé also anticipates postmodernism in his use of breaks and blanks by which he internalizes intertextual heterogeneity and puts it to work not as relation between texts but as a play of intervals and interruptions within texts. Mallarmé's intertextuality thus becomes an explicit version of the ways in which a text is never its own contemporary, cannot constitute a self-contained whole, conveys only its non-coincidence with itself. In Camus's *The Fall* there is no centre, no totality, no certainty. There is only delay, spacing, temporalizing and displacement.

V

Even then there is no reason to think that postmodernism is the last word in culture and criticism. The facts falsify the situation supposedly created by postmodernism. Serious scholars, teachers and researchers all over the world are seriously engaged in interpreting, annotating, explicating and editing texts. They are engaged in the common pursuit of knowledge in their search for sources and biographical facts, in their study on the social and historical background, in everything, in fact, that can help us to understand and enjoy the energy dynamics of a literary discourse.

SELECT BIBLIOGRAPHY

Benjamin, Walter, "The Work of Art in the Age of Mechanical Reproduction," Illuminations. Trans. Harry Zohn, New York : Schochken, 1969, The essay was first published in 1935.

Bradbury, Malcolm and James McFarlane, eds. *Modernism*, London : Penguin Books, 1976.

Brooker, Peter, ed. *Modernism/Postmodernism*, London : Longman, 1992.

Buchbinder David, *Contemporary Literary Theory and the Reading of Poetry.* South Melbourne : Macmillan Education, Australia Pvt. Ltd., 1991.

Calineschu, Matei, *Five Faces of Modernity: Modernism, Avant-garde, Decadence, Kitsch, Postmodernism*, Durham : Duke University Press, 1987.

Cohen, Ralph, *Future Literary Theory*, New York : Routledge, 1989.

Falck, Colin, *Myth, Truth and Literature : Towards a true postmodernism*, Cambridge : Cambridge University Press, 1989.

Fokkema, Douwe and Hans Bartens, eds., *Approaching Postmodernism*, Amsterdam : John Benjamins, 1986.

Hassan, Ihab Sally Hassan, eds., *Innovation/Renovation* : *New Perspectives on the Humanities*, Madison : University of Wisconsin Press, 1983.

Hutcheon Linda, A *Poetics of Postmodernism*, London : Routledge, 1988.

Karl, Frederick R., *Modern and Modernism* : *The Sovereignty of the Artist 1885-1925*, New York : Atheneum, 1985.

Lentricchia, Frank, *After the New Criticism*. Chicago : University of Chicago Press, 1980.

Levenson, Michael H., *A Genealogy of Modernism : A Study of English Literary Doctrine 1908-1922.* Cambridge : Cambridge University Press, 1984.

Lodge, David, *Working with Structuralism*, Boston : Routledge and Kegan Paul, 1981.

McHale, Brian, *Postmodernist Fiction*, London : Routledge, 1987.

Norris, Christopher, *Deconstruction* : *Theory and Practice*, London : Metheun, 1982.

Quinones, Ricardo, J., *Mapping Literary Modernism : Time and Development*, Princeton : Princeton University Press, 1985.

Schwartz, Sanford, *The Matrix of Modernism : Pound, Eliot and Early Twentieth Century Thought*, Princeton : Princeton University Press, 1985.

Sharatt, Bernard, "Eliot: Modernism, Postmodernism, and after," *The Cambridge Companion to T.S. Eliot*, Ed. A.D. Moody, Cambridge : Cambridge University Press, 1994.

4

John Dryden : Our Contemporary*

Thomas Rymer once remarked, rather sneeringly, that "till late of years, England was free from critics as it is free from wolves" (Spingarn 164). Dryden too complained in his *An Essay of Dramatic Poesy* that he had no predecessor who could guide him in the field of criticism : "I was drawing the outlines of an art without any alluring master to instruct me in it, an art which had been better praised than studied here in England.... Thus, as I may say, before the use of loadstone, or knowledge of the compass, I was sailing in a vast ocean without any other help than the polestar of the ancients, and the rulers of the French stage among the moderns, which are extremely different from ours by reasons of their opposite taste" (Ker 16-17). However, Dryden believed that "...a severe critic is the greatest help to a great art, he does the office of a friend, while designs that of an enemy and his malice keeps a poet within these bounds, which the luxuriance of his fancy would tempt him to overlap" (Ker 3). At another place Dryden succinctly sums up the functions of a good critic : "They were defenders of poets, and commentators on their works : to illustrate obscure beauties, place some passages in a better light : to redeem others from malicious interpretations : to help out an author's modesty, who is not ostentatious of his wit; and, in short, to shield from the ill nature of those fellows, who were then called *zoili* and *momi* and now take upon themselves the venerable name of censors" (Poems 422-423). It is indeed a great achievement of Dryden that during a critical period he not only excelled as a poet of outstanding calibre but could also emerge as a major critic who anticipated in many ways the twentieth

* International Conference on "Dryden and the Age of Neoclassicism", Salzburg, Austria, 1999.

century critical scenario. He anticipated quite a few of the significant aspects and schools of contemporary literary criticism : New Criticism, Pluralistic Criticism, Intertextual Studies or rewriting of earlier texts, Comparative Literature, Translation Theories and Bakhtinian Dialogism. Dr Johnson rightly described Dryden as the "father of English criticism." In fact, Elizabethan critics had dealt with the external matters of literature only. They simply classified the figures of speech, the kind of meters and the literary forms or discussed the rules of versification. Sir Philip Sidney rose above the merely rhetorical and talked about the art of poetry. Ben Jonson discussed the value of the classical literature as an aid to creation. But the essential tone of all this criticism was didactic. Dryden for the first time made criticism theoretical and comparative and established himself as the first practitioner of practical criticism. About Dryden's significance Eliot thinks that it mainly consists in his affirming at the right moment the native element in literature. In view of the quest for identity which has become a global phenomenon today Dryden's affirmation of the native seems to be surprisingly modern. In fact the affinity between Dryden and Eliot in important critical views is simply unmistakable. Extremely well-read, Dryden had, to borrow a phrase from Eliot, "the entire Europe in his bones." He had not only read and mastered the classics : Sophocles, Euripides, Theocritus and Virgil, but also Shakespeare, Ben Jonson, Beaumont and Fletcher and a host of other critics, ancient and modern. Although he was critically familiar with the French Literature he did not believe, like Arnold, that the grass on the other side of the English channel was always greener. Even at a time when French drama, in the hands of Corneille and his followers, was achieving the highest excellence Dryden does not hesitate to defend the English mainly on the ground of natural flavour and theatrical effect. The violation of the unities gives more freedom to the dramatist and results in a better dramatic effect. The subplots add to the variety of the plot structure and makes the drama more interesting as does the introduction of many characters. Thus Dryden turns the table and converts weakness into strength and in support of his arguments calls attention to the success of Shakespeare's plays. What is singularly remarkable about Dryden's criticism is that it is not only marked by a fine literary sensibility but more importantly by an unusually strong commonsense, which leads to liberalism. Even to Aristotle he would not pay a slavish homage. "It is not enough," he says "that Aristotle had said so, for Aristotle drew his models of tragedy from Sophocles and Euripides and if he had seen ours, might have changed his mind." Aristotle's judgment was certainly based on the plays that were available to him. Anybody who has witnessed the plays of Brecht or Pirandello or even Beckett, for that matter, knows how correct Dryden is.

Dryden was the first Englishman to attempt any extended descriptive criticism. It is in his criticism that literary analysis, the dominant concern of modern criticism emerges for the first time. There is no surviving analysis of an Elizabethan play and no contemporary analysis of a metaphysical poem. It is in Dryden's *examen* of *The Silent Woman* that we get the first elaborate critical analysis of a literary work in English. In this respect Dryden anticipates New Criticism.

Dryden is also a pioneer in the field of historical criticism. He recognizes that the genius and temperament differ from age to age, and hence literature in different periods of history is bound to be different. He traces the decay of literature in the pre-Restoration period to historical causes and its revival to the jubilation of the Restoration. Thus he recognizes that the Elizabethan Drama and the Restoration Drama are governed by different literary conventions. In this respect Dryden distantly prefigures as an exponent of cultural studies. At the same time in his pluralistic approach to literature he looks forward to the Chicago critics. In this connection David Daiches observes : "We must remember too that Dryden's methods shift according to the work he is discussing : he was intelligent and sensitive enough as a critic to realize that different kinds of work require different critical approaches. He would never have analysed Shakespeare the way he analysed Jonson, for he knew that they were doing different sorts of things" (Daiches 222).

Dryden is the first serious comparatist. He adds a new dimension to literary criticism by his regular employment of the comparative method of evaluation. Here is, for example, his sharp, insightful comparison of Homer and Virgil :

> In the works of the two authors we may read their manners and natural inclinations, which are wholly different. Virgil was a quiet, sedate temper, Homer was violent, impetuous, and full of fire. The chief talent of Virgil was propriety of thoughts, and ornaments of words : Homer was rapid in his thoughts, and took all the liberties both of numbers and of expressions, which his language, and the age in which he lived allowed him. Homer's inventions were more copious, Virgil's more confined. So, if Homer had not led the way, it was not in Virgil to have begun heroic poetry : for nothing can be more evident, than that the Roman poem is but the second part of the *Ilius*; a

> continuation of the same story : and the persons already formed : The manners of Aeneas are those of Hector superadded to those which Homer gave him. The adventures of Ulysses in the *Odyssey* are imitated in the first six books of Virgil's *Aeneid*; and though the ancients are not the same (which would have argued him of a servile copying, and total barrenness of invention) yet the seas were the same in which both the heroes wandered; and Dido cannot be denied to be the poetical daughter of Calypso. The six latter books of Virgil are the four and twenty *Iliads* contracted : a quarrel occasioned by a lady, a single combat, battles fought, and a town besieged. I say not this in derogation to Virgil, neither do I contradict anything which I have formerly said in his just praise, for his episodes are almost wholly of his own invention; and the form which he has given to the telling, makes the tale his own, even though the original story had been the same. But this proves, however, that Homer taught Virgil to design. And if invention be the first virtue of an epic poet, then the Latin poem can only be allowed the second place (*Poems* 269-270).

In his comparison of Ovid and Chaucer also he points out their similarities and differences, remarks that 'the figures in Chaucer are more lively and set in a better light" and then proceeds to examine the strengths and weaknesses of Chaucer in the New Critical fashion. Take another example : 'Milton was the poetical son of Spenser and Mr. Waller of Fairfax; for we have our lineal descendants and clans, as well as other families : Spenser more than one insinuates, that the soul of Chaucer was transfused into his body; and that he was begotten by him two hundred years after his decease" (*Poems* 268). What Dryden is doing, in fact, is that he is trying to define a tradition and here too he anticipates Eliot's theory of tradition. Place by its side, for example, the following comments of Eliot on Dryden : "He is a successor of Jonson, and therefore the descendant of Marlowe; he is the ancestor of nearly all that is best in the poetry of the eighteenth century" (*Dryden* 8). The same method of defining the tradition by genealogy, by "lineal descendants and clans." *An Essay of Dramatic Poesy* which is Dryden's seminal work in literary criticism is developed systematically through a comparative study of the ancients and the moderns, the French drama and the English drama, rhyme and blank verse etc. All the prefaces are marked by Dryden's fine sensibility, and his discerning critical acumen is evident in his comparative approach to the problems at hand. Whether it is a particular author or a particular piece of translation Dryden always tries to establish his point by comparison and analysis and by placing the author in a broader perspective. Although the term "Comparative Literature" is said to have been used in English for the first time in 1886 as the title of a book by an Irish Barrister named H.M. Posnet, Dryden was a practising comparatist more than two hundred years before the term came into existence, and in the twentieth century when Comparative Literature has emerged as a significant school of literary criticism Dryden deserves the credit of being an early practitioner of it.

Now Translation Studies. Translation Studies, an important branch of Comparative Literature, has started gaining ground only since the 1970s so that it has come to be seen only in recent years as a discipline in its own right, and it is amazing that writing in the seventeenth century Dryden discussed problems which we have started taking seriously only now. All his translations are prefaced by insightful essays on the various problems associated with translation. In his preface to *The Life of Lucan* Dryden writes that a translator

> ought to possess himself entirely and perfectly comprehend the genius and sense of his author, the nature of the subject, and the terms of the art of subject treated of. And then he will express himself as justly and with as much life, as if he wrote the original; whereas he who copies word for word loses all the spirit in the tedious transfusion (Bassnett 149).

The key word is "possession". The translator, Dryden argues, must possess himself of everything the author has to offer, for only then he will create something with as much life as an original. What Dryden then modestly admits that in spite of his sincere efforts he has not been able to translate Virgil satisfactorily. The reasons he assigns tells a lot about the problems of translating an author like Virgil in any modern language :

> Virgil...being so very sparing of his words, and leaving so much to be imagined by the reader, can never be translated as he ought in any modern tongue. To make him copious is to alter his character; and to translate him line by line is impossible, because the Latin is naturally a more succinct language than either the Italian, Spanish, French, or even the English (which by reason of its monsyllables, is most compendious of them)... the turn of his verse, the breakings, his propriety, his numbers and his gravity, I have as far imitated as the poverty of our language and the hastiness of my performance would allow (*Poems* 385).

Dryden then goes on to discuss the special properties of Lucretius and Ovid and shows the same critical insight as is evinced in his discussion of Virgil. The entire ***Preface to Sylvae*** is interesting in many ways. It shows Dryden's almost New critical exegesis, his comparative method par excellence, his interest in the aesthetics of sound in poetry, his workshop criticism and his insights into what is now known as translatology. I shall close this section by referring to one more important passage of Dryden where he provides theoretical categories of translation. He writes :

> All translation, I suppose, may be reduced to these three heads : First that of metaphrase, or turning an author word by word, and line by line, from one language to another. Thus, or near his manner, was Horace his *Art of Poetry* translated by Ben Jonson. The second way is that of paraphrase, or translation with latitude where the author is kept in view by the translator, so as never to be lost, but his words are not so strictly followed as his sense : and that too is admitted to be amplified, but not altered. Such is Mr. Waller's translation of Virgil's fourth *Aeneid.* The third way is that of imitation where the translator (if now he has not lost that name) assumes the liberty, not only to vary from the words and sense, but forsakes both as he sees occasion: and taking only some general hints from the original, to run division on the groundwork, as he pleases. Such is Mr. Cowley's practice in turning two odes of Pinder, and one of Horace, into English (*Poems* 509).

Dryden then discusses in detail the relative merits and demerits of these three kinds of translation — metaphrase, paraphrase and imitation — which roughly correspond to modern literalism, middle ground and free translation. Lefevere's seven strategies of translation can be seen only as an elaboration of Dryden's three.

What Dryden means by "possession" would be clear from his own practice, for after all, all Dryden's criticism is what Eliot calls "workshop criticism," a craftsman talking about his craft. Dryden writes :

> "...to be a thorough translator he must be a thorough poet. Neither is it enough to give his author's sense in good English in poetical expressions, and in musical number. For, though all these are exceeding difficult to perform there yet remains a harder task : and 'tis secret of which few translators have sufficiently thought...that is the maintaining of the character of an author, which distinguishes him from all others, and make him appear that individual poet whom you would interpret" (*Poems* 383-384).

Dryden then discusses the distinctive features of Virgil and Ovid and narrates how he, as translator, goes about the job :

> I can make the difference more plain by giving you my own method of proceeding, in my translations out of four several poets...Virgil, Theocritus, Lucretius, and Horace. In each of them I considered the genius and distinguishing character of my author. I looked on Virgil, as a succinct and grave majestic writer : one who weighed not only every thought, but every word and syllable : who was still aiming to crowd his sense into as narrow a compass as possibly he could : for which reason he is so very figurative, that he requires (I must almost say) a grammar apart to construe him. His verse is everywhere sounding the very thing in your ears whose sense it bears : yet the numbers are perfectly varied to increase the delight of the reader; so that the sounds are never repeated twice together... though he is smooth where smoothness is required yet he is so far from affecting it, that he seems rather to disdain it; frequently makes use of synaloephas, and concludes his sense in the middle of his verse. He is everywhere above conceits of epigrammatic wit and gross hyperboles. He maintains majesty in midst of plainness; he shines but glares not; and is stately without ambition, which is the vice of Lucan. I drew my definition of poetical wit from my particular consideration of him. For propriety of thought and words are only to be found in him; and where they are proper they will be delightful. Pleasure follows necessity, as the effect does the cause; and therefore is not to be put into the definition. This exact propriety of Virgil I particularly regarded as a great part of his character (*Poems* 384-385).

To pass from translation to intertext is a simple step forward, because strictly speaking, an intertextual writing, be it fiction or drama, is also a kind of translation as transcreation. Christopher Nash remarks : "...intertextual fiction is genuinely pluralistic in its orientation with reference to utterances outside it and to the material within it. The narrative at once would disintegrate previous texts...and is rendered capable of doing so by its relation to them" (Nash 152). What is true about fiction is also true about drama, and Dryden's systematic rewriting of a number of plays can be seen as early examples of intertextual writing. Although these plays have been traditionally described as adaptations some of them may more appropriately be called intertextual plays, because the adaptations are of such a radical nature that the earlier texts "disintegrate." In *All for*

Love, for example, Dryden transforms Shakespeare's epic vision ranging all over the Mediterranean world over a period of dozen years into a few events that take place in a day and night in the city of Alexandria. In the preface to *All for Love* Dryden says that his intention is "to work up the pity (of the original story) to a greater height."

Accordingly, in Dryden's play those who seem to be noble and heroic at the beginning are shown as victims of great suffering, and thus they arouse a lot of pity in the minds of the audience. Antony suffers terribly because he has to keep up his image as a king and a husband and thus fulfil his obligatory duties. Cleopatra tells Octavia : "If you have suffered I have suffered more." Though she is a queen she thinks that she would have been happier if she had been a cheerful, domesticated wife, content with her home and family. Octavia shines not as an individual but as a type. She becomes the symbol of the family and is defined by her relationships : her role as wife, as mother and as sister. She is brought to Egypt along with her two little daughters to plead her cause. Not only the characters in the play pity her; she exacts a full measure of domestic pity from her husband. In order to achieve his goal Dryden forces Shakespeare's emotional tragedy to conform to the unities of time, place and action. Dryden tries to capture a moment in Antony's life while Shakespeare covers a much longer period. Yet the vitality and naturalness of Shakespeare's play is missing in *All for Love* which ultimately remains an inspired imitation more in the line of eighteenth century sentimental tragedies than that of pure tragedies of Shakespeare.

In *Oedipus*, too, Dryden makes may drastic changes. He introduces a subplot in which Creon wants to marry Eurydice who wants to marry Adrastus, a prince whom Creon has held prisoner. The subplot is quite sensational and Dryden introduces it to make the play more interesting. In Act III Scene I the ghost of Laius appears in a chariot and accuses Oedipus of being a murderer. Jocasta kills her children before she commits suicide, Dryden's obvious intention is to make the play more sensational but in the process the pathetic irony which was there in abundance in the simplicity of Sophocles's play and Oedipus's dialogues is completely lost.

As in *All for Love* so in *Troilus and Cressida* as well Dryden's emphasis is on pity. The scene where Troilus and Cressida argue whether to surrender Cressida or not evokes more pity than honour. Troilus agrees to give Cressida up and Hector says : "I pity thee, indeed I pity thee." When in a heroic manner Hector offers to fight to keep Cressida in Troy Troilus refuses and says : "That you have pitied me is my reward." Dryden took special pains with an added scene of quarrel and reconciliation between Troilus and Hector to depict pity which Dryden considered as "the noblest and most god-like of moral virtues" (Preface to *Troilus and Cressida*). In this connection we can also refer to his dedicatory letter to the Duke of Ormond where Dryden writes : "...my Lord, though you have courage in a heroical degree, yet I ascribe it to you as your attribute : mercy, beneficence, and compassion, claim precedence, as they are first in divine nature" (*Poems* 265).

Dryden wrote 28 plays in a span of 30 years. Many of these are modelled on or influenced by earlier plays — *Tempest* and *Amphitryon* — for example, but the changes there are not so radical as to be considered as intertextual writing. And even the three plays that I have marked out as intertextual suffer by contrast with their originals in spite of, or possibly because of, their neo-classical orientation. Yet the historical importance of these plays as early instances of intertextual writing cannot be gainsaid.

There are certain other modern literary phenomena early examples of which can be traced in the writings of Dryden : Bakhtinian dialogism, carnivalesque and grotesque and Conradian perception of evil. Michael Holquist tells us that in everyday usage dialogue is "a synonym of conversation," and it suggests two persons talking to each other, and this general sense of the word may "obscure its special significance" in the idea of Bakhtin. He argues that

> ...what gives dialogue its central place in dialogism is precisely the kind of relation conversations manifest, the conditions that must be met if any exchange between different speakers is to occur at all. That relation is most economically defined as one in which differences — while still remaining different — serve as the building blocks of simultaneity (Holquist 40).

Dryden's *An Essay of Dramatic Poesy* fulfils this notion of dialogism. The four speakers offer four different points of view and the text is held together by their common interest in the state of drama. The polyphonic text of the *Essay* also illustrates the modern notion of multiperspectivity.

About the grotesque in Dryden Jean H. Hagstrum in his article "Dryden's Grotesque : An Aspect of the Baroque in His Art and Criticism" (Miner 90-119) has identified various kinds of grotesque that one comes across in the writings of Dryden : the social grotesque, the grotesque of superstition, the grotesque of power, etc. The portrait of Sir Martin in *Sir Martin Mar-all* borders on the carnivalesque. Dryden also seems to anticipate Conrad in his perception of evil. In placing Christian conquerors on the soil of the New World Dryden seizes an opportunity to reveal their essential nature. The men professing the faith of the civilized world in a loving, forgiving, self-sacrificing God are soon exposed as avaricious, sadistically cruel and intellectually tyrannical. In other words, as in Conrad so in Dryden as soon as the trappings of the society are removed men degenerate into beasts. They succumb to what Conrad calls "the triumphant forces of darkness."

What I have been trying to suggest is that Dryden has interesting affinities with many aspects of contemporary literature and criticism. The parallels between Dryden's theory and practice *vis-à-vis* the major trends in twentieth century literature and criticism should make it abundantly clear that in a profound sense Dryden is our contemporary. We are closer to him than we are to our immediate literary predecessors.

WORKS CITED

Atkins, J.W.H. *English Literary Criticism : 17th and 18th Centuries*. London : Methuen & Co., 1959.

Bassnett, Susan. *Comparative Literature*. Oxford : Blackwell, 1993.

Daiches, David. *Critical Approaches to Literature*. London : Longman, 1963.

Dryden, John. *The Essays of John Dryden*. 2 vols. Ed. W.P. Ker, Oxford : Clarendon, 1900. Cited as Ker.

Dryden, John. *The Poems of John Dryden*. Ed. John Sargeaunt. London : OUP, 1952. Cited as Poems.

Holquist, Michael. *Dialogism : Bakhtin and His World*. London : Routledge, 1990.

Miner, Earl, ed. *John Dryden*. London : G. Bell & Sons, 1972.

Nash, Christopher. *World Postmodern Fiction*. Essex : Longman Group Ltd., 1993.

Schilling, Bernard N., ed. *Dryden : A Collection of Critical Essays*. New Jersey : Prentice-Hall, Inc., 1963. Cited as *Dryden*.

Spingarn, J.E. *Critical Essays of the 17th Century*, Vol. 2. London : Group, 1908.

5

Sexuality in *The Rape of the Lock*[*]

The history of sexuality is generally viewed in terms of "The Repression Hypothesis." Foucault writes :

> The discourse on modern repression holds up well, owing no doubt to how easy it is to uphold. A solemn historical and political guarantee protects it. By placing the advent of the age of repression in the seventeenth century, after hundreds of years of open spaces and free expression, one adjusts it to coincide with the development of capitalism : it becomes an integral part of the bourgeois order (5).

But Foucault has serious doubts about the hypothesis because he thinks that the basic issue is not "whether one formulates prohibition or permission," but "the way in which sex is put into discourse" (11). And on closer scrutiny, it could transpire. Foucault holds, that "since the end of the sixteenth century, the 'putting into discourse of sex' is far from undergoing a process of restriction, on the contrary it has been subjected to a mechanism of increasing incitement : that the techniques of power exercised over sex have not obeyed a principle of rigorous selection, but rather one of dissemination and implantation of polymorphous societies..." (12). Foucault's aim is not to plead for "expression" in place of "repressions," but that sexuality cannot be defined along a single axis but as a complex of a set of effects produced through various institutions and discourses. Seen in terms of power, then sexuality operates not only by prohibition but also by subtle ways of permission.

The bourgeois culture of the new class that came into being after the Restoration (1660) and increasingly gathered strength carried its

* International Conference on Michel Foucault, Toronto, Canada, 1994.

ideological project into the public sphere by the turn of the century. Ideological projects and the social phantasy were mixed up in a manner that provided a camouflage to the expression of sexuality. It is interesting to see, in the light of this context, how Pope uses sexuality in *The Rape of the Lock* through suggestions and ambiguities. In keeping with the cultural document of the age of Queen Anne, the sexuality is often masked and is marked by ambivalence. On close scrutiny it is revealed that the poem runs simultaneously at two levels, the deeper level regularly undercutting what is said at the surface level. The superficial attitude of glorification or commendation only masks the real attitude of condemnation. The dichotomy between appearance and reality that characterizes the nature of Belinda also characterizes sexuality in the poem.

Let us see. Take the title, for example. The sexuality of the title is too obvious to be missed. But while sexuality is apparent in the word "rape" which usually means the violation of the chastity of women, the sexuality is overt in the sealed metaphor of "lock." Pope does not use the more common word "locks" for hair, but the singular "lock" which, in Freudian terms, stands for the female genital, as the key stands for the male organ. Again, in using the word "rape" in its simple sense of indecent handling of women by men he suggests something morally offensive and intertextually invokes *The Rape of Lucrece and The Rape of Helen* and incidents known to all the students of literature familiar with Shakespeare and Homer. If the "rape" is grossly physical, the "lock" is a complex symbol. As a classical scholar Pope was fully aware of the totemic use of the shearing of lock in Greco-Roman literature and culture. Euripedes, Herodotus, Callidamates and Lucian, among others, refer to the shearing of the virgin lock as a ritualistic preparation for marriage. The hair so sacrified was *crinis sacer* or the "sacred lock" as Belinda's is twice called. So what the Baron violates in *The Rape of the Lock* is not Belinda's virginity but the ritualistic sign of it. To lose the totemic lock is to be dispossessed of the rights and privileges of an unmarried woman. And, more importantly, to Belinda the sign is more important than the thing, the signifier more important than the signified; the appearance is more important than reality. The sealed metaphor of the lock yields its meaning when we come to the epigraph.

> *"Nolueram, Belinda, tuos violare capillos,*
> *Sed juvat hoc precibus me tribuisse tuis"*

(I did not want, Belinda, to violate your locks; but I am glad to have granted that much to your prayers.) It is taken from Epigram XII 84 (with change of one word) of Martial, a Latin poet of the first century. The English translation is Cunnigham's. In the context of sexuality two aspects of the epigraph deserve special consideration : (i) its enigmatic, ambivalent nature and (ii) the sexual implications of Pope's substitution of "Belinda" for the original "Polytimus."

To take the first point first. The enigmatic nature of the epigraph brings out the disparity between conscious rejection of violation and her unconscious desire for it. The reality of desire is masked by the appearance of apathy. A bride's lamentation for the loss of chastity is possibly a masked jubilation. This is perfectly in keeping with the early eighteenth century attitude to sexuality; insistence on appearance which is just the opposite of reality. Next, Pope's replacement of "Polytimus" by "Belinda." The word "Belinda" is charged with enormous significance. It is a word that contains in itself the whole history of Belus the Assyrian Sol and the ideas associated with Circe who is also referred to as the daughter of Sol. Belis is the generic name of the Danaids whose father was Belus. According to the Assyrian Myths, the Danaids used to kill their bridegrooms with a sharp pin on the wedding night. This association will be evoked later in *The Rape of the Lock* when Belinda will attack the baron with a bodkin. Belinda then would become a Danaid. Again Belus was the name of Dido's father, and Dido in spite of her vow to remain faithful to her dead husband and never to remarry, reluctantly discovered that she loved Aeneas. Belinda's association with Circe is also allusively operative in the power she wields on man. Belinda's role as the daughter of Sol is used in the poem through a close association between Belinda and the Sun throughout the poem. Belinda radiates vitality and men are energized in her presence. She is radiant and resplendent and rivals the physical sun, the lesser sun, so to speak. By using the word "Belinda" Pope is able to invoke all these associations which have a direct bearing on the character of Belinda and the role she plays in *The Rape of the Lock.*

The words "dire offence" (1.1), "amorous Causes" (1.1), "Well-bred" (1.7), "assault" (1.7), "*Belle*" (1.7), "soft Bosoms" (1.12) in the opening section of the poem provide the sexual context of the poem. "Sol" (1.13) is introduced quite early in the poem and is given human attributes. Not only that. Sol is rivalled by Belinda whose radiance is expected to out-shine the sun. The juxtaposition of "Lapdogs" (1.15) and "sleepless Lovers" (1.16) not only provides an antiromantic view to love, by equating lapdogs and lovers, but also shows Belinda's domination over her lovers. In fact, later in the poem the lapdog is also equated with the husband ("When Husbands or when Lapdogs breathe their last" III 158).

The lapdog is an apparently innocent surrogate for a husband. Keeping of a lapdog or keeping a dog on the lap has strong sexual overtones. The idea is reinforced when "Shock who thought she slept too long/Leapt up and wak'd his Mistress with Tongue" (11.115-116). Shock is a kind of Icelandic lap dog noted for its mass of hair and is thus related to sexual symbolism of the lock. Shock licking Belinda with his tongue is grossly sexual.

"The Morning Dream" (11.22-114) in which Ariel explains the Rosicrucian machinery of sylphs also highlights the lusty nature of Belinda. The dream which releases the unconscious, reveals the real person. The fact that Ariel appears as "Youth more glitt'ring" than a "Birth-night Beau" (1.23) points to Belinda's unconscious craving for a young man : and not just an ordinary young man but a well-dressed fop. Ariel knows the mind of Belinda and, therefore, assumes a form that is most likely to compel her attention. It is then noticed that Belinda's cheeks would "glow" even in sleep laying bare her real nature. Ariel addresses Belinda as "Fairest of Mortals" (1.27) eulogistically, because he knows that she is susceptible to flattery; and the speech of Ariel which is modeled on Satan's temptations of Eve in a dream, is made to make Belinda realise her own importance. He says : "Hear and believe : thy own Importance Know/Nor bound thy narrow Views to Things below" (11.35-36). "Thy own Importance know" is an inversion of the Socratian doctrine *Nosce Teipsum* that it is essential to "Know Thyself" corresponding to the Indic doctrine, *atmanam biddhi.* In place of Christian humility Ariel exhorts Pride and tells her to disdain the world below. Belinda belongs to the celestial height of the stars and she must contemptuously disregard the mundane. In terms of Belinda as sun-deity she must, like the sun, shine in isolation in a state of complete self-sufficiency. At a grosser level it would mean that Belinda should realize her importance and disregard marital needs. In that case "Things below" would refer to the sexual organs. Ariel's reference to the box at the theater and the ring in Hyde park (1.44) is a sly hint at the sexuality involved in the open air pleasures of the fashionable men and women. The next two lines (11.45-46) refer to the vanity of women in having an expensive equipage, and suggest that vanity is the immortal essence of women. Ariel's speech, then, gradually veers round the essentially carnal desires of women as evidenced in the condition of the "melting Maids" (1.71) participating in "Courtly Balls, and Midnight Masquerades" (1.72). The word "melting" is both literal and figurative. At the literal level it refers to the secretion of the sexual juice on account of the heat of passion; at the figurative level it refers to the emotional involvements leading to yielding. The courtly balls were congenial to sexual gratification of the libidinous assembly. But more important were the midnight masquerades or masked balls. The uses of mask and other disguises provided an ample opportunity for erotic action without disclosing one's identity. A mask hid the appearance and revealed the reality of a character. A mask is a device that, thus, both hides and reveals. In this context Pope's use of the word "Purity" ("the Purity of melting Maids" 1.71) is obviously ironical and indicates the ambivalence that runs through the entire gamut of the poem. The idea is further reinforced by the expressions like "warm Desires" (1.75), "warm Music softens" (1.76) "when Dancing fires" (1.76), "young Coquettes" (1.88), "mystic Mazes" (1.92) and "giddy Circle" (1.93). The expression "bidden Blush" (1.89) is a fine example of Pope's indulgent humour veiled in ambiguity. A bidden blush may be an artificial blush, a redness of cheek with the application of rouge. In that case appearance is different from reality. A blush is presented as a sign of modesty where there is none really. At a deeper level, it is Pope's dig at the ability of the young coquettes to call up a blush at will which is one of their earliest accomplishments. Pope's intention is satirical; the girls master the arts and tricks of coquetry even before they attain womanhood. The fickleness of the girls is presented under a thin cloak of simplicity and innocence. The girls must have a continuously changing succession of frivolities and pleasures. If Florio represents the elegant rhetoric of amorous dalliance, Damon stands for rustic simplicity. The way Pope views the commerce of female affections ("the moving Toyshop" 1.100) suggests that he refuses to take the women seriously. The word "Toyshop" not only means that a girl looks like a shop because of so many decorative articles that she carries on her body, but also implies that the heart is an object of light game, a toy or a frivolity. The present participle "moving" is also ambiguous. In addition to the meaning that the girls change affection it also means that the heart moves or inspires the youth. In a broader perspective the description gives us a realistic picture of the position of women in queen Anne's age : mere decorations. The line "Where Wigs with Wigs, with Sword-knots Sword-knots strive" (1.101) is important in suggesting the nature of Belinda's world. It is a world made up of conventional signs, ornamental, frivolous. It is a surrogate world, a substitute for the world of flesh and blood. It is a world where sword-knots duel instead of swords, where wigs fight with wigs. The signs are more important than the facts they signify. Throughout the poem the emphasis is on signs and tokens, on appearance, so to speak instead of actuality.

Ariel ends his speech with a note of warning : "Beware of all, but most beware of Man!" (1.114). The need for this warning is attributed to Ariel's impression of an imminent danger of Belinda. The fact that Ariel warns her to be "most beware of Man" is an indirect reference to Belinda's natural weakness for the opposite sex. This is corroborated by Belinda's complete disregard of the warning ("all the Vision vanish'd" 1.120), as soon as on awakening her eyes fell "on a *Billet-doux*" (1.118). She could not resist the temptation of reading it, and in the process felt flattered by the account of the spell she had on her lover and the burning passion of love that consumed his heart. The puffed up vanity of Belinda is enacted in the elaborate ritual of Belinda's toilet. The entire toilet scene is a solemn ceremony of paying homage to Pride, "the sacred Rites of Pride" (1.128). It has also been suggested that Pope possibly uses the word "sacred" in its Latin sense of "accursed" thereby giving the whole ceremony an ironical thrust. The "heavenly Image in the Glass" (1.125), in that case, is an expression of Romantic narcissism and explores the social phantasy associated with the sexuality of women. Belinda is both a devotee and a divinity. What she worships is her own image slowly built up through "Cosmetic Powers" (1.124). It may be interesting to note in this connection that the word "cosmetic" is etymologically derived from the word "cosmos," and it may not be wrong to say that the cosmetics constitute the cosmos of Belinda. She derives her heavenly powers from her cosmetics collected from different parts of the world. Pope's gentle sarcasm is evident in the sexual undertones of the expression like "The Tortoise and Elephant unite" (1.135), "Billet-doux" (1.138) and "purer Blush" for example. With the help of the cosmetics an artificial blush is made up to look increasingly pure. It is painted blush and the more powerful the painting, the more natural, and therefore, purer, the blush looks. As Belinda is presented as sun-deity it is only natural that the dressing table would glow with a brilliant radiance and charm.

Before we proceed further we should stop for a while and look at Du Guernier's illustrations, the engravings that faced the opening line of the five cantos of the 1714 edition of *The Rape of the Lock*. Since Pope meticulously controlled the illustrations, the plates may be said to supplement the textual information. The illustration for Canto I shows Belinda asleep with Ariel hovering above, warning her of the impending danger. There is the dressing table with a number of articles including a Bible on it. But what is intriguing is that an ambiguous form can be discerned just beneath the skirt of the table. It may be a leg of the stool which Belinda will use while dressing. But it looks very much like the cloven hoof of a satyr. The illustration thus introduces a pagan symbol and the presence of the satyr drops a large hint about the poem's erotic texture which, like the satyr in the illustration, is only half-hidden.

Canto II

Canto II begins with the reinforcement of the idea of affinity between the Sun and Belinda "the Rival of his Beams" (1.3). Belinda is "Bright as the Sun" (1.13) and "like the Sun" (1.14) her eyes "shine on all alike" (1.14). The erotic underpinning is evident as much in the use of words like "Bosom" (1.14), "Breast" (1.7) as in the comments that the "Jews might kiss the sparkling *Cross* she wore" (1.7). The Jews who are not supposed to kiss a cross, a symbol of Christianity, "might kiss this particular cross because it decorates her white Breast" (1.7) and kissing the cross would be a ruse to kiss the breast. The appearance of religious piety only hides the reality of lust. Pope's tongue-in-cheek attitude is clear in his observation that if Belinda commits some "Female Errors" "Look on her Face, and you'll forget 'em all" (1.13). Her appearance hides reality. The reality is that Belinda "to the Destruction of Mankind / Nourish'd two Locks" (11.10-20). It was a deliberate device, a snare as the word "conspir'd" (1.21) makes it abundantly clear. The voyage on the Thames is a public demonstration of Belinda's glamour and her erotic appeal to the youthful company on the boat. Pope's sarcasm at the levity of Belinda is masked in the anxiety "Whether the Nymph shall break Diana's Law or some frail China Jar receive a Flaw" (11.105-106). Pope's recurring references to a frail China jar suggest that chastity, like a China jar, may be precious but brittle. It is a negative virtue, a purely temporary state of existence, and Belinda exploits this precious possession to ensnare her lovers, and virtually becomes a *femme fatale* with power to seduce, beguile, entertain and destroy the menfolk. The unsavory reference to Belinda's petticoat with "Fifty chosen Sylphs" (1.117) guarding it is also in keeping with the erotic texture of the poem. The petticoat "Tho' stiff with Hoops, and arm'd with Ribs of Whale" (1.120) is vulnerable, because real vulnerability lies in the coquettish nature of Belinda. The richness of the description of the boat, "painted Vessel" (1.47) also reminds one, intertextually, of the "barge she sat in like a burnished throne" of *Antony and Cleopatra* (II. ii 199) and connects Belinda to Cleopatra, the great *femme fatale* of Egypt for whom Antony neglected his duty as a warrior, which, in turn, recalls the liaison of Mars and Venus in Olympus. However Pope does not use the word "barge" which was the customary passenger boat on the Thames and which was generally furnished with a band of rowing crew, but without sails. Pope, instead, uses a boat with a crew, gilded mast and sails. It may be worthwhile to note in this connection that in Pope's time the fashionable ladies often competed with one another in increasing the circumference of the petticoats. The several folds of colored cloth built upon a framework of metal rings held together by whalebones made the lady look like a sailing ship. So, it was quite common to compare a heavily dressed young woman with a sailing boat, and a woman, on account of her vulnerability was also looked upon as the weaker vessel. The "painted vessel" (1.47) which literally refers to the boat metaphorically stands for Belinda artificially made up and puffed up with pride. It is not without purpose, then, that Du Guernier designed for the plate for Canto II a passenger boat with both rowers and sail. And, interestingly, Du Guernier distorted the shape of the little boat so as to make it look like the Ship of Fools that we find illustrated in Renaissance books!

Canto III

In the dramatic structure of *The Rape of the Lock* the climax takes place when the Baron cuts the lock (11.147-154). The totemic implications of the snipping of the lock has already been discussed. The fury of Belinda that follows the violence can be explained only in terms of a totemic loss of virginity. The tragedy, interestingly, is preceded by a mood of mirth and gaiety so nicely captured by Pope in the game of cards and the coffee session. In the card game when Belinda eventually wins she sends forth in joyful triumph ringing shouts of exultation : "The Nymph exulting fills with Shouts the Sky/The Walls, the Woods, and long Canal reply" (11.99-100). Here, Pope indirectly satirizes the unmaidenly manners of Belinda. The real person comes out in the moment of impulse, and the uncivilized behaviour of Belinda shows her as anything but modest and ladylike.

The real nature of Belinda is again hinted at when Ariel suddenly discerns an earthly lover reclined in the heart of Belinda. Pope's description of the situation deserves close examination. Pope writes :

As in the Nosegay of her Breast reclin'd.
He watch'd th' Ideas rising in her Mind.
Sudden he view'd in spite of all her Art.
An Earthly Lover lurking at her Heart
(11.140-144).

The metaphor of "Nosegay" or a bunch of flowers for the breast, is veiled sexuality which is unveiled with the word "reclin'd." The visual image of the physical posture is crudely erotic. The words "rising in her Mind" refer, in Freudian terms, to the expression of the repressed libido, the release of the unconscious. What Ariel, therefore, peeps into is the innermost recess of Belinda's mind, the unconscious that contains the actual nature of Belinda. There is, however, true to her hypocritical nature, a strong effort to hide real findings. But the feelings, her weakness for the opposite sex in general and for a particular gallant at that moment of time, are so strong that Ariel can see through "all her Art." The preposition "in spite of" indicates the conscious effort on the part of Belinda to hide her weakness. We cannot be sure about the identity of the lover whom Ariel discerns in the heart of Belinda. But if it is the Baron then that will partly explain the rash action of the Baron in cutting the lock. In other words, it would mean that the Baron was made bold to take so great a liberty with Belinda only because she had given him cause to believe that he was loved by her. This would also shed a new light on the epigraph : "I did not want Belinda to violate your locks; but I am glad to have granted that much to your prayers."

There are other lines also that have an erotic underpinning in veiled metaphor. Take the following lines, for example : "From silver Spouts the grateful Liquors glide/White *China's* Earth receives the smoking Tyde" (11.109-110). Once we remember that China's earth has already been used as a metaphor for Belinda, a frail *China* Jar (I.1.106), the lines with the trigger words "Spouts," "grateful," "glides" etc. — assume a strong erotic suggestion of a sexual orgasm. Similarly, reference to the scurrilous *Atlantis* notorious for its pornographic appeal is immediately followed by an evocation of the bedroom scene : "As long as *Atlantis* shall be read,/or the small Pillow grace a Lady's Bed..." (11.165-166).

In Du Guernier's illustration of the Canto III the focus is on the moment when the Baron triumphantly holds aloft his "glorious Prize" (1.162) while in his other hand he holds the "fatal Engine" (1.149) that had done the job. While Belinda is being consoled by a man and a woman presumably Sir Plume and Thalestris — another woman, possibly Clarissa, sitting at the card-table disdainfully looks away. But it was Clarissa who had handed the Baron the scissors. Since Clarissa is clear-headed, her attitude to the whole scene has the dramatic significance of a comment on the scene. She is visibly annoyed at the fuss that Belinda makes about, because she knows Belinda's real character.

Canto IV is mainly concerned with the development arising from the cutting of the lock and Belinda's rage. Umbriel's journey to the Cave of Spleen, Sir Plume's Speech and Belinda's speeches make up the Canto. However, Pope's sarcastic references to the weakness of Belinda continue to characterize the texture of the poem. In the very first couplet we learn that "secret Passions labour'd in her Breast" where the words "secret", "labour'd" and "Breast" have erotic suggestions. Incidentally, Pope almost invariably uses the word "breast" in place of "heart." References to "scornful Virgins" (1.4) and "ancient Ladies" (1.6) reveal Pope's real attitude to sex and marriage. Umbriel's journey to the Cave of Spleen and his experience there give Pope an enormous scope to satirize women in general and Belinda in particular, in an indirect manner. The "Grotto, sheltered close from air/And screen'd in Shades from Day's detested Glare" (11.21-22) has an unmistakable affinity with the womb. Spleen is the presiding deity of the gnomes and Belinda, now forsaken by Ariel, has come under the influence of Spleen. Ill Nature and Affectation are the attendant maids. Ill Nature tries to conceal her wicked thoughts by a show of outward piety and Affectation is the personification of pretended modesty and delicacy. Here also the same pattern works : Ill nature is reality; affectation is the mask. Pope obviously exposes with great poetic skill the affectations of the ladies in that great age of affectation and Belinda is a perfect representative of the age. She embodies the spirit of the age. The behaviour of Affectation is worth noting. She always speaks in soft, broken words as if through modesty, and holds her head on one side to show how very obliging and condescending she is to all. She can easily fall into a pretended fit of swooning and strike nice attitude to attract the gaze of her visitors. She would lie prostrate on the rich counterpane of her bed to show off the delicacy of her charming limbs. She would lie on bed in a costly dressing gown apparently to keep her body warm but really to parade its costliness. Affectation, in fact, is only a type of the fashionable ladies of high society. All this only points out the difference between appearance and reality. Sexuality is indulged, but only under the mask of modesty. The lines 47-54 describe various forms to which persons suffering from diseased spleen imagine themselves to have changed. Interestingly, "*Teapots*," "Dipkin" and "Jar" are all containers. They are vessels into which liquid is poured. The subtle erotic suggestions culminate in the crude statement : "and Maids turn'd Bottles, call aloud for Corks" (1.54). The references to the "rumpled Petticoats" (1.72) and "tumbled Beds" (1.72) are strongly suggestive of the sexual act. Incidentally the two lines (71-72) were edited out by Bernard Groom in his edition of *The Rape of the Lock* (London : 1955), obviously for their strong, indelicate and erotic nature. The contents of the bag given by Spleen to Umbriel are soft passions, such as tears, nervous fears and pathetic lamentations that women are prone to indulge in when they feel helpless in their ineffectual anger. Belinda's helpless mood of anger is made worse by the provocative lament of Thalestris that in vain had Belinda taken great care to nourish her locks with hairpin, comb and oil : in vain had she submitted them to the torture of curl papers and strips of pliant lead and the curling tongs. Through Thalestris's lament Pope indirectly lays bare the various instruments of sexuality. The reason why the hair is called "scared Lock" (1.133) and the Baron is described as "The Ravisher" (1.103) is that the lock must be taken as *honoree capitis*, the sacred prenuptial lock, the social insignia of virginal independence. This precisely is the reason why Belinda would rather part with "Hairs less in sight" (1.176) or hair from some other less exposed part of her head. She would even allow the Baron "to seize...any Hairs but these!" (1.176). The sexual suggestion is quite obvious. This is the height of hypocrisy where the gap between appearance and reality is the widest. The Baron, being her lover, can take any liberty with her as he likes, but it must be done in secret. It is only an intimate lover who can "seize...any Hair" (1.176), but at the same time, he must take care to see that her appearance as a virgin remains intact. Belinda feels outraged not so much by her totemic loss of virginity as by the public exposure of it. It is quite possible that Belinda in her fury lost control on her mind and the unconscious, the real wish came out through this *faux pas*.

Du Guernier's illustration depicts two Handmaids. Ill Nature is shown as more witch-like than a witch. Sheets of paper are dimly visible in her left hand. With her stores of prayers visible and her rancoruous lampoons hidden in her breast, she is presented as a consummate hypocrite. Another interesing aspect of the illustration is that, while Du Guernier omits quite a few items, he takes care to illustrate the suggestive line. "Maids turn'd Bottles, call aloud for Corks" (1.54) and we see two bottles already corked intriguingly with men's heads.

In Canto V the conclusion is as best as Pope could manage under the circumstances. All the loose ends are neatly tied up and the characters in conflicts are appeased as much as possible. Pope, however, never abandons his strategy of ambivalent sexuality suggested through words and actions. The speech of Clarissa falls on deaf ears, because Belinda in her egoistic vanity cannot have any clarity of vision. It may also suggest that girls like Belinda are generally creatures of vanity and, therefore, are unable to see things in their proper perspective. Again, Belinda brandishing a bodkin ("And drew a deadly *Bodkin* from her Side" 1.88) resembles a Danaid. The Danaids used to kill their bridegrooms on the wedding nights with sharp pins. Belinda, though apparently sweet and charming, is unexpectedly capable of tremendous rage ("And in soft Bosom dwells such mightly Rage" 1.12) and reminds one of Juno who, though a divinity, could entertain the human passion of hatred. By bringing Juno into the ambience of the poem Pope not only wonders that anger can dwell in such a soft bosom, but also suggests Belinda's unrelenting resentment. Appearance is so deceptive that it is wellnigh impossible to realize her real nature.

Foucault has rightly remarked :

> Since the eighteenth century, Sex has not ceased to provoke a kind of generalized discursive erethism. And these discourses on sex did not multiply apart from or against power, but in the very space and as the means of its exercise (32).

The *Rape of the Lock* as a discourse is an eloquent testimony to it.

WORKS CITED

Foucault Michel : The *History of Sexuality Vol. I : An Introduction.* Trans. Robert Harley, New York : Vintage Books, 1970.

Pope Alexander : *The Rape of the Lock.* Ed. R.K. Kaul, Delhi : Oxford University Press, 1977.

6

Coleridge and the 'Inmost Ind'*

Orientalism was high in the air in the 1790s when Coleridge was in his early youth. Soon after the foundation of the Asiatic Society in Calcutta in 1784 Sir William Jones, the great orientalist wrote a series of essays that made a tremendous impact not only in England but also in Europe. In his first seminal essay "On the Gods of Greece, Italy and India" published in the first volume of the *Asiatic Researches* he suggested that India, generally regarded as uncivilized, might be historically the origin of human civilization. He also translated, among other things, *Manusamhitā*, the ordinances of Menu and *Abhijnānaśakuntalam*, a drama of Kalidas. In his third anniversary lecture he went to the extent of suggesting that both Pythagoras and Plato had drawn their inspiration from the sages of India. He also pointed out that the attitude to the soul that we find in Pythagoras and Plato is similar to what we find in Patanjali's *Yogasūtras* and the *Gītā*. In his celebrated poem, "Hymn to Narayena" Jones presented the sun as the "Eternal Mind." He had written many other hymns also, such as "Hymn to Camadeo," "Hymn to Indra," "Hymn to Lacshmi," "Hymn to Sereswaty," "Hymn to Durga" etc. But the "Hymn to Narayena" is generally regarded as his best. In brief, Jones through his creative and critical writings made the treasures of classical Indian literature accessible to Europe and made historic and momentous contribution to Orientalism. Among those who read Jones in Germany Herder and Friedrich Schlegel felt the need for the study of Sanskrit literature for a better understanding of their own literature and culture. In 1785 the first English translation of the *Gītā* made by Charles Wilkins at the instance of Warren Hastings and published from London as *Bhagavad-*

* International Coleridge Summer Conference, Cannington, U.K., 1998.

Geeta became available to the English speaking world and immediately it had its impact on the English Romantics including Blake, and the *Gītā* has been influencing the literature in English ever since. Then, Thomas Maurice's contribution to Orientalism was simply overwhelming. His seven volume *Indian Antiquities* (London, 1793-1800) and two-volume *History of Hindostan* (London, 1795-98) have been most influential on the literature of the English Romantics in fuelling their imagination. In this connection Beer writes :

> ...the Eastern tales with their great vogue in the eighteenth century, were in many ways a new literary force. Although the European romance-tradition might appear to offer a different way of approaching human experience from that offered by the rationalist and legalist philosophy which dominated intellectual life, its devotion to Christian values made it also an indirect supporter of that order. The Eastern tale...touched daemonic springs in the imagination...(Brett 45-60).

It is quite natural that Coleridge whose antennae were always out to register a new intellectual movement and who had an insatiable intellectual curiosity ranging over the entire world of knowledge at that time would be interested in India presented through the writings of Maurice, Jones and others. Jones identified the earliest school of Indian philosophy with the philosophy of Pythagoras and Plato. The question whether Pythagoras visited India was debated well into the nineteenth century and Coleridge in his *Philosophical Lectures* contended that it was quite probable that Pythagoras had travelled to India and derived his belief in metaphysics not from Egypt as Herodotus would have us believe, but from India. Coleridge, in fact, holds the position that Pythagoras, like his contemporary Buddha, was indebted to the Sankhya for his world view. Coleridge's *Philosophical Lectures* reveals that he was also familiar with other passages to India which brought the Greeks into contact with Indian Philosophy — Apollonias of Tyana and Alexander the Great. From Pythagoras to Plato is a simple step forward. Russell has rightly remarked :

> What appears as Platonism is, when analysed, found to be in essence Pythagorianism. The whole conception of an eternal world revealed to the intellect but not to the senses, is derived from him (86).

And so far as Plotinus is concerned he is the founder of neoplatonism which intensified the mysticism of Plato's teaching. For Plotinus the object of human life is to ascend to the One which is the eternal source of all beings. He also "developed mystical dialectics : the principle of opposites and their unity determines harmony and beauty, evil and ugliness in the world" (*DP 352*). The ideas are so close to the ideas of the *Upanishads* and the *Gītā* that it seems quite probable that schooled in Alexandria which was the meeting place of Greek and Indian cultures he became familiar with the sacred texts of India. We will see later how this idea of Oneness — *hen kai pan* (one and the many) and *omne ens unum* (all in one) — informs the entire literary, philosophical and religious ideas of Coleridge. Revival of Spinoza, in this context, may also be accounted for by Europe's longing for One in the Many — the Whole and the Indivisible — as Spinoza provided an answer through his majestic vision of the Substance of which Matter and Mind are both modifications. Of course, Coleridge, though "sunk in Spinoza" (*CL* I 534) for some time, went back to Plato and Plotinus and through them to Christianity. The relation between Plato and Plotinus *vis-à-vis* Christianity has been succinctly summed up by Russell: "But for him [Plato] Christians would not have thought of Christ as Word" (56). And about Plotinus Russell quotes Dean Inge approvingly : "Platonism is part of the vital structure of Christian theology with which no other philosophy...can work without friction" (289). Russell quips : "Plotinus is the man in whom Plato lived again" (285). Coleridge with his sharp critical insight clearly sees the link and takes a position that all that is valuable in neo-Platonism was ideationally present in the pre-Christian Pythagoras and Plato. The transcendent deity whether of Pythagoras and Plato or, their possible source, the Indian philosophy later materialized in the person of Christ.

II

Of all the gods of Indian pantheon the image of Vishnu as the Only One Being afloat on the cosmic ocean immensely fascinated Coleridge, for, as we shall presently see, more reasons than one. Maurice's *History of Hindostan* had a graphic showing Vishnu reposing for a thousand years. The world expands when he awakes and it contracts as he falls asleep. This image becomes for Coleridge, the objective correlative for the state in which intellect is spiritualized. Then all things counterfeit infinity and a coherent vision is obtained. This image has a significant bearing on the creative process and the esemplastic quality of Coleridgean imagination that "dissolves, diffuses, dissipates in order to recreate" (*BL* 167). In *Anima Poetae* also he appreciates the German word for imagination and remarks :

> How excellently the German *Einbildungskraft* expresses this prime and loftiest faculty, the power of coadulation, the faculty

> that forms *the many into one* — In-eins-bildung (236 emphasis added).

Coleridge's abiding interest in the image of Vishnu is evident in a series of letters and literary encounters. After the initial encounters with Vishnu through Jones and Maurice we see him going to see Bowles on 6th September 1797, and in their meeting they are likely to have discussed the deity in the context of the poems they were planning to write. On the 14th October he writes to Thelwal and in the letter he uses the image of Vishnu afloat on the cosmic ocean as a metaphor for his desired state of mind. He writes :

> My mind feels as if it ached to behold and know something great something one & indivisible — and it is only in the faith of this that rocks or waterfalls, mountains or caverns give me the sense of sublimity or majesty. But in this faith *all things* counterfeit infinity....I should much wish like the Indian Vishna [Vishnu] to float about along an infinite ocean cradled in the flower of the Lotos, & wake once in a million years for a few minutes — just to know that I was going to sleep a million years more (*CL* I 350-51).

The idea of "*one & indivisible*" on which Coleridge puts deliberate emphasis is central to Coleridge's thought. In philosophy, religion and literature he has always aspired after the "*one & indivisible*" In 1803 he writes :

> ...God is not all things, for in this case he would be indigent to all; but all things are God, & eternally indigent of God...if we add to the nature of God either Essence, or Intellect, or Beauty we deprive him of being Good himself, the only *One*, the purely & absolutely ONE (*CN* II 1680).

In this connection Jones's observations are worth remembering :

> Coleridge's strongest belief in a God "Himself in all and all things in himself" has been sustained at least as far back as *The Eolian Harp* where he affirms his belief in a God 'at once the Soul of each and God of all'... (Brett 91-122).

Even later around 1806 when he changed from Unitarianism to Trinitarianism for him Trinity was "Tri-Unity" :

> ...neither of these Three can be conceived *apart* or *confusedly* so that the Idea of God involves that of Tri-Unity (*CL* II 1189-90).[1]

Still later on 31 January 1819 he expresses his admiration for Rammohun, an Indian Advaitin and writes to Southey :

> A Brahmin who has I hear arisen to attempt what we have both so often wished — *viz.* to be the Luther of Brahmanism — and with all the effect that could be wished considering the times (*CL* IV 917).[2]

By 1824, however, Coleridge became at least formally a Trinitarian. In this connection Chambers writes :

> Coleridge was able, from 1824 onwards, to devote himself to what he had long considered to be the great task of his life, the defence of Trinitarian Christianity, both as a practical rule for conduct and for politics, as a necessity of metaphysical thought (310).

Anyway, after writing to Thelwal on 14 October 1797[3] about "the Indian Vishna" he writes to Bowles for a copy of his poem "The Spirit of Discovery by Sea" in which Vishnu figures predominantly as protecting Noah's ark at Hindu Kush or the Indian Caucasus which was then supposed to be the center of the earth. The importance given to Vishnu by an Englishman, and by extension, by the English orientalists of the time, becomes more significant when we notice that in the course of his letter to Thelwal Coleridge says that he has "put this feeling in the mouth of Alhadra," a character in his play, *Osorio*. The play was begun in March 1797 and completed before September 13, 1797. Coleridge goes on to say :

> A moorish Priest (who has been with her & then left her to seek men) had just mentioned the owl — 'It's note comes dreariest in the fall of the year' — this dwells on her mind — & she bursts into this soliloquy" (*CL* I 350).

The entire soliloquy is interesting from the philosophical point of view but the lines that immediately concern us are :

> *It were a lot divine in some small skiff*
>
> *Along some Ocean's boundless solitude*
>
> *To float for ever with a careless course.*
>
> *And think myself the only Being alive !*
>
> (*CL* I 351 emphasis added).[4]

The idea of intense repose associated with the image of Vishnu is used again in an unpublished historic drama of Five Acts, *The Triumph of Loyalty* (1801). There Earl Henry, a character in the play, remarks :

> Oh! there is Joy above the name of Pleasure,
>
> Deep self-possession, and intense Repose.
>
> No other than as Eastern Sages feign,

The God who floats upon a Lotos Leaf,

Dreams for a thousand ages; then awaking.

Creates a world, and smiling at the bubble,

Relapses into bliss (*CPW* II 1071 emphasis added).

It is noteworthy that part of the passage of this unpublished play is used in the dramatic fragment, "The Night Scene" but with a significant change in tone :

Earl Henry...Oh! there is a joy above the name of pleasure, Deep self-possession, an intense repose.

Sand (with a sarcastic smile).[5] No other than as eastern sages paint

The God, who floats upon a lotos leaf

Dreams for a thousand ages; then awaking,

Creates a world, and smiling at the bubble,

Relapses into bliss (*CPW* I 422).

Now coming back to his letter to Thelwal of 14 October 1797 we notice that Coleridge has made important changes. One change is related to the image and the other is related to the spelling. In the traditional image Vishnu is not afloat on a lotus or a lotus leaf, but on a snake. It is Brahma, the god of creation who sits on the lotus stemming out from the navel of Vishnu. But by placing Vishnu on the lotus Coleridge may be said to have bestowed the attributes of Brahma to Vishnu so that Vishnu — as in *Vishnupurana* — becomes both the creator and the preserver. The change in spelling — form Vishnu to Vishna — is possibly intended to suggest the affinity between Vishnu and Krishna, the earthly incarnation of Vishnu. Moreover, in the first chapter of the *Ordinances of Menu* which Coleridge had read — he particularly admired the first chapter[6] — the great sages are told how Brahma after creating the universe was reabsorbed into the Supreme Being. This might have led Coleridge to take the position that Vishnu appropriates Brahma and becomes The One. The mixing up of the lotus and the lotus leaf, similarly, may have been occasioned by Coleridge's memory of two literary documents. In the review of Kindersley's *Specimens of Hindoo Literature* (London, 1794) published in *Monthly Review* (1795) a reference is made to the lotus not the leaf. In the *Gītā* also in Chapter XI during the mystic vision offered by Krishna to Arjuna, Brahma is presented as sitting on a lotus rising from the navel of Vishnu.[7] The lotus leaf, however, does figure in the *Gītā* but in a completely different context. In Chapter V we are told that a man who entrusts his life to the Supreme Being remains like the leaf of the lotus unaffected by waters.[8]

There are two important aspects of the image of Vishnu which have significant bearing on Coleridge's theory of poetry. At one level, it is contemplation followed by action. Or, more precisely, infinite contemplation punctuated by brief periods of finite action. It is this dialectical relationship between the infinite and the finite, between contemplation and action, between passivity and activity that constitutes the essence of Vedanta and neo-Platonism. Jones had harped on this affinity in a series of articles and it is only natural that Coleridge would find it after his heart and accept it. Secondly, and more importantly, this dialectical relationship of opposites is central to Coleridge's theory of Imagination. The mind full of scattered fragments of memory remains inert, neutral, unchanged — passive, in a word — and then suddenly there is an outburst of creativity. In this connection Lowes observes :

> The shaping spirit of imagination sits aloof, like God as he is commonly conceived, creating in some thaumaturgic fashion out of nothing its visionary world. The ways of creation are wrapt in mystery (428).

This is how a poem like "*Kubla Khan*" is created. In the first place it was created during a period when Coleridge was in a state of repose, though on a much smaller scale, like "the Indian Vishna" :

> The Author continued for about three hours in a profound sleep, at least of the external senses, during which time he has the most vivid confidence, that he could not have composed less than from two to three hundred lines; if that indeed can be called composition in which all the images rose up before him as *things*, with a parallel production of correspondent expressions, without any sensation or consciousness of effort. On awaking he appeared to himself a distinct recollection of the whole and taking his pen, ink, and paper, instantly and eagerly wrote the lines that are preserved (*CWP* I 296).[9]

Again, within the poem itself a miracle — juxtaposition of heat and ice — is realized. "A sunny pleasure dome with caves of ice". The act of creation itself, in fact, is "a miracle of rare device" and the poem reconciling opposites including man's infinite yearnings for a finite earthly paradise with a fine dome and well-defined boundaries, acts out the miracle.

III

Now about the "cave of ice." Apart from the fact that the cave as a symbol has a long literary tradition ranging from Socrates to Forster and the psychic dimensions acquired since Freud, literally caves were abundant in ancient India. They were the dwelling places of sages and philosophers, and most sages were also philosophers. But the cave of ice that we find in "Kubla Khan" can be identified with an actual Indian cave. The reference is to the cave of Amarnath in Kashmir. In his *Notebooks* Coleridge refers to Maurice's description of the cave of Amarnath :

> In a cave in the mountains of Cashmere an Image of Ice, which makes its appearance thus — ["] two days before the new *moon* there appears a bubble of Ice which increases in size everyday till the 15th day, at which it is an ell or more in height : then as the moon decreases, the Image ["] does also till it vanishes. Read the whole 107th page of Maurice's Indostan (*CN* I 250).

And in the very next note (241) he refers to Major Rennell. It is worth noting that James Rennell in his *Memoir of a Map of Hindostan* (London, 1793) had also referred to this cave :

> The pardonable superstition of the sequestered inhabitants, has multiplied the places of worship of Mahadeo whose image it was that appeared in the cave...(143).

If the cave of Amarnath provides Coleridge with the most powerful metaphor for a poem, the landscape of Kashmir and its long philosophical tradition also contribute immensely to the poetry of Coleridge and the aesthetic and philosophical foundations of it. The dome of "Kubla Khan" which, according to Wilson Knight and others "stands for the achievement of civilization, the artefact created by man from the wilderness" (Adair 122) may have come either directly from Bernier's account of his travels in "Cashmere" where he saw it in the king's pleasure garden[10] or indirectly from Maurice's description of Kashmir as the paradise of India :

> For myself, were it consistent with sacred writ to place the seat of Paradise any where but in the immediate neighbourhood of the Euphrates, I should incline with Bernier to conclude it was indeed in India, though not in the parched land of Ceylone, but in the warm, delicious and fertile valley of Cashmere, the present Paradise of Asia... (*HH* I 365).

A great poem as it is "Kubla Khan" is amenable to many kinds of interpretations depending on the interpretations of the symbolic significance of the various objects — chasm, river, dome, cave, ice etc. — and the ways in which the images in the poem melt into one another. The fact remains, nevertheless, that the landscape in many of its details draws heavily on the landscape of Kashmir. In fact, in English consciousness and the romantic imagination Kashmir was gradually identified as the oriental paradise. Southey made use of it in *The Curse of Kehama* (1810) a book which, incidentally, Shelley liked very much and recommended to others. Moore used it in *Lalla Rookh* (1817), Shelley himself used it in *Alastor* (1816) and *Prometheus Unbound* (1820). But Coleridge is possibly the first romantic poet to make such a creative use of the landscape of Kashmir. In fact, it would not possibly be wrong to say that the physical landscape of Kashmir provides an objective correlative for a highly charged psychic landscape and the mysterious process of creation for Coleridge.

IV

In *Biographia Literaria* Coleridge names India as one of the four countries where "the analysis of mind had reached its noon and manhood" (54). It is true that Coleridge's admiration for the ancient Indian philosophy is due to his discovering its affinity with neo-Platonism of which he may be said to be an exponent. It is also true that he made a creative use of the Indian philosophy and the Indian landscape in his poetry. But it should be borne in mind that his admiration for India was never uncritical. While, for example, he admired the first chapter of the *Ordinances of Menu* as something sublime he did not hesitate to criticize the Ordinances in general, and remarked : "Menu's Ordinances exhibit a mournful picture of an hideous Union of Priest-craft & Despotism"[11] (*CL* I 252). In fact, after 1806, that is after he became a Trinitarian his interest in Indian religion began to wane and in his later years he became sarcastic — a view expressed in the extract from "The Night Scene" we have already discussed — in his attitude to what he called "Brahman Theosophy" (Muirhead 284). He, in fact, regretted his earlier reverence :

> I have myself paid this debt of homage on my first presentation to these foreign potentates by aid of the great linguists above mentioned (Muirhead 284).

The linguists "above mentioned" are Jones and Wilkins and Coleridge had a feeling that these linguists and other orientalists as well gave a highly exaggerated account of the Indian gods and goddesses and overestimated their importance. These gods and goddesses according to Coleridge

> ...dance in and out like wandering flashes, or motley aliens from a distant country, the mutes of the show, often enough to remind us of their incompatibility with the doctrines of omneity and infinity, which are the constant theme and the philosophic import of the Indian theology; but without an attempt to resolve the riddle (Muirhead 284).

He even chides Wilkins for discovering an affinity between the story of the *Gītā* and the Miltonic epic and inveighs against the opinion:

> "...if there is one character of genius predominant in Milton it is this that he never passes off bigness for greatness" (Muirhead 283).

Actually what irks Coleridge about the Indian theology is its pantheistic character. And to Coleridge pantheism tantamounts to atheism. In this connection we can refer to his letter to Rev. Joh Edwards written in March 1796. Coleridge writes :

> How is it that Dr. Priestley is not an atheist? — He asserts in thee different Places, that God not only *does*, but *is*, everything. — But if God be every Thing, every Thing is God : which is all the Atheists assert (*CL* I 192).

So, one reason for Coleridge's change of heart is related to his missionary activity and the threat that pantheism posed to the orthodox Christianity of a highly Anglican cast. He had, however, much against his will, always felt a strong pull towards pantheism. In fact as Dorothy Edmund has pointed out, he was never able to complete his philosophy of "I am" with a philosophy of "It is" (Brett 195-220). This possibly is also the reason why in his *Philosophical Lectures* Coleridge tries to dissociate Pythagoras not so much from Buddhism as from Brahmanism which to him was synonymous with pantheism.[12] Another possible reason is that the successors of Jones did not have his vision. Jones was essentially a literary man with a high originality and clear vision. Colebroke who succeeded Jones might be a better scholar but he had none of these qualities. As a result Orientalism lost its charm and attraction and soon a reaction against it also set in.

V

What I have been trying to suggest in the foregoing discussion is that in his response to Orientalism Coleridge was mainly interested in three important aspects of India : Indian landscape, Indian religion and Indian philosophy. The Indian landscape fascinated him as a romantic poet, fuelled his imagination and he made an excellent use of it in his poetry. He also maintained an admiration for "those great Priests of Nature who formed the Indian Worship in its purity, when all things, strictly of Nature, were reverenced according to their importance" (*CN* II 2600). He rejects Indian religion or more precisely the Indian pantheon and the Hindu view of gods because of his belief that Indian religion does not make a distinction between All-things-God and All-things-in-God so that there was no distinction between the Creator and the Creation (*PL* II). Here Coleridge, to my mind, suffers from a critical myopia because of his prejudice against "Brhaman Theosophy." The entire Chapter XI of the *Gītā* is concerned with Arjuna's vision of the Universal Form within the body of Krishna. We may also recall, in this connection, a dream that Coleridge had in his early youth. There is a strange affinity between Arjuna's vision of the Universal Form and Coleridge's dream. Coleridge records :

> I SAW in early youth, as in a dream, the birth of the planets; and my eyes beheld as *one* what the understanding afterwards divided into (1) the origin of the masses, (2) the origin of their motions, and (3) the site or position of their circles and ellipses. All the deviations, too, were seen as one intuition of one the self-same necessity, and this necessarily was a law of spirit, and all was spirit. And in matter all beheld the past activity of others or their own — and this reflection, this echo is matter — its only essence, if essence it be. And of this, too, I saw the necessity and understood it, but I understood not how infinite multitude and manifoldness could be one; only I saw and understood that it was yet more out of my power to comprehend how it could be otherwise — and in this unity I worshipped in the depth of knowledge that passes all understanding the Being of all things — and in Being their sole goodness — and I saw that God is the One, the Good — possesses it not, but is it (*AP* 77).

There is an unmistakable affinity in the nature and substance of Arjuna's vision of the Universal Form and Coleridge's dream. Both are marked by a sense of wonder and incomprehensibility of the vision/dream of God as many in one.

Coleridge's strongest admiration, however, undoubtedly was for Indian philosophy and the belief of the Vedanta in a Supreme Being — One and Indivisible, mainly because of its affinity with the ideas of Pythagoras, Plato, Plotinus and partly Spinoza. One single idea that colours and characterizes all his writings — philosophical, theological and literary — is his insistence on *one* harmonious whole reconciling all opposites.

Coleridge is a Unitarian not in a narrow theological sense but in a most profound sense of the term in which it covers the entire universe of discourse. It is thus that India became a part of his consciousness and left its mark on his writings.

NOTES AND REFERENCES

1. In this connection an entry in CN II (2448) 17.22 is worth noting : "Thinking during the perusal of Horsley's Letters in Rep. to D.P. objections to the Trinity on the part of Jews, Mahometans, and Infidels, it burst upon me at once as an awful Truth what 7 or 8 years ago I thought of proving with a *hollow Faith* and for an *ambiguous purpose*, my mind then wavering in its necessary passage from Unitarianism (which I have often said is the religion of a man whose reason would make him an Atheist but whose Heart and Common sense *will* not permit him to be so) thro' Spinosism into Plato and St. John/No Christ, No God! — This I now feel with all its needful evidence, of the Understanding : would to God, my spirit were made to conform thereto — that No Trinity, no God."
2. Incidentally Rammohun had a temporary alliance with the Trinitarian Baptist missionaries of Serampore and he even succeded in converting one of their members to Unitarianism in 1821. See Leask 139.
3. See *CPW* II 514 n.
4. In the play, Act V Sc. i 11 53-56 (*CPW* II 584) the initial capital letters of the nouns have been replaced by small letters.
5. It is interesting to note the direction "with a sarcastic smile," because by 1813 Coleridge had completely rejected the Indian gods.
6. "The first chapter contains sublimity" (*CL* I 252).
7. *Brahmanamiśam kamalāsanastha*" (Brahma the ruler seated on his lotus seat). See the *Gītā* Chapter XI verse 15. And Verse 9 says "*prajāpatistvam*" (You are Brahma).
8. "Padmapatramibambhasā" (As lotus leaf by water). See the Gītā Chapter V Verse 10.
9. Adair while agreeing that "Kubla Khan" came to Coleridge "unbidden in sleep" tries to relate it to "that reverie where the well-loved myths of Greece merged in his dreaming mind" (114). If the river Helicon associated with Orpheus sinks and rises again and so does the Alpheus or Alph of "Kubla Khan" we should remember that the river Saraswati, the oldest Indian river associated with Saraswati, the Indian goddess of learning also hides under the earth and rises again. Furthermore, it is also significant that *Alpha* the first Greek letter is parallelled by the first Sanskrit letter *A* which also happens to be the first letter of Rigveda and is of the same importance. It is also possible to associate the underworld with the unconscious that throws up images to the surface world, the world of the conscious, from time to time.
10. See Lowes 353.
11. It is a view that would be subscribed to by many in modern times.
12. Coleridge here fails to realize the philosophical climate provided by the Upanishads.

WORKS CITED

Adair, Patricia M. *The Waking Dream*. London. Edward Arnold, 1967.

Appleyard, J. A. *Coleridge's Philosophy of Literature*. Cambridge : Harvard UP, 1965.

Beer, John. ed. *Coleridge's Variety*. London : Macmillan, 1974.

—. *Coleridge, the Visionary*. London : Chattoa & Windus, 1959.

Brett, R.L. ed. *S.T. Coleridge. London* : G. Bell & Sons, 1971.

Chambers, E.K. *Samuel Taylor Coleridge : A Biographical Study*. London : Oxford UP, 1938, Rpt. 1950.

Coleridge, S.T. *Anima Poetae*. Ed. E.H. Coleridge. London : William Heinemann, 1896. Cited as *AP*.

—. *Biographia Literaria*. Ed. George Watson. London : Everyman's Library, 1971. Cited as *BL*.

—. *Collected Letters of Samuel Taylor Coleridge*. Ed. E.L. Griggs. 6 vols. London : Oxford UP, 1956-71. Cited as *CL*.

—. *The Complete Poetical Works of Samuel Taylor Coleridge*. Ed. E.H. Coleridge. 2 vols. London : Oxford UP, 1912. Rpt. 1975. Cited as *CPW*.

—. *The Notebooks of Samuel Taylor Coleridge*. Ed. Kathleen Coburn. 2 vols. London : Routledge & Kegan Paul, 1962. Cited as *CN*.

—. *Philosophical Lectures*. Ed. Kathleen Coburn. London, 1919. Cited as *PL*.

—. Drew, John. *India and the Romantic Imagination*. London : Oxford UP, 1987.

Leask, N. *British Romantic Writers and the East*. Cambridge : Cambridge UP, 1992.

Lowes, J.L. *The Road to Xanadu : A Study in the Ways of the Imagination*. Boston, 1927. Rpt. New York : Vontage Books, 1959.

Maurice, Thomas. *The History of Hindostan*. 2 vols. London, 1795-98. Cited as *H.H.*

Muirhead, John H. *Coteridge as Philosopher*. London : George Allen & Unwin, 1954.

Rosenthal, M. and P. Yudin, eds. *A Dictionary of Philosophy*. Moscow: Progress Publishers, 1967. Cited as *DP.*

Russell, B. *A History of Western Philosophy*. London : Unwin Paperbacks, 1984.

Srimad Bhagavad Gītā. Tr. Swami Vireswarananda. Madra : Ramakrishna Math, 1987. Cited as *Gītā*.

7

Shelley, India, and Bengali Poetry*

I

In his letter to Thomas Love Peacock written on October 22, 1821 Shelley expressed his desire to come to India as an employee of the East India Company. Peacock discouraged him : "I should not like your Indian project (which I think would agree neither with your mind nor body), if it were practicable. But it is altogether impossible. The whole of the Civil Service of India is sealed against all but the covenanted servants, who are inducted into it through established gradations, beginning at an early period of life."[1] Even in January 1822, a few months before he was drowned we find Shelley still unhappy about his inability to come to India. He wrote to Peacock in his letter of 11 January 1822 : "I wish I had something better to do than furnish this jingling food for the hunger of oblivion, called *verse* : but I have not, & since you give me no encouragement about India I cannot hope to have."[2] In this connection Peacock wrote in his *Memoirs* that Shelley "had expressed his desire to be employed politically at the court of a native prince and I had told him that such employment was restricted to the regular service of the East India Company."[3] That Shelley was serious about his intention is evident from the fact that he had already ordered James Mill's *History of British India* to equip himself intellectually for the purpose. His intention was not just to visit India but to settle here. At that time the Shelleys had already lost two children — Clara and William — to the vagaries of Italian climate, did not feel like returning to England and were seriously contemplating of settling in some unseen lands such as India.

---

* National Seminar on the occasion of the bi-centenary of Shelley's birth, Calcutta, 1992.

Shelley's interest in India can possibly be traced to his exposure to the writings of Sir William Jones, his reading of books like Edward Moore's *Hindu Pantheon*, a book which he is known to have acquired from his bookseller. There are passages in Jones which have direct bearing on the philosophy of Shelley.[4] Another instance of Shelley's interest in India is his fascination for Southey's *The Curse of Kehema* (1810), a poem depicting Indian life. Shelley wrote to Elizabeth Hitchner on June 11, 1811 that *The Curse of Kehema* was his "most favourite poem." In fact Shelley had been anxiously waiting for its publication, and on December 2, 1810 he had written to John Joseph Stockdale enquiring about it : when do you suppose that Southey's *Curse of Kehema* will come out, I am curious to see it...."[5] There is another book which Shelley approvingly referred to, around this time, in several letters. The book is Lady Morgan Sydney Owenson's (1776-1859) *The Missionary : an Indian Tale* (3 vols. 1811). Shelley wrote to Elizabeth Hitchner on 11 June 1811) : "I have just finished a novel of the day — the Missionary by Miss Owenson."[6] Again, on 19 June 1811 he wrote to Thomas Jefferson Hogg : "The only thing that has interested me, if I except your letters has been one novel. It is Miss Owenson's *Missionary* an Indian tale. Will you read it, it is really a divine thing. Luxima the Indian is an Angel. What pity that we cannot incorporate these creations of Fancy; the very thought of them thrills the soul. Since I have read this book I have read no other — but I have thought strangely."[7] Again on 20 June 1811 he urged Hogg : "Have you read a new novel, the Missionary by Miss Owenson : It is a divine thing. Luxima the Indian Priestess, were it possible to embody such a character, is *perfect.* The Missionary has been my companion for some time. I advise you to read it."[8] Shelley's interest in India was possibly reinforced in 1820 when Shelley's cousin Medwin spent some time with them in Pisa. Thomas Medwin (1788-1869) had come to India as lieutenant in the Twenty-fourth Light Dragoons, in July 1819 had been put on half pay with the rank of captain. After leaving India he spent some time in Geneva where he met Trelawny and later went to Shelley in October 1820. Medwin was a great admirer of his cousin and did a lot to advance his reputation. In his letter to Clairmont dated 29 October 1820 Shelley wrote : "I have read or written nothing lately, having been much occupied...by Medwin who relates wonderful and interesting things of the interior of India."[9] Mrs. Shelley in her "Note on poems of 1822" also refers to Shelley's favourite companion, Edward Ellerker Williams of the 8th Light Dragoons who had begun his life in the navy, and had afterwards entered the army; he had spent several years in India...."[10] The image of the exotic India had appealed to Shelley and fired his imagination, and it is significant that we so often come across oriental imageries in his poetry especially in *Queen Mab, Alastor, Prometheus Unbound and Hellas.*

II

Although Shelley could not physically come to India during his life time he came to India, one might say, with a vengeance, as a poet after the introduction of English education in India. The Hindu College was established in 1817 and by 1830, thanks to the good offices of Henry Vivian Louis Derozio, the students became acquainted with the English Romantics. Following Macaulay's Minutes on Education (02 February 1835) and the introduction of English education, the Indian community, in general, and the Bengali intellectual milieu, in particular, suddenly discovered "realm of gold" including the writings of Shelley. Shelley's philosophy of love, spirit of revolution, love of Nature, call for atheism, idea of beauty and his sensuousness captivated their mind. Shelley's romantic imagination and lyrical outbursts had an immediate appeal to the Bengali readers. Professor Francis Turner Palgrave's *The Golden Treasury of Songs and Lyrics* came out in 1861 and his generous selection of Shelley's poems — as many as 22 entries, twice as many as any other poet except Shakespeare and Wordsworth — partly monitored the taste of the reading public. It is, therefore, not surprising that the poems that have been most popular with the Bengali readers are the poems that we find in *The Golden Treasury* : "To a Skylark," "Ozymandias," "Ode to the West Wind," "Love's Philosophy," "Stanzas written in Dejection near Naples" etc. The longer poems are blithely ignored by most readers. Of course Tagore, we will see later, was a brilliant exception. It is debatable whether the poems included in *The Golden Treasury* are really representative poems of Shelley. Should we not go to the longer poems ("Hymn to Intellectual Beauty," "Alastor," "The Triumph of Life," for example) and the plays (*Prometheus Unbound, The Cenci,* for example) for a better understanding of Shelley? However, Palgrave had his limitations, because his anthology was of "songs and lyrics" so that he tried to choose the most song-like poems. Anyway the fact remains that "Ode to the West Wind" has since appeared in as many as 77 anthologies, closely followed by "To a Skylark" (76)[11]. Despite Arnold's rejection of Shelley as an "ineffectual angel" Shelley remained and continues to remain popular with the Bengali readers.

III

The people at the helm of Bengali literature felt that the knowledge and the aesthetic experience of the English poems could be profitably used for the enrichment of Bengali literature. In one issue (Vaiśākh 1266 B.S. : May 1859) of the first Bengali daily *Saṁbād Prabhākar* (1839) the editor, possibly Isvar Gupta whom Bankimchandra had accepted as his mentor[12] and who might be regarded as the literary dictator and custodian of culture of his time exhorts the readers :

> It is extremely important to keep up the habit of translating English poems [into Bengali], although it is a quite difficult job, because a good translation demands complete submission to another's psychology and intention. But once habituated and successful there is no end to joy. Please seriously try to translate the best of English poems into Bengali. Don't neglect it.[13]

Isvar Gupta's successors also never failed to appeal to the readers, year after year, to translate the best English poems into Bengali. In response to these calls many English poems including the poems of Shelley were translated. In 1859 when Isvar Gupta died English education had already spread from cities to the distant, interior villages. Students were attending colleges and the University of Calcutta had been established. The educated modern readers thirsted for a new kind of poetry. It was around this time that Madhusudan (1824-73), trained in English sensibility appeared on the scene, brought about a radical change in theme, treatment and technique of Bengali poetry, and in a significant way bridged the East and the West. In the 1840s Madhusudan was engrossed in English Romantic literature. That was the period when the English Romantics were his constant companion. The study of the Romantics suffused his sensibility in such a way that it may not always be possible to isolate or identify the influence of Shelley. But sometimes the influence is quite visible as in the case of *Tilottamāsambhab Kāvya* which can claim to be the "first stepping stone to modern poetry."[14] The treatment of the romantic beauty of Tilottama and her eternal charm bears the unmistakable stamp of Shelley.

Hemchandra Bandyopadhyay (1838-1903) whose admiration for Shelley is evident in his translation of "To a Skylark"[15] into Bengali, also drew inspiration from Shelley's hope for the revival of Greco-Roman culture and dreamt of a union of the East and the West. The poems of Biharilal Chakravarty (1835-1894) are marked by a feeling of romantic languor that is so typical of Shelley. The quest-motif and the intense longing for a union with the Ideal Beauty that we find in *Premaprabāhinī* (1870) have a striking affinity with Shelley's *Alastor*. In fact, there are passages in the fifth canto of *Premaprabāhinī* which seem to be distinct and not very distant echo of some passages of *Alastor*.[16] Biharilal's experience of the ecstatic moment also finds expression in utterances which closely parallel lines of "Hymn to Intellectual Beauty."[17] Like Shelley, Biharilal is also a mystic poet of love and beauty to whom life and love are practically synonymous. The Shelleyan Spirit of Beauty can also be discerned in some passages.[18] Tagore also identified Biharilal's "Sarasvati" as Shelley's "Spirit of Beauty."[19] Even the boat image that is central to the poem is essentially Shelleyan. Debendranath Sen (1855-1920)[20] had been brought up under the influence of Biharilal, and, accordingly, we find the same attitude to Nature and Love that characterizes the English Romantics, particularly, Shelley. His *Ãkhir Milan* (Meeting of Eyes) is perceptibly influenced by Shelley's "Love's Philosophy," Akshay Kumar Baral (1860-1919) closely follows Shelley's "Epipsychidion," particularly the fourth stanza, in his conception of the Spirit of Beauty.[21]

IV

Now we come to Tagore, the greatest poet of the century, if not of all time. Tagore was exposed to Western culture from his early childhood, as his grandfather, Prince Dwarakanath Tagore was "a partner in Empire." Tagore had an intimate acquaintance, at an impressionable age with the English Romantics whose influence can be distinctly discerned in the early poems of Tagore. The poems are full of vague ideas, immature discussion of the mysteries of creation and nebulous imagery. Poems like "Tārakār Ātmahatyā"[22] (A Star Commits Suicide), "Sṛṣṭi, Sthiti, Pralay" (Creation, Preservation, Destruction) reveal the poet's state of mind. We also learn from *Jībansmṛti* (Autobiographical Reminiscences) that the young Tagore was much impressed and attracted by the intensity of feeling and the force of expression of the Romantic poets.[23] A keen reader of *Abodhbandhu* Tagore read and was fascinated by the story of *Alastor* published in it. The story with all its romantic longing and languor had reached the deepest recesses of Tagore's psyche and was an abiding influence till his old age. We shall come to that later. Suffice it to say for the time being that the hero of *Kabikāhinī*[24] is largely modelled on the hero of *Alastor*. Then, in the early eighties Tagore wrote several essays in *Bhāratī* stressing the need for enriching Bengali poetry through a perceptive study of the English Romantics. In one of these[25] Tagore wrote :

> We have the skin of a rhino that doesn't find pleasure in a soft touch. That's why we are fond of Byron. Very few Bengali people can appreciate the ethereal imagination of Shelley, which is as soft as moonlight.[26]

He also translated some poems of Shelley. One obvious purpose was to acquaint the budding poets with the Shelleyan sensibility, and the other purpose, not so obvious, was to exploit the resources of the Bengali language, to "purify the dialect of the tribe," so to speak, and forge it into new forms.

The mood of dejection reflected in the dull, monotonous, dragging movement of the English lines is perfectly retained in the diction and the metrical pattern used by Tagore in his translation of "Stanzas written in dejection near Neples."[27] Tagore will again refer to this poem, much later in his life, in 1927 to be precise, in one of his letters written during his journey to Java. There, however, the feeling of pathos inherent in the cry of the new-born will be seen as symptomatic of a universal pathos, a cosmic cry. To come back to the point, Shelley continued to interest Tagore. On 20 March 1895 Tagore wrote to Indira Debi :

> Do you know why I particularly like Shelley more than many other great men? His character was free from any kind of conflict; he never tried to analyse himself or anybody else — his nature had a seamless totality. Children, and sometimes women, appeal to us, because of their natural simplicity, because they are not plagued by conflict or battered by theories. The beauty of Shelley's nature is not tarnished by any doubts or debates. Whatever he has become is entirely due to the influence of some inevitable creative urge from within....He is as noble and beautiful as external Nature....[28]

The admiration almost amounts to adulation. What Tagore admired in Shelley is his natural simplicity, his childlike innocence and his spontaneity of response.

Again, as late as in 1922 in his address delivered on the occasion of the death centenary of Shelley, Tagore said :

> When we carefully examine Shelley's poetry we see that he wanted to establish communication with the spirit of the universe. To him the external, physical beauty of the world was not the real thing.... Think of his skylark poem. The skylark is not just a bird; it is a source of universal beauty. What struck the poet is the affinity between the song of the bird and the essence of the infinite forms of beauty of the universe.[29]

And again :

> Shelley looked at the human life, a complex of joy and sorrow, as a veil. The fragmentary nature of life, its crudeness, hides Truth. The poet was extremely eager to tear the veil and see the image of Truth in its pristine purity.[30]

The observations point to an important affinity between Shelley and Tagore. Both wanted to tear the veil of the mundane, reveal the great cosmic force operating behind and express it in their poems. Both celebrated the glory of that great unseen power that controls our life. Shelley's quest for the unknown ended in failure. Truth eluded his grasp, and he was filled with sorrow. But Tagore assiduously pursued Truth and his absolute trust in God, his religious piety, his broad humane outlook possibly helped him in the realization of his goal in quest. He discovered God's grandeur manifest in every object and a profound significance underlying the vital interactions between Man and Nature,[31] as well as between Man and God. So while there is romantic agony in Shelley, Tagore's agony finds transcendence in his devotion to divinity.

We should never lose sight of the fact that Shelley died before he was 30 while Tagore lived to be 80. Just before his death Shelley's poetry was taking a new turn with "The Triumph of Life." There is, however, only a lightning flash of the riddle of existence as he asked : "Then, what is life?" But Shelley died soon afterwards and, therefore, had no time to search for the answer. The search and the solution, on the other hand, consumed the entire poetical career of Tagore so that only in the sixties he seems to have found an answer to the question and attain a profound serenity, sense of fulfilment, as it were.[32]

It is, therefore, natural that the influence of Shelley is most evident in the early period of Tagore in the poems of *Sandhyā Saṅgīt* (The Evening Song) and *Prabhāt Saṅgīt* (The Morning Song), for example. Even in *Sanār Tari* the poem "Mānas Sundarī" reminds one of Shelley's "Hymn to Intellectual Beauty" and some parts of *Prometheus Unbound* in celebrating the joy of union of the poet's soul and the external Nature, and in harmonizing various kinds of attractions and appeals of Nature in a musical symphony. "*Sindhupāre*" (On the Ocean Bank) reminds one of *Alastor* but unlike the Shelley of *Alastor*, here the poet discovers, at the end of the journey, the familiar figure veiled in an aura of strangeness. The obvious source of inspiration of "Varaṣaśeṣ" (The End of the Year) is Shelley's "Ode to the West Wind, though, again, there is as much difference in the nature of experience[33] as in the moral fabric of the vision. Shelley sees the West Wind as a symbol of revolution "to quicken a new birth" and as "the trumpet of prophecy." Tagore appeals for a transcendence, a glorious death which through transvaluation of values would be better than life-in-death existence : "Better put me face to face with glorious Death in a flash of lightning with a crash of thunder."[34]

Briefly, Tagore in his long, richly creative poetical career absorbed the influence of Shelley, assimilated it into his bloodstream and gradually outgrew that influence. Yet he retained an unshakable admiration for Shelley and the two poems that profoundly appealed to him are "Alastor" and "The Hymn to Intellectual Beauty," none of which had the distinction of Palgrave certificate.

Satyendranath Dutta (1882-1922), a junior contemporary of Tagore was quite fond of Shelley. He considered Shelley as one of the very few 'real' poets. In his introductory poem of *Tīrthasalil*, a collection of translations of foreign poems, he stated that his purpose was to bring a note of variety in Bengali poetry.[35] In this collection we find two poems of Shelley : "The Indian Serenade" and "To a Skylark" translated as "*Milansaṅket*"[36] and "*Cātakpakshīr Prati*"[37] respectively. A master metrician Satyendranath tried to follow the original meter. On reading the translation, Tagore remarked :

> It is well-nigh impossible to capture the original spirit. But your translations stemming from the original have flowered into lovely forms of aesthetic beauty. I think that is the rare distinction of poetic translation — it is simultaneously a translation and a new poem.[38]

Tagore further observed :

> These translations of yours are like cases of reincarnation. The soul has transmigrated from one body to another. It is not a matter of craft; it is an act of creation.[39]

In other words, translation, so far as poetry is concerned, is transcreation. Just 12 days after the death of Satyendranath (25 June 1922) Tagore, in course of his presidential address delivered on the occasion of the death centenary of Shelley, translated into Bengali the Preface to "Alastor" and he concluded his speech with a prose translation of the entire poem "Hymn to Intellectual Beauty."[40] It is a superb piece of translation worth going over again and again.

In fine, I may say that the influence of Shelley constitutes a small but significant tributary of the mighty stream of Bengali poetry, and that Shelley has been more a source of inspiration than influence, unless of course, we look upon inspiration as a function of influence.

SELECT BIBLIOGRAPHY

(I have indicated by asterisks the items which I have found most helpful.)

Bandyopadhyay, Asit. *History of Modern Bengali Literature.* Calcutta : Modern Book Agency, 1986. Cited as *HMBL.*

Bandyopadhyay, Hemchandra. *Hemchandra Racanāsambhār* (*Collected Works of Hemchandra*). Ed. Pramathanath Bishi. Calcutta : Mitra & Ghosh, 1971. Cited as *Hemchandra.*

Bandyopadhyay, Srikumar. *Bāṁlā Sāhitya Parikramā* (*A Survey of Bengali Literature*). Calcutta : Saraswati Library, n.d. Cited as *BSP.*

Baral, Akshay Kumar, *Kavya Cayanika (Selected Poems).* Ed. Shyamsundar Maity. Calcutta : Banga Bharati Granthalay, 1366 B.S. Cited as *Kāvya Cayanikā.*

Chakrabrty, Biharilal, *Bīhārīlal, Racanāsambhār* (*Collected Works of Biharilal*) Ed. Pramathanath Bishi. Calcutta : Mitra & Ghosh, 1368 B.S. Cited as *Biharilal.*

Datta, Satyendranath, *Kabi Satyendranāther Granthābalī* (*Collected Works of Satyendranath, the Poet*). Ed. Bishu Mukhopadhyay. Calcutta : Vak Sahitya, 1971. Cited as *Satyendranath.*

King-Hele, Desmond. *Shelley : His Thought and Work.* London : Macmillan, 1960. Cited as *SMP.*

*Majumdar, Ujjal Kumar. *Bāngla Kāvye Pāscātyā Prabhāb* (*Western Influence on Bengali Poetry*). Calcutta : Sanskrit Prakashan, 1968. Cited as *BKPP.*

Ridenour, George M., ed. *Shelley : A Collection of Critical Essays.* New Delhi : Prentice Hall of India, 1980.

Sen Amiya Kumar. *Studies in Shelley.* Pennsylvania : Folcroft Press, 1936; 1969.

Sen, Priya Ranjan. *Western Influence in Bengali Literature.* 3rd ed. Calcutta : Academic Publishers, 1965. Cited as *WIBL.*

Shelley, P.B. *The Letters of Percy Bysshe Shelley,* 2 vols. Ed. Frederick L. Jones. London : Oxford UP, 1964. Cited *as Letters I and Letters II.*

Shelley, P.B. *Shelley : Poetical Works.* Ed. Thomas Hutchinson. London : Oxford, Paperback, 1970.

Tagore, Rabindranath. *Rabindra Racanābalī (Collected Works of Rabindranath Tagore).* Centenary ed. 15 vols. Calcutta : Govt. of West Bengal, 1961. Cited as *RR.*

REFERENCES

1. *Letters II.* 361.
2. *Letters II.* 374.
3. *Letters II.* 361.
4. See Amiya Kumar Sen, *Studies in Shelley.* 243-270.
5. *Letters I.* 24.
6. *Letters I.* 82.

7. *Letters I*. 107
8. *Letters I*. 112.
9. *Letters II*. 242.
10. *Shelley : Poetical Works*. 676. Williams was drowned together with Shelley.
11. See Granger's *Index to Poetry* referred to by Desmond King-Hele in *Shelley*: *His Thought and Work*. 241.
12. See Asit Bandyopadhyay. *HMBL*. 38.
13. Quoted in Bengali by P.R. Sen in *WIBL*. 184.
14. *HMBL*. 165.
15. Reprinted in *Hemchandra*. 411-413.
16. *See Biharilal*. 443.
17. *Biharilal*. 449.
18. See Majumdar, *BKPP*. 166. Majumdar has called attention to the tenth stanza of Biharilal's *Māyādevī*.
19. Tagore in his essay on Biharilal (*RR* Vol. 13. 907) also identifies Biharilal's "Sarasvati" as Shelley's "Spirit of Beauty."
20. Tagore dedicated his *Sonār Torī (The Barge of Gold)* to Debendranath Sen.
21. See *Kāvya Cayanikā*. 4-5.
22. Prabhat Kumar Mukhopadhyay, however, holds that the poem is a translation of some poem by Shelley. Mukhopadhyay does not name the original poem, but Shelley's "To a Star" might be the source of inspiration. Furthermore, Mukhopadhyay argues that the star actually refers to Kadambari Debi. See Prabhat Kumar Mukhopadhyay, *Rabīndranāth O Rabīndrasāhitya* Prabeśika (*Rabindranath and an Introduction to Tagore Literature*) Santiniketan : Visva-Bharati, 1907. 118-119.
23. *See RR*. Vol. 10. 84-85.
24. *RR*. Vol. 5. 55-90.

    About *Kabikāhinī (The Tale of a Poet)* Tagore writes in *Jibansmṛti (Reminiscences)* :

    "In the first year of *Bhāratī* I published a long poem. It was written at an age when a writer, failing to see anything else in the world, only sees his own indistinct shadow in a magnified form" (*RR*. Vol. 10. 71).
25. "Bāṅgālī Kabi nay kena?" (Why is a Bengali not a poet?)
26. "āmāder ganḍacarmaman ati mṛdusparśe sukh ambhah karite pārena. eijanya āmrā bāiraṇer bhakta. śelir jyotsnār mato ati aśarīrī kalpanā khub kam bāṅgālīr bhālo lāge." (Bhārātī 1287 B.S. asadh)
27. See *RR*. Vol. 4. 860-861.
28. *Chinnapatrābalī (Torn Letters)* Letter No. 204. (*RR*. Vol. 11. 221-222).
29. The Presidential address delivered in Calcutta on 8 July 1922 published in *Bhāratī* in Āświn 1329 B.S. 523-531.

Reprinted in *Rabīndra Bīkshyā* Collection 4, Pauṣ 1384 B.S. 90-100. See Rabīndra Bīkshyā. 96-97.

30. *Rabīndra Bīkshyā*. 97.
31. "viśvaprakṛti ebaṁ mānabloker madhye nityaśacal abhijṅatār prabarttanā ... (experiential dynamics constantly operating between the world of Nature and the world of Man...).

    Bhūmika (Preface), *Sonār Tarī (The Barge of Gold) RR*. Vol. 1. 342.
32. "sāhityer lakshyai paripurṇatār saundarya" (The singular aim of literature is the beauty of fulfilment.) See *RR*. Vol. 10. 85.
33. See Majumdar, *BKPP*. 213.
34. "er ceye mahān mrtyur sāthe mukhomukhi kare dāo more bajrer āloke."
35. "omar khaiyam āsiyā mileche, eseche bhalteyār

    hayen eseche selī, sādi, kīts, barns, berānjār

    kumbha āmār bhariyā enechi śata tīrther jale

    baṅgabāir puṇyābhiṣek punah āji habe bale"

    (It is a confluence of the poetry of Omar Khayam, Voltaire, Heine, Shelley, Southey, Keats, Burns and Beranger...I have filled my pitcher with the water of hundred sacred places to let the Bengali Muse a fresh and sacred bath.) See *Satyendranath*. 205-206.
36. *Satyendranath*. 254.
37. *Satyendranath*. 219-223.
38. Quoted by Kanak Bandyopadhyay in the Preface to *Satyendranath*. 15.
39. *Satyedranath*. 16.
40. *Rabīndra Bīkshyā*. 99-100.

    [All the translations, unless otherwise stated, are by the present author.]

8

In Search of *La Belle Dame sans Merci**

My purpose in the present paper is to try to map out first the literary tradition within which Keats's poem is subsumed and suggest that it is a tradition which is not only universal but also an ongoing process in the course of which "la belle dame sans merci" has assumed an enormous symbolic significance.

To begin with the poem itself. We know that the poem is included in the *Journal Letter to George Keats* (February 1819) and that it was first published in the *Indicator* of May 1820 with a short prefatory note by Leigh Hunt stating that it was suggested by Chaucer's translation[1] of a medieval French poem "Le Belle Dame sans Merci" (1424) of Alain Chartier who was the court-poet of Charles II of France. Chaucer's own poem on the same theme is entitled "Merciless Beauty."[2] Divided into three parts — Captivity, Rejection and Escape — the poem focuses on the nature of merciless beauty of "la belle dame sans merci" :

So hath your beaute fro your herte chaced
Pitee, that me ne availeth not to pleyne;
For Danger hath your mercy in his cheyne...

Spenser's description of Phaedria in *Faerie Queene*[3] anticipates, to some extent Keats's "belle dame." Phaedria is a "Ladie fresh and faire, Making sweet solace to her selfe along." She meets Cymochles and leads him away "to a shady dale " and corrupts him. Shakespeare's "belle dame"

---

* National Seminar on the occasion of the bi-centenary of Keats's birth, Patan (Gujarat), 1995.

stanzas in *Pericles* may also have some bearing on the nature of 'la belle dame sans merci."[4]

All these prototypes — Chartier, Chaucer, Spenser *et al* may have definite contribution to the ideational content of the poem but the root of the "la belle dame sans merci" motif must be traced to the universal belief that beyond the human realm of sense perception there is a world peopled by supernatural beings who resemble humans and mate with them. There are stories in which a woman, a seductress shows ruthless disregard for the welfare of her lover. Because of the malign characteristics of the "belle dame" she is often depicted as a witch, vampire, succubus etc. It was believed that a witch could assume any form — male or female[5] — to copulate with mortals. The succubus appeared to men during their sleep in order to have sex with them. As the succubus motif merged with other demonic aspects of the "belle dame" theme we meet her in the form of demons, vampire etc., in such works as Goethe's "Die Braut Von Corinth" (The Bride of Corinth, 1997), Coleridge's "Christabel" (1816) and Poe's "Ligeia" (1840). Then there is another phrase which is often used interchangeably with the phrase "la belle dame sans merci." The phrase is "femme fatale" or fatal woman, fatal for the person who loves her. Although both "belle dame sans merci" and "femme fatale" destroy a man by robbing him of his strength and qualities and not infrequently his life, there is a genetic difference between the two. Strictly speaking, "la belle dame sans merci" is a supernatural enchantress while "femme fatale" is a mortal, a human being of flesh and blood. In the course of our discussion we shall take them together as they appear ubiquitously in legend, folklore and literature of the world. The Middle English popular ballad, "Thomas Rhymer" draws on this folklore.

Thomas Erceldoune, more commonly known as Thomas Rhymer, was a very popular poet, and seer of the fourteenth century Scotland. He is said to have received his gift from fairy and his story resembles that of other medieval visits to fairyland.[6] The story preserves the tradition of pre-Christian times, such as the injunction of silence, the shoes of green velvet, and the river of blood that separates fairy from the natural world. The passage through river may be seen as an ancient symbol of rebirth associated with the gaining of visionary insights and the beginning of a new life of religious powers! The story begins with the following lines :

True Thomas lay oer yond grassy bank,
And he beheld a ladie gay,
A ladie that was brisk and bold
Come riding oer the fernie brae.

The ballad was later developed into the medieval romance *Thomas of Ercildoune and the Queene of Elf-Land* in which Thomas asks for the love of the lady whom he takes for the Queen of Heaven and asks for pity : "And sayd, lufly ladye! rewe on mee." A mystical journey to the underworld follows and the underworld as is customary, is a cave or shadowy hollow.

ladde hym in at Fldone birke,
Under nethe a derne lee;
Where it was derk als mydnyght myrke,
And ever the water till his knee.[7]

We also learn that the lady is shape-shifter, capable of assuming different shapes — beautiful and ugly. In fact, closely related to the "belle dame" motif is the loathly lady theme handled with remarkable skill by Chaucer in "The Wife of Bath's Tale" in which the hero marries an ugly hag only to see her transformed into a beautiful lady after he has accepted her answer to the question "What thyng it is that women moost desire";[8] "Wommen desiren have sovereyntee/ As wel over hir housbond, as hir love"[9] or domination over their husbands. The withered hag is metamorphosed back to the lovely lady she originally was. We come across the same theme in the medieval ballad, "The Marriage of Sir Gawain." In this ballad King Arthur riding by Tam Wadling soon after Christmas in the forest of Inglewood met a fierce baron who offered him choice between fighting and ransom, and said, that the king must return on New Year's Day "And bring me word what thing it is/That a woman will most desire;/This shalbe thy ransome, Arthur" he says, "For I'le have noe other hier."[10]

Arthur went back, wrote several possible answers and then on the New Year's Day proceeded to Tam Wadling. On the way he met an ugly lady :

And as he rode over a more
Hee see a lady where shee sate
Betwixt an oke and a greene hollen
She was clad in red scarlett.
Then theres shold have stood her mouth,
Then there was sett her eye;
The other was in her forehead fast,
The way that she might see.
Her nose was crooked and turn'd outward
Her mouth stood foule a-wry;
A worse form'd lady than shee was,
Never men saw with his eye.[11]

The woman assured him, "Of me be thou nothing dismay'd/ Tho I be ugly to see" and offered to solve his problem, and, in return, Arthur promised to marry her to Sir Gawain or one of his knights. Then she gave the answer :

And she says a woman will have her will
And this is all her cheef desire.[12]

The answer satisfied the baron and the king on his return to Camelot told his knights that he had in the forest a bride for one of them and a number of knights rode out in his company to find her. But on seeing her they recoiled; they thought it was better to die than to marry her. At last Sir Gawain married her mainly to oblige King Arthur. The ugly lady was taken home and bedded when to Gawain's surprise she turned into a beautiful woman in his arms. Then she offered him a choice :

Choose thee, gentle Gawain,
Truth as I doe say,
Weather thou wilt have me in this likeness
In the night or else in the day[13]

Gawain left it to her "because thou art my owne lady, /Thou shalt have all the will."[14] The woman was very happy and said :

Blessed be the gentle Gawain,
This day that I thee see!
For as thou seest me att this time,
From henceforth I wilbe.[15]

Related to the Loathly Lady theme is the Animal Bride motif. There are stories in which "la belle dame" is sometimes an animal or a reptile who awaits disenchantment by her lover. The motif can take a malign form as in the stories of the supernatural Lamia. Lamia, a witch is transformed by Hermes from a serpent into a beautiful young woman. She loves the Corinthian Lycius, and he, spellbound by her beauty, takes her secretly to his house. Not content with his happiness he makes a bridal feast and invites his friends. Among them comes the sage Apollonius who pierces through Lamia's disguise and calls her by name, whereupon with a frightful scream she disappears. The story of Lamia has been popularized by Keats. Incidentally, in the French folklore there is a story of Melusina, a water sprite, something like a mermaid. She consented in the form of woman, to marry Raymond of Poitiers on condition that he should never see her on a Saturday on which day she actually reverted to her mermaidlike condition. Her husband broke the compact on a Saturday whereupon she fled. In *Undine* (1811)[16] a fairy romance, an humble fisherman and his wife have lost their child by drowning and Undine a water-sprite comes mysteriously to them and is brought up in her stead. A knight Huldbrand von Ringsteten takes shelter in their cottage and falls in love with Undine. They are married and, in consequence, Undine gets a soul. Huldbrand begins to neglect his wife and becomes attached to one Bertalda who happens to be the lost child of the fisherman. One day Huldbrand rebukes his wife while in a boat and she is snatched away by her people. Huldbrand proposes to Bertalda and they are about to be married when Undine, rising from a well goes to the knight's room, kisses him and he dies. Anderson's "The Little Maid" (1837) and Jean Giradoux's play *Ondine* (1939) are variations of the same theme.

The German story of Tannhauser is also a part of the "belle dame" tradition. Tannhauser, a German minnersinger (a lyric poet like the French troubadours) of the thirteenth century is the subject of a legend embodied in a 16th century ballad. According to this story as he rode by the Horseberg in Thrungia, he was attracted by the figure of a beautiful woman whom he recognised as Venus. She beckoned him into a cave where he spent seven years in revelry. Smitten by his conscience he then left Venusberg and went to Rome to seek absolution from the Pope. His Holiness replied that it was as impossible for Tannhauser to be forgiven as the dry staff to burgeon, and Tannhauser departed in despair. But after three days the staff broke into blossom. The Pope sent hurriedly for Tannhauser but he was nowhere to be found. He had returned to Venus. The story of Tannhauser has been widely told in England and Germany by William Morris, Swinburne, Heine, Richard Wagner and Thomas Mann, among others.[17]

To go chronologically, in the classical period we meet a number of "belles dames sans merci" in the Greek and Roman epics : Circe, the Sirens and Calypso. Circe turns her victims into beasts after their orgies of pleasure in her domain. But Calypso is dangerous only to the extent that Odysseus's infatuation for her impedes his journey back to Ithaca. Playing the role similar to Calypso's is Virgil's Dido from whom Aeneas must wrench himself to fulfil his destiny to found Rome. And it is the classical period that offers as the celebrated "femme fatale," Cleopatra. And, then, there is the archetypal "femme fatale," Helen. Although the Greek Helen is a rather passive temptress, in Rossetti's "Troy Town" (1880) she assumes quite an active, if not aggressive and demonic role.[18]

In the biblical literature — Lilith, Adams's first wife, is the most significant ancestress of "la belle dame sans merci." According to

Rabbinical tradition Lilith was the first wife of Adam whom Adam expelled from Eden supposedly for her refusal to accept his dominant role. (One of the first feminists in literature!) Lilith appears in Goethe's *Faust* (1808). In Mann's *The Magic Montain* she is associated with Clave Chauchat and Rossetti's poem, "Eden Bower" (1881) gives an account of how Lilith tempted Satan by offering her body only to ruin Adam and Eve.[19] Furthermore, the idea that all human woes are due to either the biblical Eve or the classical Pandora makes them archetypal "femmes fatales." In that case both "la belle dame sans merci" and "femme fatale" may be regarded as daughters of Eve or Pandora.

In the Middle Ages we meet "la belle dame sans merci" in many spheres. There are the dangerous witches Vivien and Morgan la fee of the Arthurian legends, the famous adultresses — Iseult and Guinivere. In fact Guinivere is to Camelot what Eve was to Eden. And then there is the adored object of the courtly lover. The lady in Courtly Love literature may be as passive as the Helen of Troy but the fact that the lover pines away or is driven to desperate acts of passion for her sake makes her a "belle dame sans merci."

During the Renaissance we meet "belles dames sans merci" in Alcina in Ariosto's *Orlando Furioso* (1616) and in Armida in Tasso's *Gerusalemme Liberata* (1581). Spenser's Acrasia also belongs to this group because she represents Temptation, the lure of false paradise. We find the knight asleep in Acrasia's embrace in complete disregard of his duties as a knight :

His warlike arms, the idle instruments
Of sleeping praise, were hung upon a tree,
And his brave shield, full of old monuments,
Was foully fazed, that none the signs might see;
Ne for them, ne for honour cared he,
Ne ought, that did to his advancement tend,
But in levd loves, and wasteful luxury
His days, his goods, his body he did spend :
O horrible enchantment, that him so did blend![20]

The condition of the knight parallels the condition of Antony who neglects his duties for his love for Cleopatra. It is always a liaison between Valour and Beauty. Tannhauser was also a "noble knight." In Keats's poem also it is, a knight-at-arms who falls victim to the temptation of "la belle dame sans merci." And behind all these stories lies the myth of Mars and Venus caught in their illicit liaison by Vulcan's net as the Olympian gods jeered at them. After the Renaissance we do not meet the "belles dames" quite often. The "belle dame" motif definitely suffered an eclipse during the age of reason but in the nineteenth century it had a powerful rebirth. It reappears as the most powerful symbol of the poetic Muse. The artist must sacrifice all his personal comforts and cultivate a spirit of dedication to the Muse, but, in return he, like the poet in *Alastor* or Gustave von Aschenbach in Mann's *Death in Venice* must be gradually emaciated and meet a miserable death. At the symbolic level, the Muse — cruel, pitiless, beautiful maiden as she is — accepts only the art and rejects the artist. This is Tagore's *jībandevatā* (the presiding genius, the poetic Muse) who, coming in a golden boat, takes away the rich harvest but leaves the poet behind.

II

The dismal, desolate landscape that we find in the poem "La Belle Deme sans Merci" thus becomes the fitting symbol of the poet's exhausted state of mind. Like the storm in *King Lear* the landscape in only an externalization of a state of mind. The poem then describes in visual terms the sense of exhaustion and deprivation caused by the poet's dedication to the poetic Muse. When the "belle dame" has finished her work — as in "Ode to Autumn" — when the harvest is done and the granary is full, the sedge withers and the birds fall silent. There is also a striking similarity between the knight-at-arms in "La Belle Dame sans Merci" and the speaker in "Ode to Melancholy." Helen Vendler has pointed out how the poems "share the paraphernalia of pallor, anguish, rose, garland, strange foods, grotto, eyes, kisses, lips"[21] etc. Keats as a poet is enthralled and disenthralled and his own will becomes powerless in the process. He must serve the Muse even at the risk of his life. This is the artist's predicament. The attraction is irresistible though the consequences are known to be disastrous. Poesy compels love and yet she is pitiless. So, it is not for nothing that Keats describes his poesy as "my *demon* poesy" (emphasis added). In "Ode on Indolence" he writes :

> The last, whom I love more, the more of blame
> Is heaped upon her, maiden most unmeek —
> I knew to be *my demon Poesy* (emphasis added).

Incidentally Mallarmé in "Don du poéme" (Gift of the poem) very powerfully describes the agony of the poet in giving birth to a poem. Heine adapts a fairy tale to express the fate of the poet who has no choice but to serve his mistress, the poetic Muse, the cruel woman, "la belle dame sans merci." The poetic Muse is not only a "belle dame sans merci" but also a "femme fatale." Both the motifs are fused in the poem. The title of this short poem is "Lorelei" i.e. Muse. Here is the poem in English translation:

> I do not know why it should be but I am so sad; there is an old time fairy tale which I cannot put out of my mind. The air is cool and the twilight is falling and the Rhine is flowing calmly by; the top of the mountain is glittering in the evening sun.
>
> Up there the most gorgeously beautiful maiden is sitting; her golden jewellery sparkles and she is combing her golden hair. She is combing it with a golden comb singing a song as she does so; it has a wonderful compelling melody.
>
> It makes a wild nostalgia possess the boatman in his boat; he pays no attention to the submerged rocks, he can only look up and up.
>
> In the end, if I remember rightly, the waves swallow up the boatman and his boat. And that is what she has done, the Lorelei and her song.

III

It may also be rewarding to see the poem in the light of biographical and psychoanalytic criticism. Physically Keats had been suffering from consumption (Feb-May 1819). Emotionally he was passionately in love with Fanny Brawne (he had first met her in October-November 1818), and at the same time he was acutely conscious of the fact that his love could never be fulfilled in a consummated marriage ("new love pine at them beyond tomorrow"). His condition is, therefore, very much like the condition of the knight-at-arms of "La Belle Dame sans Merci" : "wretched," "alone," "pale," "haggard" and "woe-begone." Fanny Brawne, his "belle dame" however was not probably "sans merci." The moving letter that she wrote on 23 May 1821, exactly three months after Keats's death is an eloquent testimony to it. She wrote :

> All his friends have forgotten him. They have got over the first shock, and that with them is all. They think I have done the same, which I do not wonder at, for I have taken care never to trouble them with any feelings of mine, but I can tell you who next to me (I must say *next* to me) loved him best, that I have not got over it and never shall..."[22]

The thirty-one letters that she had written to Fanny Keats during the period from 1820 to 1824 make one thing abundantly clear; she loved him with all her heart. In Keats's lifetime she may have enjoyed to the full parties, dancing and admiration, but after his death she led a quiet, retired life, shunning and disliking societies. That is Fanny's part of the story. So far as Keats is concerned, Fanny's popularity, viewed with the jealous eyes of a passionate man violently in love, gave him many miserable hours. He felt that Fanny was not adequately reciprocating his feelings. Though in love with him she appeared to him fickle and frivolous, volatile and inconsiderate. This might not be true but that was Keats's impression. In one of his letters to Fanny he writes :

> "I have heard you say that it was not unpleasant to wait a few years — you have amusements — your mind is away — you have not brooded over one idea as I have, and how should you? You are to me an object intensely desirable — the air I breathe in a room empty of you is unhealthy. I am not the same to you — no — you can wait — you have a thousand activities — you can be happy without me. Any party anything to fill up the day has been enough...you may have altered...if you have not — if you still behave in dancing rooms and other societies as I have seen you — I do not want to live — if you have done so I wish this coming night be my last. I cannot live without you and not only you but *chaste you; virtuous you*. The Sun rises and sets, the day passes, and you follow the bent of your inclination to a certain extent — you have no conception of the quantity of miserable feeling that passes through me in a day — Be serious! Love is not a plaything a crystal conscience."[23]

And again :

> If my health would bear it, I could write a poem which I have in my head, which would be a consolation for people in such a situation as mine. I would show someone in Love as I am, with a person living in such Liberty as you do. Shakespeare always sums up matters in the most sovereign manner. Hamlet's heart was full of such Misery as mine is when he said to Ophelia "Go to a Nunnery, go, go!" Indeed I should like to give up the matter at once — I should like to die. I am sickened at the brute world which you are smiling with. I hate men and women more (Letters II. 312).

In another letter Keats refers to an oriental story in which a group of men reach "some gardens of paradise where they meet with a most enchanting Lady; and just as they are going to embrace her, she bids them shut their eyes" and eludes their grasp. And then Keats comments : "How I applied this to you, my dear; how I palpitated at it..." (Letters II. 130).

His self-pity becomes evident in another letter :

> "I cannot be admired; I am not a thing to be admired. You are, I love you; all I can bring you is a swooning admiration of your Beauty.... I have two luxuries to brood over in my walks, your Loveliness and the hour of my death. O that I could have possession of them both in the same minute. I hate the world." (Letters II. 133)

The idea of death leads to the idea of martyrdom. He writes in another letter :

> "I could be martyr'd for my Religion — Love is my religion — I could die for that — I could die for you. My creed is Love and you are its only tenet — You have ravish'd me away by a power I cannot resist..." (Letters II, 223-224).

The poems addressed to Fanny are also marked by passionate expressions of the torments of love and uncertainty about her response to his love. In "To Fanny" (1819) he implores : "Beckon me not into the wintry air" and "pr'y thee, do not turn/ The current of your heart from me so soon." He questions: "Must not a woman be/ A Feather on the sea, / Sway'd to and fro by every wind and tide?" The poem "To-" and the poem beginning with the line "This living hand..." also express the same kind of passionate unrest that marks "To Fanny." In the sonnet, No. XXX we hear the agonized cry : "I cry your mercy — pity — love! — aye — love!/ Merciful love that tantalize not..."

A look at Keats's other letters of this period would also corroborate this view. When Keats submitted the first draft of the poem "La Belle Dame sans Merci" to George Keatses we see him referring to one of his dreams, the dream of Paola and Francesca : "*I floated about the whirling atmosphere as it is described with a beautiful figure to whose lips mine were joined at [as] it seemed for an age...O that I could dream it every night*" (Letters II. 91). The same year (1819) around July he seems to be fascinated, if not obsessed, by the metaphor of frustrated erotic experience on reading Weber's *Tales of the East* (Letters II. 130). His emotional involvement with Fanny is also expressed in imagery very close to that of "La Belle Dame sans Merci" : "*I cry to dream again,*" "*I eternally see her figure eternally vanishing,*" "*my imagination is horribly vivid about her*" (Letters II. 224, 345, 351).

And the burst of fine poetry that Keats had after he had been touched by love, during the period, say, from December 1818 (Keats first met Fanny during October/November 1818) and May 1819 or 3rd February 1820 when he left for Italy, deserves special attention. "The Eve of Saint

Agnes," all the great odes, and "La Belle Dame sans Merci" among others were written during this period. Fanny was obviously the main source of inspiration, and thus in her were fused the traditional idea of "la belle dame sans merci" and the idea of "femme fatale" as a symbol of poetic Muse.

IV

Let us now make another search of the "belle dame" in the light of an important biographical event that must have a significant bearing on the dreamlike texture of the poem: Keats's acquaintance with Coleridge. They had met on a Sunday in April 1819 and talked about "*Different genera and species of Dreams—Nightmare — a dream accompanied (with) by a sense of touch — single and double touch — A dream related — First and second consciousness — the difference explained between will and volition...*" (Letters, II. 88-99).

Now, the poem ostensibly is a dialogue. The first three stanzas suggest an interrogator, somebody finding the knight-at-arms in a miserable condition loitering about and asking him about the reasons thereof. The rest of the poem — the next nine stanzas — form the reply of the knight-at-arms to the question. He tries to give an account of how he has come to this. But what should strike us is the conspicuous absence of the marks of quotation. There is no visible indication that there are two speakers. How to explain it? One possible explanation can be found if we treat the entire poem as a dream model in terms of Freud's theory of the mind. According to this theory the personal identity is only a fiction invented to hold together chaotic impressions. Personal identity in other words, is the unifying consciousness — a matter more of convenience than conviction — a makeshift arrangement, a defensive mechanism in face of the vast and intractable incoherence of the self and the world. On account of the dark continent of the unconscious the subject never realizes itself and becomes painfully conscious of his fragmented self, the essentially schizophrenic nature of the human character. The mind is always engaged in and committed to a search, a search for meaning, a search for significance, but the search invariably ends in a delusion. What one ultimately finds is only his "other," and it is mainly in dream[24] that man dives into the abysmal depths of the unconscious, experiences reality, the primordial desires, but, fled is that dream as soon as one wakes up. The unconscious is beautiful because it is true, but it is "sans merci" because it is hard, stubborn, ruthless and unrelenting. Seen in this light the structure of the poem would imply that it is a dream within a dream, an interior monologue, the knight asking himself about his present miserable condition, and then, "la belle dame sans merci" is the Unconscious fulfilling the repressed, unfulfilled desire.

The essay proposes to halt at the frontiers of legend, folkore and psychology where the scattered fragments of memory shape into myriad forms.

The fact that the poem is amenable to so many different interpretations that sustain and reinforce one another, goes a long way to suggest that the poem itself has become a metaphor. Metaphorically the poem "La Belle Dame sans Merci" is the "belle dame" that eludes our grasp and, therefore, is "sans merci."

NOTES

1. See Skeat. *Chaucerian and Other Pieces* xvi. quoted by C.S. Lewis *Allegory of Love* (London : Oxford UP, 1936, pp. 244-247). Chaucer's poem begins with the lines "Half in a dreme, not fully wel awaked,/ The golden sleep me wrapped under his wing." Incidentally Chaucer's translation has 864 lines. Keats's poem has just 48 lines.
2. *The Works of Chaucer* Ed. A.W. Pollard (London : Macmillan & Co. Ltd., 1960) p. 634.
3. Edmund Spenser. *The Faerie Queene* II. 6, 3, 14, 7.
4. The stanzas 10 and 11 where Pericles is going to risk his life to win the King's daughter, and Antiochus warns him about the merciless nature of the princess, a "death's net."
5. The only difference between a witch assuming the form a woman and a real mortal woman is that a mortal has a soul which a witch does not have. Paracelsas holds that a witch could acquire a soul only by living as a mortal, experiencing human suffering, and thereby be spared of some punishment.
6. Incidentally, Thomas spent "seven years" with the faery. Thomas Becket spent seven years abroad before he came back to Canterbury. 2. J.E. Housman ed. *British Popular Ballads*.
7. In John Spiers, *Medieval English Poetry* (London : Faber & Faber, 1957) p. 73.
8. *The Works of Geoffrey Chaucer* ed. Alfred W. Pollard (London : Macmillan & Co. Ltd., 1960) p. 168.
9. *Ibid.*, p. 168.
10. *The Oxford Book of Ballads ed.* Arthur Quiller-Couch. (London : Oxford UP, 1955) p. 89.
11. *Ibid.* p. 91.
12. *Ibid.* p. 93.
13. *Ibid.* p. 95.

14. *Ibid.* p. 96.
15. *Ibid.* p. 96.
16. Published in 1811 by Fredrich, Baron de la Motte Fouque (1777-1843), a German officer and a prolific writer of poetry, drama, and fiction.
17. Heine's poem "Tannhauser : A Legend" begins with a warning : "Good Christians all, be not entrapped/In Satan's cunning snare/I sing the lay of Tannhauser/ To bid your souls beware. Brave Tannhauser, Venusberg/ Seven Years he bode therein."
18. In Rossetti's poem Helen goes to the shrine of Venus, and prays for the fulfilment of her "heart's desire." Venus grants her prayer and then "Cupid looked on Helen's breast,.../Saw the heart within its nest,/Saw the flame of heart's desire-/Marked his arrow's burning crest." And then, "Cupid ... took another dart...Fledged it for another heart,/ Winged the shaft with the heart's desire..." and "Paris turned upon his bed."
19. The jilted Eve invited Satan : "...today, thou master of Lilith,/Wrap me round in the form I'll borrow/And let me tell thee of sweet to-morrow/ ...Fold me fast, O God-snake of Eden!/... What more prize than love to impel thee?/ Grip and lip my limbs as I tell thee!"
20. Edmund Spenser, *The Faerie Queene* II xii st. 80.
21. Helen Vendler, *The Odes of John Keats* (Cambridge, Massachusetts : Harvard UP, 1983) p. 334.
22. See *Letters of Fanny Brawne to Fanny Keats, 1820-1824* Ed. Fred Rdgcumbe. (Oxford UP, 1937).
23. The *Letters of John Keats, 1814-1821* Ed. Hyder Edward Rollins, Vol 2. (Cambridge: Cambridge UP, 1958). Subsequently referred to as *Letters* II. p. 304.
24. The knight says : "I met a lady." According to S.O.D. the O.E. verb "mete" meant to dream; and "met" is the past participle. O.E. Maetan M.E. mete. Me mette = I dreamt (S.O.D., p. 1242). So, I met a lady = I dreamt a lady.

9

The Legacy of Matthew Arnold*

Modern criticism may be said to have started very well with Eliot's "Tradition and the Individual Talent" (1919) (*Selected Essays* 13-22). In 1941 John Crowe Ransom in his epoch-making book *The New Criticism* hailed Eliot as one of the pioneers of New Criticism, because among other things, Ransom wanted that criticism must become more scientific, or precise and systematic. The immediate occasion for this pleading was Ransom's dissatisfaction with the philosophical, historical, biographical and impressionistic criticism. The reason for this dissatisfaction was that all these kinds of criticism diverted the attention away from the literary work to something which was not strictly literary. In other words, critics often focussed their attention not on the literary work but on the various factors or circumstances leading to the work and their subjective reaction to it. The work for these critics was only the starting point, and that was precisely a point of departure. But Eliot, way back in 1919, very emphatically insisted that "honest criticism and sensitive appreciation are directed not upon the poet but upon the poetry" (*Selected Essays* 17), and he had seriously tried to "divert interest from the poet to the poetry..." (*SE* 22).

Eliot is now regarded as one of the most important critics, if not *the* most important critic, of the twentieth century, and Eliot's denigration of Arnold is now common knowledge. By quoting Arnold's famous statement, "Poetry is at bottom a criticism of Life," Eliot had very sarcastically remarked : "At bottom that is a great way down; the bottom is the bottom. At the bottom of the abyss is what few ever see..." (*The Use of Poetry and the Use of Criticism* 111). But by using the words "at bottom"

* 1995

Arnold simply meant "on ultimate analysis"; on ultimate analysis poetry takes its origin from life and it illuminates life; it sharpens our perception of life.

However, in spite of Eliot's antagonism to Arnold a comparison of Arnold and Eliot as critiques would reveal many interesting points of affinity between the two. Despite Eliot's denial of Arnold's legacy he would appear as a continuator of the Arnoldian tradition, although it must be admitted that as a critic Eliot is more systematic and more perceptive than Arnold.

Eliot's criticism of Arnold is contained mainly in two essays "Arnold and Pater" (*S.E.* 431-443) (1930) and "Matthew Arnold" (*UPUC* 103-119) (1932-1933). Eliot's main contention is that Arnold is the "poet and critic of a period of false stability," and all his writing in the kind of *Literature and Dogma* is "a valiant attempt to dodge the issue, to mediate between Newman and Huxley" (105-106). According to Eliot, Arnold fails as a critic mainly because his criticism is "very much influenced by his religious attitude" (110) and partly because "he was an educator" (110). Nevertheless, Arnold is the only Victorian critic. Eliot finds worth discussing in detail, and he admits that however "well-nourished we may be on previous literature and previous culture, we cannot afford to neglect Arnold" (105).

What draws Eliot to Arnold is the similarity of situation in which he is historically placed. But first let us see what the situation is :

> From time to time every hundred years or so, it is desired that some critic shall appear to review the past of our literature, and set the poets and the poems in a new order. The task is not one of evolution but of readjustment... (108).

Now this is a situation which disables Arnold, according to Eliot, to become a critic, and turns him into a propagandist of criticism. But Eliot at the outset of his critical career found himself in an exactly similar situation and felt that if Arnold "were our exact contemporary, he would find all his labour to perform again" (*The Sacred Wood XI*). If Arnold had to face a whole chaos of literary values and principles so is the case with Eliot. He also faces a similar chaotic situation and has to attack the uncritical and put forward the real aims and objectives of literary criticism. We find Arnold engaged in a lifelong campaign against the "Philistines" and wasting his energy in educating the public to look for "the best that is known and thought in the world and thus to establish a current of fresh and true ideas" (*Essays in Criticism* First Series 4). Eliot also begins as a Jeremiah. In "The Imperfect Critic" Eliot calls attention to the debris that has accumulated in the name of English literary criticism. And so Arnold's famous manifesto, "The Function of Criticism at the Present Time" (1865) is parallelled by Eliot's "The Function of Criticism" (*S.E.* 23-34) in which Eliot repeats Arnold's censure of the Englishman's extreme individualism and antipathy to criticism. The English character remains at bottom obstinately "humorous" and "nonconformist." Again, Arnold's excursions into more general fields, mainly as a critic of life, in *Culture* and *Anarchy* (1869) anticipate Eliot's similar excursions in his *Idea of a Christian Society* (1939) and *Notes towards the Definition of Culture* (1948). Arnold's role as an "educator" and his interest in education are parallelled by Eliot's essays on "The Aims of Education" (*To Criticize the Critic* 61-124). The wide range of Arnold's intellectual interests clearly indicates a profound concern for a total cultural pattern, for a qualitative improvement of life. It may be true that at times Arnold mistakes compromise for integration. His *Literature* and *Dogma*, for example, appears to Eliot as "a valiant attempt to dodge the issue." Yet, Eliot would possibly agree with Arnold when he writes :

> But first let us ask ourselves why the demand for an intellectual deliverance arises in such an age as the present, and in what the deliverance itself consists? The demand arises because the present age has around it a copious and complex present, and behind it copious and complex past; it arises because the present age exhibits to the individual man who contemplates it the spectacle of a vast multitude of facts awaiting and inviting comprehension. The deliverance consists in man's comprehension of this present and past (*Essays, Letters and Reviews* 5-6).

And again a few lines down :

> The spectacle of facts, presented for the comprehension of the present age are immense.... The spectacle is the collective life of humanity. And everywhere there is connection, everywhere there is illustration, *no single event, no single literature, is adequately comprehended except in its relation to other events, to other literatures*. The literature of ancient Greece, the literature of the Christian Middle Age, so long as they are regarded as two isolated growths of the human spirit, are not adequately comprehended : and it is the adequate comprehension which is the demand of the present age. (6)

In reading such passages one remembers Eliot's notions of "historical sense" and "simultaneous order" and the affinity seems to be quite close.

Arnold believed that a current of living ideas is necessary if literature is to flourish. For that the writers must look outside as well as inside their mother countries. It may be borne in mind in this connection that most of the major influences of Eliot are either American or French.

Apart from the similarities in views regarding the equipment of a writer and a critic, there is a striking similarity between Arnold and Eliot in matters of some important critical principles as well. Arnold repeatedly advocated for a detached objective standpoint. If it is to be meaningful, criticism must essentially be the exercise of an openminded curiosity. An ideal critic must try to view an object, a literary work, "as in itself it really is" (*Essays in Criticism*, Second Series 7). Eliot also believes that a perfect critic, or any critic attempting at perfection should not be carried away by instant feelings. A literary critic should have no emotions except those immediately provoked by a work of art (*SW* 12). And again :

> ...the critic needs to be able not only to saturate himself in the spirit and the fashion of a time — the local flavour — but also *to separate himself suddenly from it in appreciation of the highest creative work* (37). (Emphasis added)

In critical methods also Eliot prescribes and practises what Arnold repeatedly recommended : comparison and anaysis. While discussing the critical position of Charles Whibley Eliot comments : "He exercises neither of the tools of the critic : comparison and analysis" (37). In judgment also Arnold and Eliot have enough agreement. Arnold considers Shakespeare and Milton "as our poetical classics" (*EC*, Second Series 35). Eliot, after his initial denigration of Milton in "Milton I" (1936) (*On Poetry and Poets* 138-145) and partial recantation in "Milton II" (1947) (146-161) ultimately arrives at the conviction that "Shakespeare and Milton are our two greatest poets" (*TCC* 148). Interestingly, if Eliot in "Milton II" points out the pernicious influence of Milton as a model. Arnold had already hinted at it :

> Thompson, Cowper, Wordsworth, all of them good poets *who have studied Milton, followed Milton, adopted his form, fail in their diction and rhythm...* (*EC*, Second Series 62). Emphasis mine.

And in his famous 1853 Preface (*English Critical Essays* ed. Edmund Jones 304-322) Arnold, in spite of his great admiration for Shakespeare, "a name never to be mentioned without reverence" warned the practising poets about the dangers of using Shakespeare as their model :

> I will venture, however, to express a doubt, whether the *influence* of his works, excellent and fruitful for the readers of poetry, for

> the great majority, has been of unmixed advantage to the writers of it (*ECE* 313).

Again, if Arnold rejects Shelley, so does Eliot, though the processes of rationalization are different. Arnold's criticism of Shelley is biographical in the sense that he takes an account of the biographical details relating to the life of Shelley and establishes that Shelley had no sense of humour and that he suffered from self-deception. After bringing this point home Arnold just brackets Shelley the poet with Shelley the man and makes a smmary assessment : "The man Shelley, in every truth, is not entirely sane, and Shelley's poetry is not entirely sane either" (251). It is really a matter of regret that Arnold does not examine the poetry of Shelley nor does he make any close criticism, nor does he even follow his own "touchstone" method. Eliot also rejects Shelley. But he takes up some passages and shows us convincingly how Shelley at times descends to "just bad *jingling*" (*UPUC* 91-92) and how the bad parts of a poem "can contaminate the whole so that when Shelley rises to the heights, one enjoys his poetry only with regretful pleasure" (92). It appears that although Eliot also finds Shelley the man "quite difficult to accept" (89) he rejects him on the ground of immature and false sensibility. Later, however, Eliot in his "Preface to Leon Vivante" (1950) slightly revised his opinion about Shelley in the light of Vivante's distinction between "poetic thought" and "thought of the poet." Arnold's rejection is apparently largely motivated by a moral bias which was almost an obsession with him.

About Keats, Eliot explains what Arnold suggests. Arnold writes :

> No one else in English poetry, save Shakespeare, has in expression quite the fascinating felicity of Keats, his perfection of loveliness. I think, he said humbly, shall be among the English poets after my death. He is : he is with Shakespeare (*EC*, Second Series 119).

Eliot also considers Keats a great poet, a "singular poet in a varied and remarkable period" (*UPUC* 100) and finds an affinity between Shakespeare and Keats in the kind of greatness :

> Keats seems to me also a great poet.... But I am not so much concerned with the degree of his greatness as with its kind; and its kind is manifested more clearly in his Letters than in his poem; and...it seems to me to be much more the kind of Shakespeare (100).

About Byron, however, both Arnold and Eliot feel that Byron is not a great poet. Arnold subscribes to the views of Goethe : "The moment he reflects, he is a child...*sobalder reflectirt ist er ein kind*" (*EC*, Second Series 185) Byron is careless, diffuse, repetitious; he lacks in criticism of life. Eliot also believes that Byron suffers from a defective sensibility :

> The imperceptiveness of Byron to the English word — so that he has to use a great many words before we become aware of him — indicates for practical purposes defective sensibility (*OPP* 201).

But neither Arnold nor Eliot rejects Byron altogether. While Arnold finds in him "the splendid and imperishable excellence of sincerity and strength" (*EC*, Second Series 193) Eliot's discovery is that "at a lower intensity he gets a surprising range of effect" (201). Even in style, in tone, and in argument one is often surprised to find a striking affinity. Compare, for example, the following two passages, one from Arnold and the other from Eliot:

1. Gray, a born poet, fell upon an age of prose.... Born in the same year with Milton Gray would have been another man... coming when he did and endowed as he was, a man born out of date, a man whose full spiritual flowering was impossible (*EC*, Second Series 91-93).
2. Nothing that was done in this period [referring to the Romantic Period] was of the nature of what Arnold was able to do, because that was not the time when it could be done (*UPUC* 110).

To sum up the relation between Arnold and Eliot: Eliot formulates into a very logical system of principle what Arnold only vaguely suggests. It is preposterous to say that such and such idea was first propounded by such and such persons, because it is almost impossible in the field of literature to trace an idea back to its origin. Eliot says in his essay on Byron that Byron abuses Coleridge from whom he learned a great deal. So is the case with Eliot. He always abuses Arnold but from Arnold he has learnt a great deal.

II

According to Ransom, besides Eliot the other pioneer of New Criticism is I.A. Richards. Arnold's influence on Richards can be discerned when Richards, out of a belief that arts are supremely valuable as stimuli, as preparations for more competent living, writes :

> The arts are our storehouse of recorded values. They spring from and perpetuate hours in the lives of exceptional people

> when their control and command of experience is at its highest hours when the varying possibilities of experience are most clearly seen and the different activities which may arise are most exquisitely reconciled.... The arts record the most important judgments we possess as to values to experience.... But subtle or recondite experiences are for most men incommunicable and indescribable.... In the arts we find the record in the only form in which these things can be recorded of the experiences which seemed most worth having to the most sensitive and discriminating persons (I.A. Richards 32).

Arnold anticipates Richards's insistence on the saving power of poetry with its capacity for moulding our aesthetic responses and impulses. Arnold's distrust of the "personal estimate" (*EC*, Second Series 6) anticipates Wimsatt's warning against *affective fallacy* (Wimsatt 21-39), as in his insistence on the "real estimate" he anticipates the objective approach to literary criticism so strongly advocated by the New Critics. His opinion of poetry as "criticism of life" is close to Winters's observation that "a poem (or any other work of literature) is a statement in words about a human experience" (*In Defence of Reason* 26), and "the poem is good in so far it makes a defensible rational statement about a given experience" (7). In his moral bias Winters has an interesting affinity with Arnold. When Arnold writes in "The Study of Poetry,"

> But for supreme poetical success more is required than the powerful application of idea to life; it must be an application under the conditions fixed by the laws of poetic truth and poetic beauty (*EC*, Second Series 48)

one can discover an affinity between Arnold's views on the relation between form and content with the views of the neo-Aristotelians.

Again when Blackmur writes :

> Poetry is life at the remove of form and meaning; not life lived but life framed and identified. So the criticism of poetry is bound to be occupied at once with the terms and modes by which the remove was made and with the relation between — in the ambiguous stock phrase — content and form; which is to say with the establishment, and *appreciation of human or moral value* (Blackmur 69) (Emphasis added)

it sounds like a distant but distinct echo of Arnold. The influence of Arnold on Lionel Trilling and F.R. Leavis is conspicuous in their conviction of the moral role of literature, its openness to life. When Arnold pleads that the business of a poet is with the inward man, the "flickerings of the innermost flame" to borrow a phrase from Virginia Woolf, he makes room for what is described by Elizabeth Wright as psychoanalytic criticism of a character. Arnold's untiring emphasis on style as an important criterion for judging a poem has now developed into the branch of criticism known as Stylistics.

F.R. Leavis was wiser than he knew when in 1938 he, by way of a rejoinder to Eliot's labelling Arnold as more a propagandist for criticism than a critic, endorsed Hopkins's views, that Arnold is "a rare genius and a great critic" (*Scrutiny Vol. 7,* 319-332).

Arnold is certainly the most important critic of the second half of the nineteenth century, although the immediate influence of Arnold on the English literary criticism was not very happy. A (deliberate) misinterpretation of his idea of "disinterestedness" led Walter Pater, Oscar Wilde and their followers to plead for primacy of art to life and a gradual rejection of life altogether in the manner of Gautier's theory of "art for art's sake." Literature during the aesthetic movement was practically cut off from life. But across the Atlantic the writings of the exponents of New Humanism — Irving Babbitt and Paul Elmer More, for example, showed perceptible influence of Arnold in the broad cultural perspective in which literature was placed. In the subsequent generation of critics, both in England and in America, Arnold is a major influence. His profound influence on Eliot, Leavis and Trilling, among others, and his affinity with some of the major schools of contemporary literary criticism constitute a valuable legacy of Arnold as a critic.

WORKS CITED

Arnold, Matthew. "The Function of Criticism at the Present Time," *Essays in Criticism*, First Series. London : Macmillan & Co., 1865.

——. "The Study of Poetry, "*Essays in Criticism* Second Series. 1880; London : Macmillan & Co., 1990.

——. *Essays, Letters and Reviews.* 1865; London : Oxford University Press, 1960.

——. *Preface* to 1853 volume of Poems. Reprinted as "The Choice of Subjects in Poetry," *English Critical Essays Nineteenth Century*, ed. Edumnd Jones. 1916; London : OUP, 1959.

Blackmur, R.P. "A Critic's Job of Work," *The Double Agent: Essays in Craft and Elucidation*. New York : Arrow Edition, 1935.

Eliot, T.S. "Tradition and the Individual Talent," *Selected Essays* Rev. ed. London : Faber and Faber, 1951.

——. *The Sacred Wood.* 1920; London : Methuen & Co. Ltd., 1966.

——. "Preface," *English Poetry and its Contribution to the Knowledge of a Creative Principle* by Leon Vivante. London : Faber and Faber, 1950.

——. *On Poetry and Poets.* 1957; London : Faber and Faber, 1961.

——. "The Aims of Education," *To Criticize the Critic.* London : Faber and Faber, 1965.

——. The *Use of Poetry and the Use of Criticism.* 1933; London : Faber and Faber, 1964.

Ransom, J.C. *The New Criticism. New York* : New Directions, 1941.

Richards, L.A. *Principles of Literary Criticism.* 1924; London : Routledge & Kegan Paul, 1963.

Scrutiny Vol. 7, 1938-39; 319-332.

Wimsatt, W.K. Jr. *The Verbal Icon.* 1954; New York : The Noonday Press, 1958.

Winters, Yvor. *In Defence of Reason.* 1947; Denver : Swallow, 1960.

10

Thomas Hardy as a War-Poet*

War is not a life : it is a situation....

—Eliot

Better known as a novelist than as a poet Hardy is, nevertheless a war-poet as well of great significance. Hardy is certainly not a war-poet in the sense Owen is a war-poet, because Hardy never fought in a war. Rupert Brooke, Julian Grenfell, Francis Ledwidge, Siegfried Sassoon, Wilfred Owen *et al*, are warrior-poets. Yet Hardy's attitude to war as evinced in his war-poems has a striking affinity with the attitude of soldier-poets. In fact, it will not be an exaggeration to say that with a remarkable prescience Hardy had anticipated the sentiments of the soldier-poets and appropriated them in his war-poems. Hardy's attitude to war is all the more interesting because it is congruent with his tragic vision that saw man as living and loving, labouring and perishing against the background of some inscrutable and inexorable forces. Its significance also lies in the fact that it is so different from the current sentimental attitude to war — an attitude that we find in the poems of Tennyson and Rupert Brooke — a kind of romantic conception of the soldier as a knight-errant, and glorification of war as an occasion for demonstrating patriotic feelings and self-sacrifice. Hardy does not deny that patriotism is a noble sentiment; he would only widen the idea of patriotism to cover the entire world. Again, Hardy has also the highest regard for the endurance and fortitude of a soldier who willingly suffers for the sake of his 'country.' But with a profound humanitarian outlook, moving compassion and fine perception Hardy sees a soldier not just as

---

* National Seminar on the occasion of the 150th birth anniversary of Thomas Hardy, Midnapore (W.B.), 1990.

a soldier but as a *man* and prizes the warmth of human relationship as something supremely valuable. "I am happy to say that not a single one is Jingo or Imperial," Hardy remarked about his war-poems.

The war-poems of Hardy which constitute only a small part of his total *oeuvres* can be broadly divided into two groups related as they are to the second Boer War (1899-1902) and the first World War (1914-1918). *The Dynasts* (1903-1908) is also concerned with war, with Napoleon as the central figure. But there is a difference — and a vital one — between *The Dynasts* and other war-poems. While Hardy actually lived through the Boer War and the first World War, in *The Dynasts* he only imaginatively recreates a historical situation of the past. But there are many passages in this great epic-drama which foreshadow Hardy's attitude to war reflected in the war-poems written on the occasions of the second Boer War and the first World War.

Wilfred Owen, the most celebrated war-poet of the twentieth century, who died on 4 November 1918 wrote about his poems in an unfinished Preface :

> This book is not concerned with Poetry
> The subject of it is War and the Pity of War
> The Poetry is in the pity.

Owen's avowed position harks back to one of Hardy's poems, "The Pity of It," composed in February 1915 and published in April 1915. In this poem Hardy contends that the common soldiers are just puppets of sinister warmongers comprising possibly a group of oligarchs and munition makers. Like Owen Hardy was also horrified at the senseless slaughter of war. The soldiers, whether German or British, have no real enmity between them. The thematic affinity between "The Pity of It" and Owen's "Strange Meeting" ("Whatever hope was yours / Was my life also") is unmistakable. Hardy, in fact, goes to the extent of asserting that the Germans and the English are "kin folk kin tongued." The poem ends with a terrible curse imprecated on the war-lords :

> "Whosoever they be
> At root and bottom of this, who flung this flame
> Between kin folk and kin tongued even as are we
> Sinister, ugly, lurid, be their fame :
> May their families grow to shun their name,
> And their brood perish everlastingly."

The racial homogeneity between the Germans and the English is also the theme of his poem, "England to Germany in 1914" where Hardy appeals to the German war-lords by pointing out that the Germans and the English are from the same racial extraction. Moreover, he also reminds them that the English have always admired the German landscape :

> We have loved your burgs, your pines' green moan
> Fair Rhine-stream, and its storied towers;
> Your shining souls of deathless dowers
> Have won us as they were our own;

The complex feeling of compassionate regret and unequivocal protest that characterizes Hardy's poems associated with the first World War can be distinctly discerned in the earlier cluster of poems occasioned by the second Boer War declared in October 1899 as a reaction to Paul Krieger's ultimatum. It may be recalled in this connection that Paul Krieger, son of a Boer farmer came to be recognised by 1883 as the top man in South African Republic and he was elected President. Krieger dreamed of a Boer Empire. But his vision was matched and counteracted by Cecil Rhodes, an Englishman and the son of a county clergyman who went to South Africa, became fabulously rich and believed passionately in the idea of British imperialism. Rhodes dreamed of British influence from "Cape to Cairo." The British Empire at war with small republics in South Africa clearly laid bare Britain's imperialistic designs. As the troops began to leave for South Africa from Southampton Hardy records his feelings in "Embarcation." Like Marlow in *Heart of Darkness* Hardy draws historical parallels and associates Southampton with three wars of imperial conquests. He parallels the South African war with Roman and Saxon conquests and wonders why nobody questions the war : "None dubious of the cause, none murmuring." Hardy could clearly see through the mask of patriotism and felt distressed at the misery of the commonfolk on account of the diabolical greed and scramble for power of a few war-lords. He also regrets that even in a 'civilized' age people could "argue in the selfsame bloody mode." Is civilization only a superstructure, and man basically a savage?

In keeping with his general world-view Hardy thinks of internationalism as the only possible solution to the problems that gave rise to war. In a letter to Galsworthy Hardy wrote : "The exchange of international thought is the only possible solution for the world." In "Departure" Hardy wonders why patriotism cannot transcend its parochialism and "include earth and seas." In 1917 Hardy wrote that "nothing effectual will be accomplished in the cause of Peace till the sentiment of Patriotism be freed from the narrow meaning attaching to it...and be extended to the whole globe."

In a tone of pity distilled of war Hardy points out that the common soldiers are mere "puppets in a playing hand" and asks in a tone of violent bitterness :

When shall the saner softer polities
Whereof we dream, have sway in each proud land
And patriotism, grown Godlike, scorn to stand
Bondslave to realms, but circle earth and seas?

The idea of internationalism is also echoed in a later poem, "His Country," where it dawns on the *persona* that his country is not confined to any particular region. He muses :

"What is there to bound
My denizenship? It seems I have found
Its scope to be world-wide."

In "The Colonel's Soliloquy" the colonel, a professional soldier, realizes, rather late in the day, the folly of war. The undertone of disillusionment that marks the poem actually emanates from Hardy's life-long concern and solicitude for the ordinary mortals, the commonfolk. Instead of glorifying war he focusses on the damages done by war to the warm human relationships and tender domestic sentiments. In "The Going to the Battery" it is the wife's lament and the pathos of departure that bring the band music and pealing of bells into an ironical relationship with the situation. The illusory jubilation is completely undercut by real sorrow. In "A Wife in London" Hardy highlights how the dreams of a young couple are ruthlessly shattered by war. In this poem which is ironically structured, first comes the "flashed news" of the husband's death in war away from home in a foreign land; and next day arrives the letter — obviously posted long before the casualty — in which he writes at length about his plans for the future. The letter only adds poignancy to the agony of the girl already widowed by war at the prime of her youth. In "The Souls of the Slain" Hardy provides a realistic perspective to the poem in which the dead soldiers realize that the glory of war is only an illusion, and, caught in a mood of nostalgia they wonder what their wives would probably live by :

"And our wives? quoth another resignedly,
"Dwell they on our deeds?"
...."Deeds of home, that live yet
Fresh as new...deeds of fondness or fret;

And their mothers also would not prize their military valour, but

"...Muse sadly and murmur
Your doings as boys....
Of your babyhood's innocent days.

Significantly, "Song of the Soldiers' Wives and Sweethearts" captures the mood of the jubilation of the wives and the sweethearts as the soldiers return home, but maintains a meaningful silence about their heroism or glory.

War blights possibilities. It uproots "by the night-gun's stroke / Of what the Yester moonshine brought to flower," Hardy says in "In Time of Wars and Tumults." In "Cry of the Homeless" the people rendered homeless after the Prussian invasion of Belgium, curse the Conqueror :

'May thy love he slighted, blighted
And forsaken," be it said
By thy victims,
'And thy children beg their bread!'

But then comes the "richer malediction" :

"Nay : a richer malediction!...
Rather let this thing befall
In time's hurling and unfurling
On the night when comes thy call;
That compassion dew thy pillow
And bedrench thy senses all
For thy victims,
Till death dark thee with his pall."

Modern warfare is different from earlier warfares of days of chivalry when warriors strictly followed the code of honour. But, now, in any war, honour is the first casualty, and as a natural consequence, innocent civilians and children are mercilessly slaughtered. By 1914 war in the air and under the water had developed enormously. Old weapons were either drastically modified or replaced by newer and more sophisticated ones. The weapons became more and more deadly and diabolical. In the first World War gas, artificial fog, liquid and tanks were brought into operation. Modern warfare reminds Hardy of Herod's killing of children :

Herod breathes : "Sly slaughter
Shall rule! Let us by modes once called accurst,
Overhead, under water,
Stab first."

When the armistice was signed at last on 11 November 1918 Hardy, then 78, wrote a poem, "And There was a Great Calm." The poem is remarkable as an expression of Hardy's bitter hatred of war and the stark realism in which that hatred is verbalized. The evil of war has "a brute-like blindness" about it and Hardy sees the period of the first World War as "the four years' dance / of Death." The poem ends on the question raised by the Spirit of Pity : Why the War "had to be." It is only a few power-hungry war-mongers who incite the common men, drag the simple, peaceful men into war, uproot them from their sweet domestic environments and slaughter innocent civilians including women and children; even the animals are not spared. The colossal waste of life and love is the gift of war!

It is true that Hardy never fought in a war. But there is hardly any aspect of war that escaped his notice and contemplation. The soldier-poets in the battlefield only realized the profound truth of Hardy's perceptive and prophetic utterances. In a way the soldier-poets practically carried on, with courage and conviction, the war on War so powerfully waged by Hardy even before the first World War had broken out.

11

Yvor Winters's Theory of Form*

Yvor Winters is not primarily a theoretician, because he believes that "theory in itself is insufficient."[1] His theory of form, therefore, has to be developed from the various observations he has made on different occasions. While it is true that the observations are partly occasioned by the immediate context in which they are made, there is a broader pattern within which these observations can be reconciled. It can be seen, then, that Winters's theory of form is quite consistent and well-defined. While discussing the theory of form we have confined our discussion to the poetic form only, keeping in view Winters's remark that "the poem exhausts more fully than any other literary form the inherent possibilities of language."[2]

Winters is an avowed moralist.[3] Rejecting what he calls the "didactic," the "hedonistic" and the "romantic," he says he is most in sympathy with a fourth theory, which, "for lack of better term," he calls the "moralistic" theory.[4] I propose to examine how Winters's theory of form is related to his idea about the moral nature of literature and his belief that the poet is a moral agent. It can also be seen that Winters's theory of form has a strong affinity with the tradition of Indian thought as expounded in Sanskrit poetics.

To begin with, there are two aspects of a poem : (1) the subject matter or the material provided by the life-experience; and (2) the way the material is structured into an authentically personal and unified art-form. The material governs and is subsequently governed by the structure in the poetic process. Winters writes :

---

* International Conference of ICLA, New York, 1982.

"The poem is a statement in words about human experience,"[5] and again : "I believe that a poem (or other work of artistic literature) is a statement in words about a human experience. I use the term statement in a very inclusive sense, and for a lack of something better."[6] The statement referred to, however, is a rational statement, because words are concepts, and language itself is essentially rational. So Winters qualifies :

> The poem is good in so far it makes a defensible rational statement about a given human experience (the experience need not be real but must be in some sense possible) and at the same time communicates the emotion which ought to be motivated by that rational understanding of that experience.[7]

But the poetic statement is different from a statement of purely cognitive nature.[8] Winters writes : "A poem is first of all a statement in words. But it differs from all such statements of a purely philosophical or theoretical nature, in that, it has by intention a controlled content of feeling."[9] The "content of feeling" refers to Winters's theory of language and the word "controlled" refers to the role of the poet, while both the aspects, at bottom, are inextricably interlinked with the issue of the morality of poetry.

Thoughts and feelings are couched in words, and words have dual roles to play :

> My theory rests on the observation that language, if one disregards for the present its phonetic values, is dual in nature; that each word is both conceptual and evocative, denotative and connotative, and that the feeling, evocation, or connotation is directly the result of the concept and dependent upon the concept for its existence.[10]

And again :

> These terms, however, all suggest certain loose possibilities in the way of perception and feeling; and the poet's business is so to relate them, that a single and definite idea emerges.[11]

The poet exploits the denotative and the connotative aspects of a language in transmitting meanings and feelings. In other words, he uses words to generate referential meanings but he also uses the emotional connotations (or the feeling-contents) associated with the words. The referential sense of any statement is its motive and the connotations form its emotion. The relation between motive and emotion as far as I understand these terms, is similar to, if not identical with, the relation between denotation and connotation. Furthermore, there is a close relation between motive and emotion, as there is between thought and feeling. If the concept happens to be trite or imprecise, the feeling will be enfeebled and the harmony will be disturbed.

What is important in regard to a poem is a just feeling, and not necessarily an intense feeling. The feeling, to be just, must be properly motivated. A poem can be successful only when the poet is able to strike the perfect balance between motive and emotion. This balance can be achieved by a judicious application of the tools for the evocation of the proper feeling. Some of the tools such as imagery, diction, syntax, etc., are subjective, while others such as rhythm, meter, etc., are objective. The blending can be perfect only when the poet has a perfect command of the resources of language, the varying levels of denotation and connotation and the rhythmic potentialities.[12] But a command of the language is not enough. Since a poetic statement has a "controlled content of feeling," and also because a poem must make "a defensible rational statement about human experience," reason must function as a moderator of the consciousness of the poet and also as the ultimate controlling principle. Reason is of paramount importance in Winters's theory of form.[13] The rational quality of language calls for the central function of reason both in the understanding and evaluation of the human experience, the raw material of a poem, and also in the composition of poetry. It brings the human character of the poet into full activity in his poetic expression : "The poet, then, understands his subject in rational terms, and he so employs language that he communicates simultaneously that understanding and the feelings which it properly motivates."[14] When the poet tries to understand his experience in rational terms, as a man *qua* man he is equipped with a world-view; he has his personal passions and prejudices. His experience originates from an interaction between the given situation and his highly developed sensibililty. The poet is, then, in "semi-intuitive contact with experience," as Winters observes in his note to the poem "Heracles."[15] In a way, one's view of reality determines one's view of consciousness.[16] The point is that the poetic reaction to life-experience becomes significant only when the total personality of the poet — the rational, the emotional and the sensuous — is involved in the response. It is through reasonable control in the organization of the perceived material that the poet achieves the desired balance in his completed poem,[17] for it is not the material but the perception, organization and structuring of the material that makes a poem successful. Quite often the forms of individual poems vary in quality because of the varying powers and interests of the poets. Winters traces, for example, the source of the Romantic disintegration in the Romantics' abandonment of logic.[18]

Since the content of poetry is human experience, moral evaluation of human experience will inevitably creep into the texture of the poem. The poet draws the emotion from the rational understanding of the human experience; he evaluates his experience and records it in the light of the rational understanding derived from the tenable human experience. This is an act of moral judgment. If the poet can hit upon the right form which can best control the logical content and evoke the proper feeling toward the subject, then the poem becomes aesthetically moral. This is not an easy task. Winters writes : "The act of moral judgment so considered is far more difficult, is a much fuller experience, than an act of classification; it is a full and definitive account of a human experience."[19] Moreover, "The feeling is particular and unparaphrasable...is inseparable from what we call poetic form or unity, for the creation of form is nothing more nor less than the act of evaluating, and shaping (that is, controlling) a given experience."[20] A similar idea is expressed elsewhere : "The poetic content inheres in the feeling, the style, untranslatable and can be reduced to no formula save itself."[21] The form inheres in the feeling and embodies the poet's perception of life, the evaluation of the perception through reason and emotion as revealed in the completed poem. When the evaluation of experience is communicated through all possible variations of versification and rhythm, it makes poetry "a means of enriching one's awareness of human experience...and strengthen the moral temper."[22] Moreover, "if art is moral," Winters contends,[23] "there should be relationship between art and human action." Winters concludes that poetry is thus "a civilizing influence : it trains our power of judgment and should, I imagine, affect the daily judgments and actions."[24] And again : "We regard as greatest those works which deal with experiences which affect human life most profoundly, and this criterion is not merely one of the intensity of the experience but of the generality or exclusiveness of the implications."[25] This, in a way, completes the circuit by pointing out the way in which poetry can and should influence the course of human action. The morality of poetry is not confined to the poet or the act of composition of poetry; it encompasses and involves the reader as well.

While discussing the form of poetry, Winters suggests that any successful poem is a complex of meaning with two distinguishable features : a logical structure and a texture made up of sound through meter and musical phrasing; the rational structure and the rhythmical progression :

> What we speak of loosely as the "form" of a poem is probably, at least for the most part, two-fold; we have on the one hand the rational structure of the poem, the orderly arrangement and progression of thoughts; and we have on the other a kind of rhythm broader and less easily measurable than the rhythm of the line — the poem exists in time, the mind proceeds through it in time, and if the poet is a good one he takes advantage of this fact and makes the progression rhythmical.[26]

What Winters means by "rhythmical" may be understood from his explanation of the term in the context of his own poems : "These poems are rhythmical not merely from line to line but in total movement from beginning to end, and that the relations between the meanings of the part is an element in the rhythm, along with the sound."[27] The rhythmical progression results from the ordering of a poem's rhythm, meter, pace and cadence. Winters starts with the assumption that "meter or rather the total phonetic quality of material language is in some way or degree expressive."[28] Music expresses emotion. A particular kind of music expresses a particular kind of emotion. Although the material language is no substitute for music, it shares with music the property of rhythm : "And metrical language, if we understand the language, is not pure sound; the sound is merely one quality of the total meaning, but it contributes, or can be made to contribute to the meaning."[29] And again: "If the total rhythmic structure can affect the total feeling of the poem, it is only reasonable to suppose that there is a similar relationship within the details."[30]

Winters believes that a well-formulated metrical technique is essential to the art of poetry, although Winters would hasten to warn us that a monotonous meter invariably enfeebles the rhythm. Within the general frame of metrical reference, it is the variations from the metrical norm that gives rhythmic vitality to a poem. An appropriate meter with careful variations can enhance and strengthen the total rhythmic structure in its capacity to transmit both motive and emotion, which together comprise the philosophical structure of the poem. This becomes evident in the audible reading of poetry. In the individual poem the meter serves as the metrical norm; but the rhythm is the broad, prevailing accentual sound pattern of the actualized poem. The metrical technique is thus a necessary controlling instrument of all kinds of poetry. It helps the poet to relate his rational understanding to his emotion and enable him to qualify his emotion more precisely than in any other form of statement. What is more important, it provides the poet with an opportunity to bring his poem close to a true judgment of rational choice because, "the total phonetic value of metrical language has the power to qualify the expression of feeling through language."[31]

> He [the poet] is not endeavouring to invent a logical argument, then meter it, then confuse argument and meter in the interests of excitement. He is seeking to state a true moral judgment; he is endeavouring to bring each word as close to a true judgment as possible; and he has it in his power to modify the values of words within certain limits.[32]

And again :

> Meter has certain phonetic values of its own, and it clarifies, identifies, and even modifies the phonetic values of unmetered language. And the total phonetic value of metrical language has the power to qualify the expression of feeling through language. Since the expression of feeling is a part of the moral judgment as I have defined it, the meter has moral significance, for it renders possible a refinement in the adjustment of feeling to motive which would not otherwise be possible.[33]

We have earlier seen that the rational structure of poem is aesthetically moral, and now we see that the rhythmical progression or the texture made up of sound through meter and metrical phrasing is also of moral significance. Thus the form of a poem which integrates the logical and the metrical structures is moral par excellence, and in Winters's aesthetics this integration is achieved not through any esemplastic imagination[34] but by an act of moral judgment.[35] The form must be sensitive to and improve upon the configuration of reality.

Incidentally, in his poem "Dedication For a Book of Criticism" addressed to W.D. Briggs, Winters says that the task of a scholar is very difficult indeed. Winters writes :

> Strong the scholar is to scan
> What is permanent in man;
> To detect his form and kind
> And preserve the human mind;
> By the type himself to guide,
> Universal wisdom bide.[36]

I believe that Winters has satisfactorily performed the task he had set upon himself[37] and there is every reason to hope that the prayer that Winters made in his poem "To Herman Melville in 1951" would be granted without pain :

Saint Herman grant me this that I may be
Saved from the worms who have impested thee.[38]

Winters's concept of form as related to the circuit of poetic experience has a close affinity with the tradition of Indian thought. Sanskrit poetics clearly delineates the circuit of poetic experience. The modality of poetic experience is similar to life-experience in terms of stimulus and response. The circuit begins in the world itself, the primary source and the ultimate reservoir of all experience. The next link is the poet, who reacts intensely to the life-experience and recreates that experience in an art-form which becomes the objective correlative for the experience. This form is the third link. The fourth link is the reader, the *sahṛdaya* of Sanskrit poetics. The circuit becomes complete only when the aesthetic experience of reading a poem refines the sensibility of a reader and heightens his perceptivity. Similarly, Winters's concept of form as inhering in the logical and the metrical structures is congruent with the concept of *kāvyaśarīra* or the poetic tissue. Critic after critic in Sanskrit poetics has called attention to the distinctive quality of poetic expression which is distinguished by the supremacy of utterance (*uktipradhāna*). The poetic tissue (*kāvyaśarīra*) is qualitatively different from and superior to other verbal structures. Abhinava Gupta[39] interprets poetic utterance as an ideal structure (*utkriṣṭa sangaṭhana*) and derives it directly from poetic action. Utterance here does not refer to the verbal tissue alone. It is the perfect balance of all the elements of poetry. Abhinava Gupta contends that the ideal poetic structure integrates the idea and the image, the sonic and the semantic. Bhamaha[40] also meant the same thing when he defined poetry as *śabdarthasahitau kāvyam* : the sonic and the semantic together constitute the body of poetry. According to Sanskrit poetics there is a precise genetic relation between feeling and expression. Rhythm as an intrinsic feature of expression is determined by feeling. In other words, the feeling creates its own rhythm and determines the meter. The metrical structure of a poem must be organized in such a way that it points out the highlights and deepens the shadows. Expression, sound and rhythm arranged in an ideal pattern would require us to obey a certain order and development of thought, imagery and emotion. All these are poetical devices for the concretization of feeling.

The analysis of meters in terms of their efficacy to be the vehicles of feeling can be traced to the third century B.C., if not earlier, in Sanskrit poetics. Katyayana[41] is certainly one of the oldest writers in the field. He discusses the appropriateness of certain meters to certain subjects and situations. The situations, in his view, should forge their own meter (*arthānurūp chanda*). Meter is only an abstract pattern of the rhythm. Formal analysis can indicate the precise shape of this pattern. But in any actual poem, if it is a good specimen of poetic vitality, the component rhythms will certainly be found to vary from the abstract scheme, for the simple reason that rhythm is really the undulation of poetic feeling as it flows into the linguistic tissue and moulds it. The pulse of feeling cannot be expected to be mechanically regular.

As in Winters, so in Sanskrit poetics, every link in the poetic circuit is of profound moral significance. The writings of Bharata,[42] Anandabardhana,[43] and Mahima Bhatta,[44] to mention only some of the exponents of this theory, would abundantly illustrate the point. Poetry takes its origin from life and, it must, in a profound sense, illuminate life. The poetic form in its new integral reality provides the relevant means.

NOTES

In my reference to the works of Yvor Winters, I have used the following abbreviations :

IDR — *In Defense of Reason*, 3rd ed., Denver, Swallow, 1947.

FC — *The Function of Criticism : Problems and Exercises*, Denver, Swallow, 1957.

UER — *Uncollected Essays and Reviews*, edited and introduced by Francis Murphy.

CP — *Collected Poems*, rev. ed., Denver, Swallow, 1960.

FD — *Forms of Discovery: Critical and Historical Essays on the Forms of Short Poem in English*, Denver, Swallow, 1967.

1. Introduction to *The Early Poems of Yvor Winters*, 1920-28, Swallow, 1966, reprinted in *The Poetry of Yvor Winters*, with an introduction by Donald Davie, Swallow, 1978, p. 16.
2. IDR, p. 11.
3. Stanley Edgar Hyman writes : "In all these welter of comparison, dictum, evaluation, and posturing Winters retains one constant point of view, that of morality" : *The Armed Vision* (New York, 1948; rev. ed., 1955), p. 54.
4. IDR, p. 3.
5. *Ibid.*, p. 5.
6. FC, p. 26.
7. IDR, p. 11.
8. In a recent article, "The Language of Poetry : Materiality and Meaning" published in *Essays and Criticism*, Derek Attridge discusses at length the nature of the language of poetry and observes that "the organization of the linguistic substance in poetry acknowledges and enforces the fact that literary language is not the language of daily discourse."

9. IDR, p. 363.
10. *Ibid.*, p. 502.
11. *Ibid.*, p. 503.
12. "It is not with idea that one makes sonnets, but with words" Mallarme wrote in a letter to Degas. What he meant is that the poetic tissue consists of words, but words charged with evocative power : see Henri Mondor, *Vie de Mallarme* (Gallimard, 1941), p. 684.
13. The very title of his monumental work. *In Defense of Reason*, indicates the primacy of reason in Winters's critical theories.
14. IDR, p. 503.
15. CP, p. 146.
16. Cf. G.E. Powell, "Some Key Concepts in the Poetry of Yvor Winters," *Southern Review*, 11 (1975), pp. 838-54.
17. Keith F. Mekean is of the opinion that, in Winters's critical *oeuvre*, balance is more important than control: *The Moral Measure of Literature* (Denver : Swallow, 1961), p. 100.
18. I am inclined to agree with Andor Gomme (cf. *Attitudes to Criticism*) when he says : "It is through Winters's understanding of form that he is able to penetrate to the heart of the disease which he calls romanticism in which there is a special concentration on 'feeling' at the expenses of a properly motivated situation."
19. IDR, p. 503; my emphasis.
20. *Ibid.*, p. 20.
21. UER, p. 224.
22. IDR, p. 29.
23. *Ibid.*, p. 371.
24. *Ibid.*, p., 372.
25. FC, p. 27.
26. IDR, p. 12.
27. CP, p. 16.
28. IDR, p. 545.
29. *Ibid.*, p. 546.
30. *Ibid.*, p. 547.
31. *Ibid.*, p. 551.
32. *Ibid.*, p. 550; brackets mine.
33. *Ibid.*, p. 551.
34. Winters, in fact, is not quite sure what imagination means, because during the past hundred and fifty years it has been used so variously and so illusively as a term of sophisticated criticism; cf. IDR, p. 7.
35. As René Wellek has pointed out in his brilliant essay, "Yvor Winters : Rehearsed and Reconsidered" published in *Denver Quarterly*, 10 (1975-76).

36. CP, p. 145.
37. Winters carries conviction when he remarks with complete and candid confidence : "My critical and moral notions are derived from the observation of literature and life, and my theism is derived from my critical and moral notions. I did not proceed from the opposite direction"; IDR, p. 14.
38. CP, p. 137.
39. Abhinava Gupta (10th c.) : *Locana*, Comment on Manmatha's verse.
40. Bhamaha (7th c.) *Bhāmahālankāra* (Bombay, 1909).
41. Cf. V. Raghavan : "Winters quoted in the Abhinava Bharati," *Journal of Oriental Research*, Vol. 6, Pt. 3, p. 223.
42. Bharata (2nd c. B.C.); cf. *Nātya Sāstra*, Kavyamala Series, Vol. 42 (Bombay, 1894), and A. Sankaran : *Some Aspects of Literary Criticism in Sanskrit*, Ch. III, Madras University, 1929.
43. Anandabardhana (9th c.); cf. *Dhanyāloka*, Kavyamala Series (Bombay, 1928).
44. Mahima, Bhatta (11 c.); cf. *Vyākti Viveka*, edited by T. Ganapati Sastri, Trivandrum Sanskrit Series, 1909.

12

Reaction Against Joyce*

James Joyce is perhaps the most talked about novelist of the present century. Quite often he is regarded as the greatest influence on the twentieth century novel. The stream of consciousness and the interior monologue which Joyce used as the rhetorics of his fictions represented really a new starting point for the novel. But Joyce not only initiated a fresh approach to the form of novel, but also as a very serious and capable artist he perfected the form to the fullest realization of all its potentialities, and in the process, practically left it dry. While *Ulysses* pushes the novel form to its limit. *Finnegans Wake* pushes the English language beyond its limit.

In all the three major works — *A Portrait of the Artist as a Young Man* (1916), *Ulysses* (1922) and *Finnegans Wake* (1939) — Joyce tries to capture reality in terms of a continuous aesthestic quest. Stephen's containment within the world of forms continues into *Ulysses* in which he takes a subordinate position. And in *Finnegans Wake* he fades away into an impersonal and distant world — a world made and held together by its own language. *Ulysses* seeks the modern version for the Odysseus myth and the result is modernism *par excellence*. Even before *Ulysses* was fully published Virginia Woolf hailed it as a great masterpiece in her now famous essay on Modern Fiction.

It is really surprising that Joyce has ceased to have any hold on the novelists writing today. The symposium on the state of fiction recently conducted in the U.K. (1978) in which eighty living novelists participated reveals the position that Joyce has among our contemporaries. He is rejected, or at best, held in awe.

---

* 1982.

A. Alvarez says :

> The experimental novel, I think, has less to do with the art of fiction than with the problems of prose aspiring to the condition of poetry. Beckett, for example, is a great genius — perhaps the only one around writing in English — but his prose works seem to me a quite deliberate attempt to complete what Joyce began : the formal assassination of the traditional novel.[1]

And Iris Murdoch remarks that the "impressionistic realism" of James Joyce and Virginia Woolf is no more than a "mood of intellectual play manipulating ideas, spinning fantasies and experimenting more light-heartedly with language."[2]

If this is the position of Joyce in England, the picture is no better in the continent. There also Joyce is rejected completely. In an essay on the trends of the contemporary French novel Henri Peyre does not find any influence of Joyce in the writings of the contemporary French novelists, perhaps because "Joyce's interior monologues once revered as the paragons of subtlety, wear off their freshness and appear crude and tricky."[3] Even Eliot, while commending *Finnegans Wake* as a "monumental book" remarked that "one book like this is enough."[4]

Yvor Winters, the noted American critic, points out with a sharp critical insight the peculiar merit of *Finnegans Wake* :

> In *Finnegans Wake*, by James Joyce, the dream convention is unmistakable. It permeates the entire texture of the work, not only the syntax but the words themselves, which are broken down and recombined in surprising ways.[5]

But he argues that Joyce suffers from the fallacy of imitative form. Winters writes :

> Mr. Joyce endeavours to express disintegration by breaking down his form, by experiencing disintegration before our very eyes, but this destroys much of his power of expression. Of course he controls the extent to which he impairs the form, but this merely means that he is willing to sacrifice just so much power of expression — in an effort to express something — and no more.[6]

And again :

> The romantic antithesis of moods is the central theme of Joyce's *Ulysses*, which, at the same time, is rendered diffuse by a stream-of-consciousness technique and by the fallacy of imitative form. The book has great virtues, which its admirers have long since

> enumerated, but it lacks final precision both of form and feeling. It is adolescent as Laforgue is adolescent; it is ironic about feelings which are not worth the irony.[7]

I think that Joyce's failure is largely due to the fact that his novels become increasingly dissociated from life. In *Finnegans Wake* we have everything except life. So, though it attains a type of technical perfection, it fails to impress and involve us. Literature must owe its allegiance to life. As it takes its origin from life, it must, in a profound sense, be committed to life; otherwise, literature becomes dead. Joyce perhaps apprehended this failure. In *A Portrait of the Artist as a Young Man* Stephen says to Cranly :

> You made me confess the fears that I have. But I will tell you also what I do not fear. I do not fear to be alone or to be spurned for another or to leave whatever I have to leave. And I am not afraid to make a mistake, a lifelong mistake and perhaps as long as eternity too.[8]

On the one hand, we have the supreme self-confidence of Joyce in his commitment to the religion of an artist, and, on the other hand, there is a stark realization, almost tragic in its intensity, about the possible rejection of him by posterity.

The foregoing discussion would lead us to conclude that Joyce does not belong to the main tradition of the English novel, though as an experimentalist he will forever remain an indispensable classic.

NOTES AND REFERENCES

1. *The New Review*, Vol. 5, no. 1; Summer, 1978, p. 15.
2. Iris Murdoch : *Sartre* : *Romantic Rationalist*, p. 31.
3. *Contemporary Literature*, Ed. By Richard Kostalanetz, New York; 1964, p. 1.
4. T.S. Eliot : *On Poetry and Poets*, Faber, 1956, p. 108.
5. Yvor Winters : *In Defense of Reason*, Denver, Third edition, 1943, p. 60.
6. *Ibid.*, pp. 61-62.
7. *Ibid.*, p. 72.
8. James Joyce : *A Portrait*, Chapter 5, section C, p. 247.

13

T.S. Eliot : The Indic Influence*

In the "East Coker" section of *Four Quartets* (1943) Eliot says : "In my beginning is my end" (*CP* 196). If we leave out the early poems of Eliot his first major poem is *The Waste Land* published in 1922. The next major poem is *Ash Wednesday* published in parts between 1928 and 1930. *The Waste Land, Ash Wednesday* and *Four Quartets* are said to parallel Dante's *Inferno, Purgatorio* and *Paradiso*. But what is more important is to try to discover the pattern that emerges from his poetry, and its main thrust. So, taking cue from Eliot's remark "In my beginning is my end" let us go back to *The Waste Land* briefly.

In the concluding section of *The Waste Land* Eliot draws on the *Brihadaranyaka Upanishad* (5.1-3) in the three-fold message of the Thunder — Da Da Da which stand for Datta (give), Dayadhyam (sympathise) and Damayata (control). About this message Kuppuswami Sastri in his Introduction to Sankaracharya's commentary on the Brihadaranyaka Upanishad writes :

> The most striking message of this Upanishad in the ethical side is embodied in the lesson which every mediator is asked to read in the dental rumblings of the three *das* of a thunder clap, which are suggestive of self-restraint (*dama*), self-sacrifice (*dāna*), and, merciful benevolence (*dayā*). This great ethical teaching is embodied in the text.[1]

This message is symbolic in the context and sums up the cryptic mode of Prajapati's teaching to the three kinds of his disciples — gods,

---

* Revised and enlarged version of the talk given on BBC in 1988 on the occasion of the birth-centenary of T.S. Eliot.

men and demons — as to how they should behave. The virtues exhorted by Prajapati are essential to break through the prevailing rainlessness and the resultant sterility of the devastated land of the Fisher King.

Now, on Eliot's own testimony, it is generally believed that Dante is the greatest influence on Eliot. In the first place, The *Waste Land* is dedicated to Ezra Pound with the words *il miglior fabbro*, the better craftsman, which is actually Dante's tribute to Arnaut Daniel in *Purgatorio* (XXVI 117). Very often it is believed that what Virgil was to Dante, Dante is to Eliot and there is no doubt of the fact that the influence of Dante permeates Eliot's poetry.[2] In his Preface to *For Lancelot Andrews* (1928) Eliot declared himself as a "classicist in literature, Anglo Catholic in religion, royalist in politics." Eliot was a pious Christian. Who but a very devoted and almost dogmatic Christian could write *The Idea of a Christian Society* in 1939 when the entire world was in the grip of the holocaust of a war? Eliot believed, and sincerely, that Christianity, a community of Christians could really save the world from destruction and avert the impending global crisis. In fact, even before the publication of *The Idea of a Christian Society* Eliot gave a radio talk on "The Churches' message to the world." In 1948 in *Notes towards the Definition of Culture* he reiterated some of the points. It may be worthwhile to remember in this connection that all these ideas were discussed in the meetings of the society of intellectuals called 'The Moot.' The members of 'The Moot' included Eliot, Karl Manheim and Middleton Murry, among others. Even in the two Coriolan poems — "The Triumphal March" and "Difficulties of a Statesman" — Eliot emphasizes the imperative need to spiritualize politics. The atmosphere of suffering and pessimism that we find in "Prufrock" (1915). "Gerontion" (1919), *The Waste Land* (1922) and "The Hollow Men" (1925) is basically secular — the non-spiritual atmosphere of the modern world. Eloise Hay in her book *The Negative Way*[3] has tried to establish that Eliot gives a Buddhist support of Christianity. Eliot's reference to the still centre and many Buddhist concepts that are scattered throughout the entire gamut of his writings possibly drive her to such a conclusion. But a closer scrutiny would reveal that in a broader perspective the message — *datta, dayadhvam, damayata* — seem more central. What constitutes the core of Eliot's total vision may be surmised on the search for their significance.

Eliot's interest in Hindu philosophy goes back to the period of his second stay at Harvard (1911-1914) when he read Sanskrit and Pali and studied the ancient classics of India. Eliot joined the graduate programme of the department of philosophy in the fall term of 1911. Next year he attended James Houghton Woods' lectures on Indian philosophy and Masaharu Anesaki's course on Buddhism. He read selected portions of the Vedas and Upanishads in Sanskrit in the copy of *Twenty Eight Upanishads* edited by Vasudev Laxman and Shastri Phansikar. The book was presented to him by Charles Lanman, Harvard's senior orientalist. In the copy Lanman had marked out some eleven passages that called for special attention. It is interesting to note that these included the section from *Brihadaranyaka Upanishad* which Eliot so meaningfully used in *The Waste Land.* Eliot also procured a catalogue of books on Vedanta and in 1913 purchased Paul Deussen's *Upanishads des Veda* and *Die Sutras des Vedanta.* This provided Eliot with German translations of primary sources plus scholarly commentary on the work of Shankara, the founder of the Vedanta school. The two works that claimed his particular attention were Patanjali's *Mahabhasya* and the *Gita.* Of the two years of his study of oriental classics he was engrossed for one year in "the mazes of Patanjali's *Mahabhasya*" (*ASG*). His exposure to the *Gita*, however, was more crucial and profound. It is not for nothing that Eliot called it "the next greatest philosophical poem to the Divine Comedy within my experience" (*SE* 258). Kearns believes that its stance represented an equilibrium he sought in personal life and philosophical thought" (Kearns 50). Incidentally, as Prof. Sati Chatterjee has pointed out in a recent article[4] "another channel of Eliot's communion with the mind of ancient India" was his close association with Josiah Royce, Professor of the History of Philosophy. "An extra-ordinary philosopher," his appearance suggested Asia. He was a living legend. It was believed that no country in Europe could produce such a superman, a sage who was "wiser than Europe, more abstract, more Himalayan" (Howarth 210). Royce who was Eliot's teacher, and who made, in his lectures, detailed analysis of Hindu mysticism of the *Upanishads* and traced the origin of mystical philosophy in the Indian scriptures, was a major factor in Eliot's reception of Eastern thought. Royce tried to establish a vital relation between religion and philosophy and made a detailed study of the polemics of assertion through negation in Yagnyavalka's teachings to his wife, Maitreyi, and in his first major work *The World and the Individual* he mentioned the central spiritual axiom of the Chandogya Upanishad (3.14), *tat tvam asi*, "that art thou." It implied for Royce the transcendence of all distinctions in the final recognition of truth. In the supplementary essay to *The World and the Individual* Royce wrote : "The Peace that passeth understanding fulfils all the needs of understanding." "The Peace which passeth understanding" is also the equivalent given by Eliot to *Shantih* in the Notes on *The Waste*

Land. Southam writes : "Eliot's interpretation derives from the words of Paul to the early Christians : "And the Peace of God, which passeth all understanding, shall keep your hearts and minds through Christ Jesus" (Southam 95). Despite the fact that Eliot's translation and possible implications are under expert fire[5] the use of *shantih shantih shantih* is both Vedic in origin and Upanishadic in its contents as suggested by Eliot in his Notes. We may recall, in this connection, that Eliot had reviewed Sri Ananda Acharya's *Brahmadarshan or Institution of the Absolute Being: An Introduction to the Study of Hindu Philosophy.* The review was published in *International Journal of Ethics* in April 1918.

Eliot's next major poem *Ash Wednesday* trembles on the verge of mystic revelation. Part I invokes the mood of weeping. Part II manifests the exhilaration attained by the death of the body, death of worldly hopes and death of carnal love. In Part III the aspirant has covered some distance in his flight and looks back at the twisted shape of his hope and despair. Part IV begins with the presentation of the glory of the Lady in Mary's colour. Part V opens with adoration, edification of the Word. Part VI presents the speaker in the toil of his struggle between memory and desire, flesh and spirit. He has relinquished all hope — "Although I do not hope to turn..." Desire is not disappearing; even memory intrudes. The speaker prays to the "blessed sister," "holy mother" : "Suffer us not to mock ourselves with falsehood." He wants to learn "Our peace in His will," and totally submit to God "And let my cry come unto Thee." The agony of suffering and penitence have not yet yielded the expected result. We must look forward to Eliot's last major poem *Four Quartets* (1943) for an answer. And it is not Christianity but the *Gita* that provides the answer.

Four Quartets is divided into four sections : "Burnt Norton," "East Coker," "The Dry Salvages" and "Little Gidding," dealing mainly with air, earth, water and fire respectively. Each section is further divided into five sections and there is a remarkable structural ordering in the poem. The poem shows that great poetry can be made out of philosophy. Now coming back to the influence of the *Gita* here. In "The Dry Salvages" section of the poem Eliot makes direct references to the *Gita* : "I sometimes wonder if that is what Krishna meant" (*CP* 209). And again, "so Krishna" as when he admonished Arjuna "On the fields of battle" (*CP* 211). Gordon thinks that here Eliot takes up the challenge of autobiography. It is "his climactic effort to fuse past and future in a single pattern" (Gordon 115). "The Dry Salvages," according to Gordon, "is about the frontiers of action where a significant life is made. There are two struggles, first with the ghosts of the past, then with the ghosts of the future. Memories, expectations : these impede the new life, and must be dissolved in the timeless pattern of spiritual autobiography" (Gordon 119). Eliot refers to three possible attitudes to action : one is attachment in which a person gets emotionally involved in self, things and persons. Then there is complete indifference in which one does not take any interest in a thing or self or person. And, then, there is still another attitude, that of detachment, in which one does one's job to the best of one's ability but avoids becoming emotionally involved. This detachment or dispassionate work — *Niṣkām karma* is the main wisdom imparted by the *Gita*. Krishna, therefore, advises Arjuna to fight, but fight with equanimity, with the right combination of insight and detachment. This is the only way to avoid being caught up in the world of karma and illusion. *Four Quartets*, Eliot's last major poem, is also "his greatest poetry of search" (Gordon 260) and upholds detachment as the best possible attitude.

One may think that this amounts to an undue overemphasis on one particular aspect of the poem. But that is not so. A close look at the symbols and images and even archetypes used by Eliot in the poem would reveal that it is not a matter of surface; it goes deep down into the heart of things. The *Gita* definitely informs considerably Eliot's thought and poetry. The Upanishadic tropes — the figures of fire, light, darkness, lotus, river and sea — are creatively used to project the fabric of Eliot's vision.

In "Burnt Norton" section of *Four Quartets* Eliot refers to the lotus : "And the lotus rose...." (*CP* 190). Lotus is the symbol of heart while the sun is the symbol of blissful knowledge. Just as the rays of the sun falling on a lotus make it bloom so the human heart suffused with true knowledge attains bliss. Lotus, in Indian thought, is a complex of symbols. We have it in the beginning of creation when Brahma appeared sitting on a lotus that came out of the navel of Vishnu. The iconographic image of *Krishna* also presents him with a lotus in one of his hands. In the Tantra, the occult, a yogi makes his journey from *mūlādhār* through *swādhisthān, manipur, anāhata, bisuddhāksha to sasrār*, in the thousand petalled rose. Finally, the lotus is a symbol of detachment as enunciated in the *Gita*. We are told —

One who performs his duty without attachment, surrendering the results unto the Supreme God, is not affected by sinful action, as the lotus leaf is untouched by water.[6]

[brahmaṇyādhāya karmāṇi sangam tyaktv̄a karoti yaḥ lipyate na sa pāpena *padma-patramivāmbhs̄a* 5.10]

The relevant verses on non-attachment are the following :

[Karmanyevādhikaraste mā phaleṣu kadācana

mā karmaphalaheturbhūrmā te sango'stvakarmaṇi 2.4]

You have a right to perform your prescribed duty, *but you are not entitled to fruits of action*. Never consider yourself to be the cause of the results of your activities, and never be attached to not doing your duty.

[Sukhaduḥkhe same kṛtvā lābhālābhau jayājayau

tato yuddhāya yujyasva naivam pāpam avāpsyasi 2.38]

Do thou fight for the sake of fighting, without considering happiness or distress, loss or gain, victory or defeat — and, by so doing, you shall never incur sin.

[Vitarāga bhaya krodhā manmayā māmupāsritāh

bahavo jnānatapasā pütā madbhāvamāgatāḥ 4.10]

Being freed from attachment, fear and anger, being fully absorbed in Me many persons in the past became purified by knowledge of Me and thus they all attained transcendental love for Me.

And here is Eliot's summing up : "For us there is only the trying. The rest is not our business." (East Coker, *CP* 203)

Fire is a major symbol in "Little Gidding." The poet talks of Pentecostal fire which glows more intense "than blaze of branch of brazier" (*CP* 214). The refining fire is the fire of divine love and mercy in its disciplinary manifestation, whether as the burning pyre of sacrifice on which the selfish self is immolated, or as the purgatorial flames through which an unappeased spirit has to pass. Eliot says : "The only hope, or else despair / Lies in the choice of pyre or pyre / To be redeemed from fire by fire" (*CP* 221). Again, "We only live, only aspire / Consumed by either fire or fire." And finally, "And all shall be well and / All manner of things shall be well / When the tongues of flames are infolded / Into the crowned knot of fire"... (*CP* 223). One feels this fire is different from the Buddhistic or Augustinian fire ("burning, burning, burning" of *The Waste Land*). The fire of lust ultimately becomes the fire of purgatory. The *Gita* is eloquent about the renunciatory and illuminating nature of fire. Lord Krishna says :

[Yathaidhāṁsi samiddho 'gnirbhasmasātkurute 'rjuna

jnānagniḥ sarvakarmāṇi bhasmasātkurute tathā 4.37]

As the blazing fire turns firewood to ashes, O Arjuna, so does *the fire of knowledge burn to ashes all reactions to material activities*. In Chapter 11 of the *Gita* fire is equated with God Himself.

[mayā prasannena tavārjuuedaṁ rūpaṁ paraṁ
darsitāmatmayogāt
tejoṁayaṁ visvamanatamādyāṁ yanme tvadanyena na
dṛṣṭapūrvam 11.47]

My dear Arjuna, happily do I show you this universal form within the material world by My internal potency. No one before you has ever seen this unlimited and glaringly effulgent form.

Eliot's concept of fire is suffused with the Upanishadic overtones. Closely related to the idea of fire is the idea of darkness. Darkness had been used in many different ways in philosophical systems. In the *Gita* Lord Krishna refers to the darkness of the soul which is most used by the enlightened :

[Yā nisa sarvabhūtanāṁ tasyāṁ jāgarti samyaṁi
yasāṁ jāgarti bhūtāni sā nisā pasyato muneḥ 2.69]

What is night for all beings is the time of awakening for the self-controlled; and the time of awakening for all beings is night for the introspective sage.

Eliot talks of darkness "to purify the soul" (*CP* 192). And again : "Descend lower, descend only / Into the world of perpetual solitude.... Internal darkness, deprivation/ And destitution of all property" (*CP* 123).

The idea comes very close to the idea of *nirvikalpa samādhi*. Eliot says in 'East Coker' — "So the darkness shall be the light" (*CP* 200).

Here are some other ideas which have close affinity with the ideas expressed in the *Gita*. The idea that "human kind / Cannot bear very much reality" (*CP* 190) is also vouched by the *Gita* : "O all-pervading Vishnu, I can no longer maintain my equilibrium. Seeing your radiant colours fill the skies and beholding your eyes and mouths I am afraid." This idea can also be traced to *Keno-panishad* (1.3) and *Kathopanishad* (2.9). Similarly "the still point of the turning world" (*CP* 191) may be seen as an echo of the *Gita* where Brahma is seen as the still point of the wheel (9.10). Again, the idea that "on whatever sphere of being / The mind of a man may be intent at the time of death" (*CP* 211) we find in the *Gita* :

[Nabhaḥspṛsaṁ dīptamanekavarṇaṁ vyāttananam
dīptavisālanetram dṛṣṭvā
hi tvām pravyathitāntarātmā dhṛtiṁ na vindāmi samaṁ ca
viṣṇo 11.24]

Whatever state of being one remembers when he quits his body, that state he will attain without fail.

[Yaṁ yaṁ vāpi smaranbhavaṁ tyajatyante kalebaram
tam tamevaiti kaunteya sadā tadbhāvabhāvitaḥ 8.6]

Coming back to the theme of the search for significance, those who seek significance must acquire "The inner freedom from the practical desire / The release from action and suffering, release from the inner / And the outer compulsion, yet surrounded / By a grace of sense..." (*CP* 191). Their virtues include endless humility, dispossession, complete simplicity, forgiveness and unassailable calm[7] achieved through the three *das* mentioned in *The Waste Land: datta, dayadhvam, damayata* — give, sympathise, control. It is through these disciplines that one can dispense with the ego and thus with the illusion of power, control and dominance it creates.

The same search of significance may be said to constitute a major theme of Eliot's plays as well. The necessities of drama, in fact, bring the problem of action and choice under sharp focus. In *Murder in the Cathedral* Becket, like Arjuna, faces a battle involving violence and shedding of kin's blood. But he must stick to his vocation of a priest. He must avoid choosing a kind of martyrdom that is prompted by pride. In order to be a real martyr one must rise above the temptation of being a martyr. That is why Becket is surprised at the appearance of the fourth tempter ("Who are you / I expected three visitors not four"). *Murder in the Cathedral* in which Eliot portrays the fulfilment of spiritual election in martyrdom, is also his "most extended evocation of the imaginative force and moral implications of the doctrine of karma..." (Kearns 41). In *The Family Reunion* (1939) Eliot traces the way in which a man discovers such an election, and it is only when Harry is able to abandon his family he is liberated from the human wheel. Gordon believes that *The Family Reunion* is also structured out of autobiographical elements. "The description of the wife in *The Family Reunion* is an accurate picture of Vivienne as others saw her at this time : an excited, irresponsible woman who would never leave her husband alone" (Gordon 64). Harry, according to Gordon, "exists from the explicit medium of the theater into the individual drama of spiritual autobiography" (Gordon 93). The theme of *The Cocktail Party* is again that of identity and significance, of the necessity of acceptance and of the salvation of choice. The two paths that Reilly describes to Celia are the different paths of a devotee and a sage, and one must make a choice between them. In *The Confidential Clerk* (1954) the theme is fundamentally the same as in the earlier plays. Colby is seeking his identity. In *The Elder Statesman* (1958), the protagonist is old and a fallen man of power. Plagued by the agents of the past he seeks for sanctuary. Practically in all the plays Eliot is preoccupied with the importance of spiritual values in search of significance. Becket in *Murder in the Cathedral*, Harry in *The Family Reunion*, Celia in *The Cocktail Party*, Colby in *The Confidential Clerk and Lord* Claverton in *The Elder Statesman* work out their destinies in different ways but the central theme is the same search for significance for which selfless detachment is essential.

It is possible to see Eliot's critical doctrine of impersonality so loudly professed in his seminal essay "Tradition and the Individual Talent" as having an affinity with the idea of detachment as enunciated in the *Gita*. In a "remarkably honest letter" to E.M. Forster written in 1929 Eliot acknowledged "private motives underlying the doctrine of 'impersonality'" (Gordon 230). A critic must develop detachment and must look at a poem as one looks at the leg of table.

It is not necessary but it is also possible to see Eliot's personal life as an illustration of the doctrine of detachment. The fact that his first marriage was a miserable failure and the fact that yet he was able to write some of the best poetry at this time, shows how remarkable was his power of detachment. Gordon has shown how in *The Cocktail Party* Eliot transmutes the power-play of his marriage into a fictitious comedy. Intense was his search for significance through search for self.

To say all this does not mean that the assimilation of the message of the *Gita* is the be-all and end-all of Eliot's literary achievement. Eliot is a major poet, a significant poet and the credit lies in his ability to absorb all kinds of influences : the *Gita* and St. Augustine, St. Paul and the Buddha. It is a very complex pattern and this complexity is its richness, and the Eastern influence or the wind from the East makes a very important, very significant contribution to the growth of his poetry.

REFERENCES

Eliot, T.S., *Collected Poems*, Faber and Faber, London, 1963 [CP].

——, *On Poetry and Poets*, Faber and Faber, London, 1957 [*OPP*].

——, *After Strange Gods : A Primer of Modern Heresy*, Faber and Faber, London, 1934 [*ASG*].

——, *Selected Essays*, Faber and Faber, London, 1963 [*SE*],

Gordon, Lyndall, *Eliot's New Life*, London, [OUP] 1988.

Howarth, Herbert, *Notes on Some Figures Behind T.S. Eliot*, Chatto and Windus, London, 1965.

Kearns, Cleo McNelly, *T.S. Eliot and the Indic Traditions : A Study in Poetry and Belief*, Cambridge University Press, 1987.

Southam, B.C., *A Student's Guide to the Selected Poems of T.S. Eliot*, Faber and Faber, London, 1974.

1. *The Brihadaranyaka Upanishad* with the commentary of Sankaracharya, Trans. Swami Madhavananda, with an introduction by Professor S. Kuppuswami Shastri, Advaita Ashram, Almora, 1924, p. xv.
2. However, by 1951 Eliot seems to have outgrown the influence of Dante. In "Poetry and Drama" (1951) Eliot writes : "...it is ultimately the function of art, in imposing a credible order upon ordinary reality, and thereby eliciting some perception of an order in reality, to bring us to a condition of serenity, stillness, and reconciliation; and then leave us, as Virgil left Dante, to proceed towards a region where that guide can avail us no farther."
3. Eloise Knapp Hay, *T.S. Eliot's Negative Way*, Cambridge University Press, 1982.
4. "Josiah Royce, T.S. Eliot and the Upanishads : A Note" in *Prospects of Comparative Studies in Indian Departments of English*, Sambalpur University, Orissa, 1987.
5. *See* Christopher Ricks, *T.S. Eliot and Prejudice*, Faber and Faber, London, 1988, pp. 194-197.
6. My emphasis.
7. Eliot talks of "serenity, stillness and reconciliation" in 1951.

14

Mallarmé and The Indian Theory of *Dhvani*[*]

Although Stéphane Mallarmé (1842-1893) and Anandavardhana (ninth century AD) are separated by about ten centuries and by continents one finds, on close scrutiny, a striking affinity between the poetic theory of Mallarmé and the Indian theory of *Dhvani* as expounded by Anandavardhana, the greatest exponent of the school. It is all the more interesting because there is no evidence of Mallarmé's familiarity with the theory of *Dhvani*, although he uses some Indian themes in his writings, the story of Nala and Damayanti, for example. But both Mallarmé and Anandavardhana are highly original as theoreticians, some early influences notwithstanding. Both are revolutionary in their attitude to poetry, in their rejection of their predecessors as superficial and insignificant, in their emphasis on the unexplored potentialities of language which, eventually, is the tool of any poetry, in their assumption that the value that inheres in poetry is not the "beautiful" in the conventional sense but rather arises out of the fact that a linguistic structure can alter and satisfy certain emotional needs, and above all, in their emphasis on the suggestive or evocative power of poetry in preference to the descriptive power of poetry. But while Anandavardhana developed his theory into an elaborate system, almost a scientific treatise, with meticulous care and consideration of the minutest semantic categories so that the methodology was systematic and exhaustive, working from parts to whole rather than *vice versa*, Mallarmé's theory is to be developed from the various critical comments and observations scattered throughout the

[*] FILLM, Guelph, Canada, 1987.

entire corpus of his writings. Both anticipate some of the major critical interests of modern times.

About eleven hundred years of Indian poetic tradition preceded Anandavardhana's appearance on the literary scene, and the origin of the *Dhvani* school, like any other school of poetry, is lost in obscurity. But it is Anandavardhana who expounds the theory of *Dhvani* as an elaborate system, assimilating in the process all the earlier theories of poetry such as *Rasa Siddhānta, Alaṃkar Siddhānta* and *Rīti Siddhānta*. It may be worthwhile to give some idea of the theory of *Dhvani*, particularly for the benefit of Western readers, before comparing it to the poetic creed of Mallarmé.

Starting with a theory of expression, the *Dhvani* school is mainly concerned with the semantic problems of the function of words and their meanings. But the theory, nevertheless, reaches out to phenomenological problems of discerning the affective response of a perceptive reader. The doctrine is based on the three-fold power of the world *Abhidhā* (denotation of word), *Lakṣanā* (the figurative power) and *Viyanjanā* (the suggestive power), yielding respectively in three kinds of meaning, namely *Vācyārtha* (the literal meaning), *Lakṣanārtha* (the figurative meaning) and *Vyanjanārtha* (the suggested meaning). *Vācyārtha* is the literal meaning in terms of common parlance; it is the primary meaning. *Lakṣanārtha* is the secondary or figurative meaning developed through a trope and *Vyanjanārtha* or *Dhvanyārtha* (Dhvani) is the suggested meaning, the emergence of which annihilates the first two meanings. The *Vyanjāna* does not consist in the utterance of something new but in suddenly revealing, almost in a lightning flash, what is already there, like the revealing of the already existing jar by the lamp. *Vyanjanārtha* or the suggested sense to which the name *Dhvani* is applied is held as the soul of poetry, the *poeisis* of a poem. *Dhvani* is defined in the following words :

> yatrārthah śabao vā tam artham upasarjanīkrta-svārthau vyaktah, kāvyaviśeṣah sa dhvanir iti sūrlhih kathitah. (The learned call that particular kind of poetry *dhvani* in which the expressed word and sense, subordinating themselves, manifest that [other suggested] sense.) (De 158)

A close analysis of the minutest details of the *Dhvani* theory reveals, as Visvanatha has shown, 5355 subdivisions of suggestive poetry. The figure is a testimony to the scientific rigour with which Anandavardhana developed the theory, taking into account all the possible variations and ramifications. Anandavardhana follows the binary division, the most modern scientific approach, in his analysis. First *dhvani-kāvya* is divided into two broad categories : *avivakṣita-vācya* and *vivakṣit ānyapara-vācya*. In the first case the expressed sense is not intended, and in the second case it is certainly meant but ultimately amounts to something else or the unexpressed. The first is based on *lakṣanā* or indication, and the second on *abhidhā* or denotation. The *lakṣanā*-born *dhvani* is again of two kinds : *arthāntarasaṃkramita* (suggestion where the expressed sense passes into another sense) and *atyanta-tiraṣkṛta* (suggestion where the expressed sense disappears entirely). Either of these, again, may be *padaprakāśya* (manifest in a word) or *vākyaprakāśya* (manifest in a sentence). *Abhidhā*-born *dhvani* is also subdivided into two categories : *asaṃlakṣya-krama* (that in which the suggested is of an imperceptible process) and *saṃlakṣyakrama* (that in which the suggested is of a perceptible process). The main difference between *asaṃlakṣya-krama* and *saṃlakṣya-krama* is that the former includes the suggestion of *rasa* or relish or some bhāva or emotional state suggested in a particular way. The latter includes the suggestion of *vastu* (matter / fact) and *alaṃkāra* (figure). The credit goes to Anandavardhana for reviving the concept of *rasa* first enunciated by Bharata (living sometime between the second century BC and the second century AD) in *Nāṭya Sāstra* (Treatise on Dramaturgy) and extending it to literature in general and poetry in particular. The process by which the *rasa* or the affective response of the perceptive reader is manifest is, according to Anandavardhana, basically a process of suggestion. The *vyānjanās* (suggestors) are the objective correlatives of the response of the reader. *Saṃlakṣyakrama* has two varieties : *śabdaśaktimūlaka* (suggested by a particular word) and *arthaśaktimūlaka* (suggested by fact or figure). This thus is of two kinds : *vastu-dhvani* (suggestion of fact) and *alaṃkāradhvani* (suggested by a figure of speech). The distinctions go on almost endlessly, but Anandavardhana takes adequate care to illustrate different kinds of *dhvani*. Space does not permit me to quote examples, but suffice it to say that the main thrust of the theory of *dhvani* is that the language of good poetry is emotive, ambiguous, non-logical and open to multiple interpretation. It is the supreme glory of language that creatively used, it can yield an infinite variety of meaning, so that poetry can transcend the descriptive and become suggestive and evocative. But this should not lead us to think that the concept of *dhvani* is something mystical aiming at leaving the unexpressed to be darkly gathered. Anandavardhana takes care to point out that the *dhvani* is not something mystical, but it is something that can be scientifically defined and satisfactorily grasped. The unexpressed is ideally linked with the expressed, without which it cannot exist. But it is wrapped up so mysteriously that it needs a *sahrday*, a perceptive reader of disciplined sensibility, to unravel the mystery, comprehend its subtlety and enjoy it. And the entire treatise is based on the solid foundation of faith that good poetry must suggest and not simply describe.

Mallarmé does not develop his doctrine so systematically or so scientifically. More a poet than a critic, Mallarmé does not really care to develop his theory of poetry at any great length. But his critical observations would show that he is at one with Anandavardhana regarding some of basic assumptions about poetry. He believes, for example, that the power of poetry consists not in description but in suggestion. Mallarmé writes :

> Les jeunes sont plus pres de l'idéal poetique que les parnassiens qui traitent encore leurs sujets à la façon des vieux philosophes et des vieux rheteurs, en présentant les objects directement. Je pense qu'il faut, au contraire, qu'il n'y qu'allusion. La contemplation des objects, l'image s'envolant des rèveries suscitees par eux, sont le chant : les parnassiens, eux, prennent la chose entièrement et la montrent : par la ils manquent de mystère; ils retirent aux espirits cette joie delicieuse de croire qu'ils creent. *Nommer* un objet, c'est supprimer les trois-quarts de la jouissance du poeme qui est faite de deviner peu à peu : la *suggérer*, voila le rève. C'est le parfait usage de ce mystère qui constitue le symbole; èvoquer petit à petit un objet pour montrer un état d'âme, ou, inversement, choisir un objet en dégager un etat d'âme, par une serie de déchiffrements... (*Oeuvres Complètes* 868-69).

The passage just quoted implies the following assumptions : First, poetry should not present things directly, descriptively or even fully. It should present things suggestively so that the desired state of mind is gradually evoked and what is unexpressed becomes slowly, stage by stage, expressed. Second, poetic enjoyment comes from divination. Finally, the suggested object is ultimately valuable because, charged with feeling, it reveals the state of soul.

Like Anandavardhana, Mallarmé opposes direct expression, prefers the suggested image (*alaṃkāra dhvani*) to an image clearly outlined, and prefers by implication *vastu-dhvani* to photographic or accurate description of an object.

The passage may be regarded as the *locus classicus* of the theory of *dhvani*. What Mallarmé says in the passage, incidentally, is not an *obiter dicta*, or just a passing remark. There are enough echoes of it in the personal letters and other writings of different periods to suggest a growing conviction. In his letter to his friend M. Cazalis, Mallarmé writes:

> Avec terreur, car j'invente une langue qui doit nécessairement jaillir d'nue poétique très nouvelle, que je pourrais définir en ces deux mots: Peindre, non la chose, maisl'effet qu'elle produit... (*Correspondance* 137).

In his letter to Francois Coppee, dated 5 December 1866, Mallarmé expresses this unambiguously : "Le hasard n'entame pas un vers, c'est la grade chose. Nous avons, plusieurs, atteint cela..." (*Correspondance* 234). His criticism of Zola also points in the same direction, as it grows out of his conviction about the true nature of great literature. Mallarmé writes :

> J'ai une grande admiration pour Zola. Il a fait mois, à vrai dire, de veritable littérature que de l'art évocatoire, en se servent, le moins qu'il est possible, des éléments littérataires; il a près les mots, c'est vrai, mais c'est tout; le reste provient de sa merveilleuse organasation et se répercute tout de suite dans I'espirit de la foule. Il a vraiment des qualitiés puissantes.... Mais la littérature a quelque chose de plus intellectual que cela : les choses existent; nous n'avous pas a les créer; nous n'avons pu'a en saisir les rapports; et ce sont les fils de ces rapports qui forment les vers et les orchestres... (*Oeuvres Complètes* 871).

The idea finds a much clearer articulation in a passage in "Crise de Vers";

> Decadante, Mystique, les Ecoles se déclarant ou étiquéttés en hâte par notre presse d'information adoptent, commee rencontre, le point d'un Idéalisme qui (pareillement aux fuges, aux sonates) refuse les matériaux naturels et. comme brutale une pensée exacte, les ardonnant; pour ne garder rien que la suggestion. Instituer une relation entre les images exactes, et que s'en détache un tiers aspect fusible et clair presente à la divinations... (*Oeuvres Complètes* 365).

What Mallarmé refers to as the third element (*tiers aspect*) is *vastu-dhvani* in Anandavardhana's theory of poetry. Again :

> Les monuments, la mer, la face humaine, tous leur plenitude natifs, conservant une vertu autrement attrayante que ne les voilera une description, évocation dites, *allusion* je sais, suggestion (*Oeuvres Complètes* 366).

Suggestion and resonance are generated when words with various denotations and connotations, the sonic and the semantic qualities, are creatively welded and patterned into organic, artistic wholes of verbal artifacts. Then we can realize the pleasure dome that Coleridge so longed to create in *Kubla Khan*. With the alchemy of genius the hard contours of the lexical items, in such a poetic context, melt in the suggestions they develop, as the charm of a youthful maiden arises out of the physical features and yet remains distinct of them. But this new power of words, Mallarmé insists, like Anandavardhana, is as real as the other ordinary powers of word. The suggestive power or *vyanjana vrtti* is a real power of language and can be realized only when language is creatively exploited. This is the reason why both Mallarmé and Anandavardhana insist on the impersonality of poetry. Both believe, like Poe, Flaubert and Eliot, in the depersonalization of the artist in the creative process so that the end product should not contain any trace of the poet. It means, by implication, and reinforces the idea that the poetic relish comes not from any "intentional fallacy" committed on the basis of our knowledge of the poet, but it actually arises out of, and is ensured by, the literary artifact, the poem itself. This further re-affirms that the suggestive power of the words or the suggestive meaning of poetry arises actually out of the language of poetry. Mallarmé shares with Anandavardhana this concern for language and the need for purifying the dialect of the tribe by exploiting the resources of the language. In this connection René Wellek observes :

> He (Mallarmé) is, as far as I know, the first writer who is radically discontent with the ordinary language of communication and attempts to construe an entirely separate poetic language.... He described and exploited systematically most of the traditional devices for separating poetic language from ordinary speech (454).

It is true that Mallarmé began his critical career under the visible influence of Edgar Allen Poe, whom he practically worshipped, and derived from him continual insistence on calculation and effect and contested the view that a poet is "a great epileptic whom one depicts unkempt with haggard eyes, haphazardly pouring forth his facile and incoherent verse on one stream" under the inspiration of some "talkative Muse." Poetry, for Mallarmé, as for Poe, is more a matter of perspiration than inspiration. It is a matter of labour and polishing file. It is also possible to trace the theory of suggestion in Western criticism in the writings of Poe. Poe seems to indicate that suggestion is an undercurrent of meaning, a product of imagination, and lends a kind of indeterminateness to the meaning of a poem. The insights of Poe, however, constitute only in an embryonic form the theory of suggestion. Mallarmé picks them up and develops them along lines which come very close to Anandavardhana's theory of *dhvani*. In other words, one may say that Mallarmé starts under the influence of Poe, outgrows the influence and becomes the greatest exponent of the nineteenth century French theory of suggestion.

It remains to the seen how Mallarmé and Anandavardhana, though independently, anticipate some of the recent tendencies in contemporary literary criticism in the West. It may be worthwhile to bear in mind in this connection how the western approach to poetry differs, historically speaking, from the Indian approach to poetry. In the West the emphasis, from the very beginning, was on rhetorics or the art of speech, which was as much a tool for argumentation and persuasive conversation as for the study of literature. In the course of time some of figures of speech — particularly metaphor and later allegory — acquired a literary status. Metaphor eventually became the figure of poetry but the relationship between poetic form and poetic meaning was never explored linguistically. Poetry was looked upon as a violation, or at least a significant departure, from common language. In India, on the contrary, rhetorics and poetics were never separated. The art of speech was, at bottom, an art of literature, and poetry was seen to be just language, but language exploited in full. In this respect, Mallarmé's preoccupation with language is worth noting. "Ce n'est point avec des idées qu'on fait des sonnets, Degas, c'est avec les mots," said Mallarmé to Degas.

The interest in the nature of words that constitutes the most important element of poetry in Mallarmé and Anandavardhana is echoed in the New Criticism's concerns for the formal aspects of poetry. The New Critics made a distinction between the language of literature and the language of science and defended literature as a unique mode of cognition different from and superior to science. The New Critics evinced interest in *vastu-dhvani*, the suggested meaning as realized in the achieved structure of the work. *Rasa-dhvani*, on the other hand, has been one of the main interests of phenomenological criticism. The reader-response theory is only a detailed ramification of *rasa-dhavani*, depending on the authority of *sahrday*, the perceptive reader, who is seen as the co-author. The meaning of a literary work emerges out of a vital interaction between the "text" or the written material which is supposed to be largely open and the reader who is to fill it with meaning. According to Roland Barthes the indeterminate text arises out of the mode of interaction in the Nietzschean sense which "posits the images of a triumphant plural unimpoverished by any constraint." The text is just interweaving, a web without a centering spider, and according to Stanley Fish, a kind of empty container waiting to be filled with meaning. According to Wolfgand Iser, the leading reader-response critic, an abundance of indeterminate elements is a characteristic feature of modern writing. All these ideas can be traced back to the aesthetic implications of *rasa-dhvani*.

To say that there are distinct echoes of the theory of poetry as enunciated by Mallarmé and Anandavardhana in contemporary literary criticism is not to suggest that contemporary literary criticism is derived either from Mallarmé or from Anandavardhana, but only to focus on the contemporary relevance of these two highly original thinkers, who worked independently and yet arrived at certain insights into the literary universals which we would love to share.

ACKNOWLEDGEMENT

I am grateful to the authorities of Bibliothèque Nationale for allowing me to use the library during my brief stay in Paris in 1984. I am particularly indebted to Andree Lhritier, of la Salle des Catalogues et de Bibliographies for providing valuable bibliographical information.

WORKS CITED

De, S.K., *Sanskrit Poetics*, Calcutta, 1976.

Mallarmé, Stephane, *Correspondance* 1862-1871, Gallimard, 1959.

——, *Oeuvres Complètes*. Ed. Henri Mondor and Jean Aubrey, Gallimard, 1945.

Wellek, René, *History of Modern Criticism* (1750-1950), London, 1970, Vol. 4.

15

Use of Source Material for the Development of the Theme of Martyrdom : Eliot and Tagore : A Comparative Study*

It is interesting to note certain similarities between *Murder in the Cathedral* and *Naṭīr Pūjā,* products as they are of two masterminds of the present century. Both Eliot and Tagore, in their personal lives, had a strong religious conviction in the will of God, although their faith found different expressions in their works. Eliot was a Catholic and had the highest regard for Christ. Tagore, on the other hand, was a Brahmo by birth and the Upanisads and the personality of the Buddha were the major influences on the philosophical background of his writings. The similarities between the teachings of the Buddha and Christ are obvious and need not be laboured. Both Eliot and Tagore had passed through the horror of the First World War and experienced the crisis of civilization. In one of his famous addresses delivered at the Calcutta Mahabodhi Society on the occasion of the birth anniversary of the Buddha, Tagore remarks :

> *kichudin pūrvei pṛthivīte ek mahāyuddha haye gelo. ek paksher jai hala, se jai bāhubaler. kintu yehetu bāhubal mānuṣer caram bal nay, ei janye mānuṣer itihāse se jai niṣphal hala, se jai natun yuddher bīj bapan kare caleche. mānuṣer šakti akrodhe, kṣhamate, ei kathā bujhte dei nā se paśu ye ājo mānuṣer madhye mareni. tāi mānuṣer satyer prati śraddhā kare mānaber guru balechen; krodhke jai karbe*

* Indian National Comparative Literature Association, Jadavpur (W.B.), 1983.

> *akrodher dvārā, nijer krodhke ebaṁ anyer krodhke. e nā hale mānuṣ byartha habe, yehetu se mānuṣ.*[1]

Historically, both *Murder in the Cathedral* and *Naṯīr Pūjā* are enacted against the backdrop of a great national upheaval. The quarrel between the Papacy and the Crown shaped the subsequent history of Europe. In *Naṯīr Pūjā* also we get glimpses of the great national upheaval that shook the country particularly in the spheres of religion and society after the advent of Buddhism. Bimbisara was a contemporary of the Buddha. They met for the first time when Bimbisara was thirty and the Buddha thirty-five. Bimbisara was the founder of the ancient empire of Magadha and the epithet *śreṇika* given to him reflects his encouragement of trade and commerce, which was certainly a new development at that time.

Yuan Chawang credits him with the construction of roads and causeways which served as avenues for commerce as well. According to one historical version he was killed by his son, Ajatasatru, who usurped the throne. According to another version Bimbisara abdicated the throne in favour of Ajatasatru and lived at a distance from the capital. Tagore draws on both the versions. He accepts the abdication theory, because it helps him in glorifying the character of Bimbisara in the light of the Buddhist doctrine of renunciation. He also subscribes to the idea of parricide, though in a modified form (*sabāi anumān karche, pather madhye orā bimbiṣār mahārājke hatyā kareche. NP* 68)[2] because it serves him well in revealing the violent and fanatic nature of Brahminism in contrast to the non-violent, pacifist Buddhism. Apart from Nanda's "*ki bhayaṁkar garjan ekī rāṣṭrabiplab?*" (NP 48)[3], the character of Lokeshwari voices the conflict between orthodox Brahminism and the liberal but austere Buddhism. She complains with intuitive feminine sentiment and impassioned human appeal :

> *e dharme mā cheler pakshe anābaśyak; strīke swāmir prayojan nei. Yārā nā putra nā swamī nā bhāi se sab gharchadāder ektukhāni bhikshā debār janye samasta prāṇke śukiya phele āmrā śūnya ghare pāde thākba? mallikā, ei puruṣer dharma āmader mereche, āmrao eke mārba.*[4]

Nor does Buddhism, according to her, allow a man to discharge his social responsibility :

> *āryaputra bimbisār, kshatriya rājā, rājatva to tār bhoger jiniṣ nay, tātei tār dharmasādhana. kintu kon marur dharma kāne maṇtra dila amni kata sahajei rājatva theke tini khase paḍlen — astra hāte nā, ranakshetre nā, mṛtyur mukhe nā (NP 41).*[5]

In *Murder in the Cathedral* the fundamental conflict is between the Papacy and the Crown, or more particularly, between the State and Religion. Tagore dramatizes the same kind of conflict in *Sacrifice*.[6] But in *Naṭīr Pūjā* the conflict is between two religions — Brahminism and Buddhism — prescribing two sets of values which are not compatible.

In *Murder in the Cathedral*, towards the end of the play, the Knights directly address the audience, because Eliot wants to shock the audience into an awareness of the contemporary relevance of the situation. Tagore, however, does it subtly with the help of a song :

hiṃsāy unmatta pṛthvī, nitya niṭhura dvandva

ghora kutila pantha tār lobhajatila bandha. (NP 59)[7]

The Chorus in *Murder in the Cathedral* says :

I have smelt them, the death-bringers, senses are quickened By subtle forebodings; (*MC* 53)

In *Naṭīr Pūjā*, as well, death is looked at from different angles (mṛtyur siṁhadvār diyei janmer jayayātra. NP 53).[8] In *Naṭīr Pūjā* there is no Chorus, but the cluster of characters represented by Basabi, Nanda, Ratnavali, Ajita and Bhadra perform the role of the Chorus. They voice the popular reaction and confused feelings, and constantly comment on the action. These characters mark different stages of conflict, from direct hostility to profound sympathy in regard to Buddhism. Both Eliot and Tagore use night as a very powerful symbol of spiritual darkness. The priest talks of "another night and another dawn", and the Chorus speaks of "the loneliness of the night of God" (*MC* 71), and also that "the darkness declared the glory of light" (*MC* 70). In *Naṭīr Pūjā* the play opens early in the morning :

purvagaganbhādge

dīpta haila suprabhāt

taruṇāruṇa rāge. (*NP* 7)[9]

Murder in the Cathedral ends with the following lines invoking the spirit of Christ :

Lord, have mercy upon us.

Christ, have mercy upon us.

Lord, have mercy upon us.

Blessed Thomas, pray for us. (*MC* 72)

And *Naṭīr Pūjā* ends with the following lines :

buddhaṁ saranaṁ gacchāmi

dhammaṁ saranaṁ gacchāmi

saṁghaṁ saranaṁ gacchāmi (NP 85)[10]

It is possible to point out many other similarities between *Murder in the Cathedral* and *Naṭīr Pūjā* in terms of history, theme, organization and execution. The similarities, however, should not blind us to the vital differences between Eliot and Tagore *vis-à-vis* their use of source materials and the development of the theme of martyrdom.

II

Eliot closely adheres to the eyewitness accounts of the murder of Thomas Becket in *Murder in the Cathedral* and concentrates on the "death and martyrdom". In Part II, the Chorus in deploring that "the peace of this world is always uncertain unless men keep the peace of God" (*MC* 41) harks back to Becket's Christmas sermon ("now think for a moment about the meaning of the word 'peace'") and reinforces the theme of martyrdom. And when the Chorus says that the "War among men defiles this world; but death in the Lord renews it" the utterance becomes proleptic. The priests keep up the theme and dilate on it. The choric speech of the Knights closely adheres to and is a summary of the charges Reginald Fitzurse levels against Becket. He charges him with grave misconduct and utter ingratitude towards the King. Becket's reply as given in one eyewitness account,

> *Non nego quin me factum sit, sed supra me est, et meae prorsus non congruit dignitati, quos dominus papa ligavit absolvere. Ipsum adeant, in eujus redundat injuriam quod me et matrem suam ecclesiam Christi Canturiae Contempserunt.*[11]

becomes in Eliot's play

> I do not deny
> That this was done through me. But it is not I
> Who can loose whom the Pope has bound.
> Let them go to him, upon whom rebounds
> Their contempt towards me, their contempt towards the
> Church shown. (*MC* 51)

Not merely modelled on the eyewitness account, but almost a free translation of it. The only significant change is that "matrem suam ecclesiam Christi Canturiae" (their mother, the church of Christ at Canterbury) has been replaced by "the Church". Significant, because it helps Eliot generalize the conflict which the play highlights. The conflict, only on the surface, is between Becket and Henry. Deep down, the conflict is between the Church and the State.

Again, when the panic-stricken priests enter the Cathedral and hasten to bar the doors of the church for personal safety Becket commands in the voice of thunder :

> *Ad quos coversus athleta mirabilis imperat ecclesiae januas eperiri, "Non decet" inquiens, "orationis domum, ecclesiam Christi, turrem facere, quae, etsi non claudatur, suis sufficit ad munimen; et nos patiendo potium quam pugnando triumbhabimus hostem, qui et pati venimus non requgnare."*[12]

Eliot clearly sees that there are two issues involved in Becket's command to unbar the door : (i) it is not seemly to make a tower of the house of prayer, the church of Christ, and (ii) by suffering rather than by fighting can the clergy triumph over their adversary. Eliot uses both the issues, but separately, in two speeches of Becket. In the first speech Becket indicates,

> I will not have the house of prayer, the church of Christ, The sanctuary, turned into a fortress. (*MC* 58)

The second speech provides, the moral explanation :

> We are not here to triumph by fighting, by stratagem, or by resistance.
> Not to fight with beasts as men. We have fought the beast
> And have conquered. We have only to conquer
> Now, by suffering (*MC* 59)

and asserts that the Law of God is "above the Law of Man."

Again, when the Knights accompanied by Hugh Mauclerc rush in with swords unsheathed they exclaim in a spirit of mad fury

> Ubi est Thomas Beketh, proditor regis et regni?[13]

And the first line in the address of the Knights is

> Where is Becket, the traitor to the King? (*MC* 60)

This is almost a literal translation of the eyewitness account. Becket's reply :

> I am here.
> No traitor to the King. I am a priest. (*MC* 60)

literally translates the eyewitness account : "Ecce adsum, non regis proditor, sed sacerdos." By breaking this single sentence into three short sentences, Eliot has achieved a dramatic wonder. The short line, "I am here" with just three monosyllables, drives home Becket's undaunted demeanour, his supreme self-confidence, almost Promethean in dimension. "No traitor to the King" is an assured and emphatic rebuttal of the charge, and "I am a priest" is an assertion of his identity and the nature of his vocation.

Becket's last speech too is a verbal reconstruction of the eyewitness account according to which, bending his neck as though for prayer he joined his hands and raised them upward in supplication and commended his cause and the Church's cause to God, St. Mary and the martyr St. Denys. The account reads :

> *inclinata in modum orantis cervice, junctis pariter et elevatis sursum manibus, Deo et sanctae Marine et beato martyri Dionysio suam et ecclesiae causam commendavit.*[14]

III

Coming back to Tagore, the story of Srimati in the *Avadānaśataka* provides the source material for *Naṭīr Pūjā*, But Tagore had written a poem, "Pūjārinī", on the same theme and drawing on the same material in 1899. "Pūjārinī" was recast in the dramatic form of *Naṭīr Pūjā* in 1926.[15] While on the one hand it indicated Tagore's continuous interest in and reverence for Buddhism — the spirit of the Buddha, in fact, is invoked time and again in his poems, plays and songs — the change of form, from the poetic to the dramatic, brings to a sharper focus the dramatic elements contained in the story. There is an obvious shift in the emphasis as well, from the martyr to martyrdom.

Interestingly, even while following the outline of the story Tagore significantly deviates from the source. In *Avadānaśataka* Srimati acts on her own : "*sa svakam jivitamaganayitva Buddhagunamscanusmrtya kesanakhastupam sammriva dipamalamakarsit* /"[16]. Srimati, a devotee of the Budhha is undaunted by the fear of death. This speaks of her moral courage. But the courage is contaminated by chauvinistic insolence and egoism, and a flagrant transgression of authority inadequately motivated. The note of headstrong insolence is completely removed in the play where Srimati is entrusted with the task of worshipping by the Lord.

> *āj basantapūrṇimāy bhagabān bodhisatver janmotsav. aśokbane tār āsane pūjā-nibedaer bhār*
>
> *śrīmatīr upar* (*NP* 32)[17]

And the bhikshu Upali's instruction in the beginning of the play that she should offer her best (*tomār ya ṣreṣṭha dān NP* 8) suggests the nature of the worship.

Another significant change that occurs in the play is the rejection of the episode of altercation between Ajatasatru the King and Srimati, a palace-maid. In *Avādanáśataka*, Ajatasatru notices from the palace-top a row of lamps lighted on the *stūpa*. He wants to know who has lighted the lamps, and is told that Srimati, a palace-maid, has done it. He then sends for Srimati and asks her why she has transgressed the order of the King. Srimati replies that although she has transgressed the order of the ruling king she has not violated — in fact, she has obeyed — the dictates of Bimbisara, the pious king, or the real king.

yāvadajātāstrurūpriprāsādātālagatastamudaramavabhasam drstvā papraccha kimidamiti / yāvadanyāyā kathitam Śrīmatyā kesanakhastupe dipamālā kṛteti / tatah Śrīmatimahūya kathayati / kimartham rājaśāsanamatikramasiti / sā kathayati / yādyapimayā tava śāsanamatikrāntam kim tu dharmarājasya mayā Bimbisārasya śāsanam nātikrantamiti /[18]

The lines just quoted present Srimati as an inspired votary of the Buddha no doubt. But at the same time the way she answers Ajatasatru, shows her proud demeanour, though occasioned by the intensity of her devotion to the Buddha and high regard for Bimbisara. This pride, albeit religious, has a touch of fanaticism and egoistic overtones. In the play, on the other hand, the dedication is achieved through gradual but determined self-effacement. The basic emotion that informs the character of Srimati is not pride but humility. The change, therefore, has a direct bearing on the theme of martyrdom as envisioned by Tagore.

In the source, Srimati is killed abruptly by Ajatasatru who flies into a rage at the insolence of the girl :

tatastena kupitena cakram kṣiptvā jīvitad vyavaropitā /[19]

Reacting sharply to what he considers her audacity the King strikes her dead at once in a fit of fury. In the play Srimati is warned, time and again, by the guards who also suffer from conflicting feelings and are half in sympathy[20] with Srimati before she is actually killed.

And the dance she performs at the *stūpa* is at the instance of Ratnavali who has procured an order from the King to that effect to humiliate Srimati by compelling her to vilify the Buddhist shrine. In the source there is no mention of any dance. Srimati, there, is only a palace-maid and not a court-dancer. The dance is Tagore's innovation. This dance which indirectly reveals the character of Ratnavali — her jealousy and rancour — gives Srimati an opportunity to offer her best to the Buddha in the form of the dance. The dance which begins on a materialistic plane (*pātakini āpādamastak alaṁkār padeche NP* 77)[21] ultimately transcends the mundane and reaches out to wider spiritual domains. The discarding of the ornaments and the gorgeous outer garments — one by one — and the gradual revelation of the nun's yellow robe (*bhikshuṇīr pītavastra*) symbolically suggest the abandonment of the external to the revelation of the internal, rejection of appearance in favour of reality, and finally affirm the eternal truth : supremacy of spiritual complacence over carnal pleasures.

In *Avadānásataka* after her death Srimati becomes an angel:

atha Śrimatī devakanyā samantayojānām divya-

prabhāmandālavabhāsita devasamitimupasamkranta /[22]

Tagore does not include this part of the legend in his play. One possible explanation is that while Tagore revered Buddhism and had the highest regard for the teachings of the Buddha, as a Brahmo he found it difficult to accept angelhood as part of the religious doctrine. But more importantly, the idea of Srimati being transfigured after her death and becoming an angel is inimical to the theme of martyrdom as Tagore develops it. The faith in angelhood, a kind of reward for the services rendered on earth considerably minimizes the significance of the sacrifice. The drama, therefore, meaningfully ends with the death of Srimati and its effect on the characters around. The recitation of the Buddhist hymn (*buddhaṁ saranaṁ gacchāmi / dhammaṁ saranaṁ gacchāmi / samghaṁ saranaṁ gacchāmi NP* 85) by Ratnavali is an indication of the changes that are afoot.

IV

It would be evident from the foregoing discussion that in spite of many similarities between *Murder in the Cathedral* and *Naṭīr Pūjā* there is a marked difference between Eliot and Tagore in their use of the source-material. While Eliot closely adheres to the source material, Tagore completely transmutes it so that the simple story of Srimati is invested with a profound significance that encompasses the meanings of life and death and tackles the riddle of existence in very clear and unequivocal Buddhist terms. The story of *Avadānásataka* provides only the starting point and that is precisely the point of departure, leading to an imaginative recreation of the story in a consummate dramatic form.

Becket, the former Chancellor to the King and the Archbishop of Canterbury is a person of towering personality and belongs to the highest stratum of society. Srimati, by contrast, is only a court-dancer (palace-maid in the source) and belongs to the lower stratum of society.

āmi ye abhāgī.

prabhur bhikṣhāpātre āmār dān kunṭhita habe (*NP* 8).[23]

In the beginning of the play she is acutely conscious of her low social status and therefore would not give the alms with her own hand but would call a princess instead. Tagore seems to be of the view that it is not necessary that a martyr must come from the higher strata of society commanding respect and adoration of the multitude. The greatness of matyrdom consists in the greatness of the vision and in realization of its value by the sacrifice of one's life, and by affecting a transvaluation of values. Unlike Srimati, Becket has to overcome the temptation of becoming a martyr[24] before he faces death boldly with matchless equanimity. Tagore while omitting the episode of direct confrontation with Ajatasatru for reasons already stated, retains the spirit. When Nanda points out that the road to the *stūpa* is blocked because of the King's order (*bodh hacche rājār niṣedh NP* 47)[25] Srimati promptly retorts that there is, nevertheless, the sanction of the Lord (*kintu prabhur ādeś āche NP* 48)[26] and again, when Bhadra asks whether Srimati will be able to get over the royal obstacle (*rājār bādhāo sarāte pārbe! NP* 50)[27] Srimati replies with confident assurance that that is beyond the jurisdiction of the King (*sekhāne rājār rājdanḍa pāuchaynā NP* 50).[28] The exclusion of the direct confrontation but retention of the spirit — the courage of conviction and the moral strength — has a direct bearing on Tagore's idea of martyrdom.

In contrast to the majestic bearing and proud demeanour of Becket the character of Srimati is marked by humility. In the beginning of the play she alone is awake (*ei purīte āj ekā kebal tumii jege? NP* 7).[29] Metaphorically she alone is in readiness to receive the message of the Buddha. Throughout the play day and night, light and darkness, sleep and wakeful state are charged with symbolic significance (*sahasā nabīn uṣā āse hate āloker jhāri, / dey sāḍā ghana andhakāre. NP* 31)[30] (*ye mor ālo lukiye āche / rāter pāre / tāke dekhte dāo NP* 54).[31]

Once awakened, Srimati by her sincerity and devotion transcends her own social standing and vindicates the majesty of her spirit. Her glory consists in her ability to rise above her social status by drawing sustenance from the soul, and dedicate herself to the will of the Buddha. In this connection Tagore writes :

jibaner yeṭā caram tātparya, yā tār nihitārtha, bāireyā kramāgata pariṇāmer dike rūp nicche tāke bujhte pādchi se tār prāṇasya prāṇam, se prāṇer aṇtaratara prān... preranā anusāre pratyek mānuṣer pather ṁūlyagaurȧb svatantrȧ. 'naṭīr pūjā' nātikāy ei kathāṭāi balbār ceṡṭā karechi. buddhadeb ke naṭī ye arghya dān karte ceyechila ṡe tār nṛtya. anya sādhakrā tāke diyechila yā chila tāderi antaratara satya, naṭī diyeche tār samasta jībaner abhibyakta satyake. mṛtyu diye se satyer caram mūlya pramāṇ kareche. ei nṛtyake paripurṇa kare jagiye ṫulechila tār praṇmaner madhye tār prāṇer prāṇ.[32]

The distinction that Tagore makes between the sacrifice of the other disciples and that of Srimati epitomizes the difference between Becket and Srimati as martyrs. The way Tagore has given a new dimension to the concept of martyrdom through his delineation of the character of Srimati within the framework of the play is really remarkable.[33] Though *Naṭīr Pūjā* is not a dance drama, the dance of the Nati constitutes the essence of this drama.[34] From the very beginning the whole drama inevitably moves towards this final dance when the simple devotion of Srimati is gradually worked up and heightened to a pitch of extraordinary richness and splendour culminating in the death of Srimati.[35] The dance of Srimati functions as the objective correlative for Tagore's idea of martyrdom.*

REFERENCES

1. *Murder in the Cathedral* (subsequently referred to as *MC*): First published in 1935. All the references are to the April 1961 impression of the Faber and Faber edition.
2. *Materials for the History of Thomas Becket*. Ed. by James C. Robertson and for Vol. VII J.C. Robertson and J.B. Shepperd. 7 Vols. Rolls series 1875-85. Subsequently referred to as *Materials*.
3. *Naṭīr Pūjā* : First published in 1926. All references are to the 1981 reprint by the Visva-Bharati. Subsequently referred to as *NP*.
4. *Avadānáataka* : Ed. by J.S. Speyer, Photomechanic, reprint 1958.
5. K.R. Kripainai: "*Naṭīr Pūjā* : An Appreciation", *Visva-Bharati Quarterly* (April, 1943).
6. Pramathanath Bishi : *Rabindranatyaprabaha*, Calcutta, 1966.
7. K.P. Jayaswal: *Imperial History of India in a Sanskrit Text*, Calcutta, 1934.
8. Sudhakar Chattopadhyay : *Bimbisara to Asoke*, Calcutta, 1934.
9. R.L. Mitra : *Sanskrit Buddhist Literature of Nepal*, rpt., Calcutta, 1973.

* I am grateful to my colleague, Dr Mihir Kumar Sen, for suggesting the topic. I am also indebted to Professor Venkata Ramanan and Professor Prabodh Chandra Sen of Santiniketan for their valuable suggestions.

NOTES

English renderings of the excerpts from *Naṭīr Pūjā* are based on Marjorie Sykes's translation of *Naṭīr Pūjā* published as "The Dancing Girl's Worship" in *Visva-Bharati Quarterly*, Vol. V, 1927. Passages left out by Marjorie Sykes are translated into English by the present author.

1. *Rabindra Rachanavali*, Govt. of West Bengal, 1961, Vol. 11, p. 472 :

   "The world saw the end of a terrible war the other day. The victory that crowned one group of belligerents was victory of armed might; but because brute force is not man's supreme source of strength, that victory has proved unfruitful and is only sowing the seeds of fresh dissension. Man's strength lies in mercy and compassion. The brute in man that has not yet perished does not allow him to realize this truth to which the Master paid homage when he said that all anger, whether one's own or of others, must be conquered by non-anger. Unless man follows this junction his life is bound to be a failure." (trans. Somnath Maitra)
2. "People say that Maharaja Bimbisar has been murdered on his way to the capital."
3. "Hark! That terrible tumult! Can it be a revolt?"
4. "I have realized it today, Mallika, that this is a man's religion. In it the woman is nowhere — the son has no need of his mother, the husband no need of his wife. And yet, in order to give alms to these begging bhikshus — neither sons, husbands, nor brothers, forsakers of their homes — we must cling to our empty homes with withered lives! This man's religion has destroyed us : We must destroy it."
5. "My husband, Bimbisar, once a khastriya king, held his kingship as a religious duty, not as a means of self-enjoyment. But a voice like the scorching desert wind touched his ears, and as a dead leaf he dropped from his throne, — not with arms in hand, not in the battlefield, nor to meet his death."
6. The conflict between Govindamanikya and Raghupati is, essentially, a conflict between the State and the Religion, between two sets of values which are not compatible. Tagore, of course, has woven a number of other strands — violence versus non-violence, magnanimity versus meanness, truth versus falsehood — into the thematic pattern of the play. But the play remains, at bottom, a study in conflict between the State and the Religion for supremacy of power.
7. "The world today is wild with the delirium of hatred, / The conflicts are cruel and unceasing in anguish, / Crooked are its path, tangled its bonds of greed...."
8. "The triumphant procession of the New Birth passes through the gate of death."

9. "The eastern sky is flushed at dawn by the aura of the rising sun." (translation mine) In a similar way "the morning slowly breaks" in *Prometheus Unbound* suggests the end of the darkness of Prometheu's soul.
10. "My refuge is in the Buddha, / My refuge is in the Dharma, / My refuge is in the Sangha."
11. *Materials*, Vol. II, p. 432.
12. *Ibid.*, p. 435.
13. *Idem.*
14. *Ibid.*, p. 437.
15. The immediate occasion, however, was casual. On his return from a two-month tour in East Bengal he finds (March 1926) that preparations are going on at Santiniketan to present a dumb-show of "*Pūjārinī*" as part of the birthday celebrations of the poet. Tagore at once decides to dramatize the poem. The result is *Naṭīr Pūjā*. But the occasional need is subservient to the impelling aesthetic needs, as it would be evident from a letter of Tagore (written to Pramatha Chaudhuri). Tagore writes : "I started writing under a pressure. But now the internal pressure (the demand of art-author) has surpassed the external pressure." The internal pressure is due to the dramatic form inhering the theme.
16. *Avadānaśataka*, p. 308.
17. "This is the birthday of our Lord, the night of the full-moon of spring, and it will be Srimati's duty this evening to place the offerings on His altar beneath the Asoka tree."
18. *Avadānaśataka*, p. 309.
19. *Idem.*
20. Partly like Mercury in Shelley's *Prometheus Unbound.*
21. "The shameless sinner has decorated her whole body with ornaments." (translation mine)
22. *Avadānaśataka*, p. 309.
23. "Alas, Sir, I am but an unfortunate creature. Any offering of mine will be shamed amidst the alms gathered for the Lord."
24. I am indebted to Sri Phanindra Kumar Mitra of Kalyani University for calling my attention to this point of difference between Becket and Srimati as martyrs.
25. "Does it not mean that our passage is forbidden by the King?"
26. "But we have our Master's order."
27. "Can you thrust aside the King's own barrier?"
28. "The King's sceptre cannot reach the shrine."
29. "Are you alone awake in this palace?" (translation mine)
30. "Suddenly the young dawn appears with a basket of light and dispels the dense darkness." (translation mine)

31. "Please allow me to see the light of my own which lies hidden in the depth of night." (translation mine)
32. *Atmaparichay*, 1940, pp. 97-98 :

    "I can now realize the ultimate significance of life, the central motif that constantly moves towards the final shape. This constitutes the life of life, the innermost, recess, the core of the heart.... Depending on inspiration every one has his own individual way and valuation of life. I have tried to say that much in the playlet, *Naṭīr Pūjā*. What the Nati wanted to offer to the Buddha was her dance. Other disciples offered only the deeply felt truth. But the Nati offered the whole truth manifest in her life. By paying the price of life she only proved how extremely precious that truth was. The deepest urge found the fullest expression in her dance." (translation mine)
33. It should be remembered that the orthodox form of Buddhism does not admit of martyrdom. It is only in its later developments such as the Mahayana that we find some form of saint-worship recognized.
34. Cf. Pramathanath Bishi : *Rabindranatyaprabaha*, Vol. 1, Calcutta, 1953, pp. 91-92.
35. The orgy of her dance as an expression of the agitation caused by her realization of truth is comparable in some respects with "Nirjharer Swapnabhaṅga."

16

Nineteenth Century Western Fiction and Bankimchandra*

There is a widely prevalent notion that Bankimchandra is the Scott of Bengal. Soon after the publication of *Durgeśnandinī* critics noticed its striking affinity with Scott's *Ivanhoe* in terms of plot, characters, mood and spirit. There are in fact many parallels between the two novels. Normans and Saxons, Moguls and Pathans, Ivanhoe and Jagatsingha, Rebecca and Ayesa, Rowena and Tilottama, Bois Gilbert and Osman, for example, are close parallels. In both the novels the story is enacted in the backdrop of history with crowded incidents, sudden turns of events, changing situations and display of powerful emotions. It is these similarities that later led Rajendralal Mitra to remark that Bankim has successfully imitated Scott, an eminent British novelist.[1] There is no doubt that the shadow of *Ivanhoe* has fallen on *Durgeśnandinī*,[2] although Bankim claimed not to have read *Ivanhoe* before he wrote *Durgeśnandinī*[3]. It is, however, quite possible that "we might trace its influence on him through filtration by means of his eldest brother who used to tell stories from English authors to his younger brothers in the evenings at home."[4]

A close scrutiny of Bankim's novels, however, clearly reveals that the novels of Bankim are basically different from and superior to the novels of Scott in terms of theme, treatment and technique. Similarities are confined to the surface only. In the first place, Bankim's use of history is very different from Scott's. Scott is mainly interested in depicting certain historical and social forces operating through his characters. But he lays so much dull stress on environment, social setting, the fabric instead of

* 150th birth-anniversary of Bankimchandra, Calcutta, 1987.

the substance that reality is crowded out. The emphasis in Bankim's novels as is evident even in his premature writing — *Rajmohan's Wife* — is on character and the flickerings of the innermost flame, which dominate a man's destiny. Even in his historical novels Bankim has his eye fixed on the character and the inner workings of the mind. In his last work, *Sītārām*, a novel with a historical background, Bankim says that the novelist should concentrate on the internal and should not waste time in dilating on the external; the historical data.[5] Devoid of both artistic detachment and passion. Scott, on the other hand, fails to create convincing characters. Of physical love Scott practically says nothing. There is no romance of love but only the general romance of history in his novels as he prefers the statuesque unreality to psychological realism, and thus evinces signal weakness in the portrait of young lovers, while in Bankim the novel gains momentum as soon as the lovers appear on the scene. Moreover, the mechanical rapidity of production which Scott was obliged to perform because of his financial difficulties, flaws his stories as well. Scott had no time for revision, while Bankim revised his novels again and again, so much so, that it is difficult to imagine how different the original editions were from their current editions. S.C. Sengupta has rightly remarked[6] that *Ivanhoe* does not have any character like Bimala, and there are more differences than similarities between Ayesa and Rebecca. Moni Bagchi also jibes at the critics who thought that *Durgeśnandinī* was modelled on *Ivanhoe* : "Do they not know that Scott's women characters are nothing but dolls made of wax?"[7] Kshetra Gupta has correctly assessed that "the British fiction only awakened Bankim, but could not provide him with a model."[8]

II

Bankim's first novel, *Rajmohan's Wife* the present version of which "comprises Bankim's own original English from Chapter IV to the 'Conclusion' and an English rendering of Bankim's Bengali version from chapter I to III"[9] is marked by visible signs of immaturity but it is important in signalling some of the essential characteristics of Bankim as a novelist. It is a domestic novel and after the historical romances Bankim would return to domestic novels — *Biṣabṛksha* and *Krṣṇakānter, Uil* — which according to the present author are his masterpieces. The setting of the novel is highly dramatic and Bankim's novels are generally more dramatic than descriptive. In this respect Bankim has closer affinity with Shakespeare than with any British or European novelist. Like Shakespeare quite often he uses double plots where the main plot is reinforced by the subplot. He uses freely and competently, some of the Elizabethan dramatic conventions such as mistaken identity, letters, dreams, disguise, miracles etc. One is reminded not only of Shakespeare but also the plays of Corneille and Racine. Even in the historical romances a common human predicament is combined with ostensibly historical forces through manifestation of strong passions. An otherwise simple life of Pratap and Saibalini, for example, is caught in the vortex of history in *Candraśekhar*. Not infrequently Bankim abandons description in favour of dialogues,[10] and quite often the characters are revealed through actions.[11] In a very perceptive criticism of *Biṣabṛksha* Srikumar Bandyopadhyay pointed out the dramatic nature of the novel in the treatment of the origin, growth and denouement of the internal conflict.[12] In the pace and sweep of *Kapālkundalā* he discovered an affinity with a Greek tragedy.[13] But we must hasten to add that Bankim does not subscribe to the tragic vision of the Greek masters or of Shakespeare. Although as in Shakespeare so in Bankim 'character is destiny' Bankim does not have the Shakespearean detachment. Bankim, the moralist, looked for a way out, and consequently the novels are invested with a moral fabric. Arabindo Poddar rightly contends[14] that the art of Bankim is not just art; it is a moral propaganda. Bhabatosh Chattopadhyay also holds[15] that outside his creative self Bankim had another important role : the role of a social reformer.

The role of the moralist notwithstanding Bankim's novels have an unmistakable affinity with the Shakespearean plays and Greek tragedies rather than with the nineteenth century Western fiction.

III

Letters constitute an important component of Bankim's novels. Although the novels are not epistolary novels in the sense in which the novels of Richardson, Goethe or Laclos are epistolary novels, the letters in Bankim's novels play a very important role in the development of plot as well as in the revelation of characters. The short almost telegraphic letter[16] of Suryamukhi in *Biṣabṛksha* throws a lightning flash on the deepest recesses of her character. The letter is a desperate cry of an agonized soul. In *Durgeśnandinī* the identity of Bimala kept in suspense for a long time is ultimately disclosed through her long letter[17] which also clarifies the relation between Tilottama, Bimala and Birendra. The short letter of Katlu Khan changes the subsequent course of action. The letters exchanged between Ayesa and Jagat Singha[18] show their real feelings to which the reader would not have access in any other way. In *Mṛṇālinī* a letter[19] raises suspicion about the legality of the relationship between

Mṛṇālinī, Girijaya and Hemchandra. In *Rājsiṁha* it is Cancalkumari's letter[20] which largely governs the plot of the novel. Similarly the short letter[21] of Brāhamanbeśī in *Kapālkundalā* leads to fresh developments. There is no point in multiplying examples. Suffice it to say that Bankim does not use letters mechanically or even conventionally. He makes an extremely creative use of letters and makes them serve purpose which otherwise would not be possible. The letters, in brief, are functional, and it is in this respect that Bankim significantly differs from Diderot, Laclos, Richardson, Goethe and Wilkie Collins. Richardson uses letters as a substitute for the narrative and, consequently his novel suffers from the deficiencies of an epistolary novel. Wilkie Collins in *The Woman in White* uses not only letters but also diaries, memoirs, papers etc. for verisimilitude, but the abuse of the narrative machinery only produces boredom. Bankim's imaginative and functional use of letters in his novels makes him shine in isolation from the writers of the Western fiction.

IV

In narrative technique Bankim shows a remarkable range and variety. In *Biṣabṛksha* the omniscient narrator sometimes identifies himself with the reader[22] and sometimes converses with the reader.[23] At times, again Bankim consciously breaks the prevalent narrative convention and strikes a highly original note which anticipates some of the major preoccupations of modern fiction. Statements like "The reader may feel annoyed, but the story begins late, only now"[24] or "A few years after this an incident took place. I cannot describe it now, nor can I decide whether I should describe it later"[25] remind one of Sterne who constantly keeps on commenting on his art of narration, and by common consent Sterne is acclaimed a 'modern' writer. In *Durgeśnandinī* while describing the beauty of Ayesa the omniscient narrator becomes captivated by her beauty, luxuriates in her charm and becomes emotionally involved.[26] As narrator, Bankim would sometimes pretend not to be quite omniscient. He would assume familiarity with all the characters but at the same time would pretend not to have absolute knowledge.[27] As a result the narrative becomes charged with suggestions and creates an atmosphere of suspense and mystery for the captivated reader. Sometimes again he would tightly control the narrative thread and hold back information.[28] On other occasions the omniscient narrator would intrude in the manner of Fielding, Scott and Dickens and philosophize on the riddle of existence. This is particularly evident in *Kapālkundalā*.

An important aspect of Bankim's narrative method is his use of what is known as flashback technique which telescopes the past and the present and brings the past into a significant relationship with the present. Furthermore, in Bankim's novels the technique simultaneously reveals the unconscious and strengthens the plot and contributes to the dramatic qualities of the novels. We rarely come across such creative use of flashback technique in the nineteenth century Western fiction.

Like the modern novelists Bankim uses multiple points of view. Two descriptions[29] of Dalani, for example, are marked by two different points of view. In the first passage the omniscient narrator adores the resplendent and immaculate beauty of Dalani; in the second Dalani is seen through the eyes of Mohammed Taki who scans her only as a potential bed-fellow. Saibalini is seen through the eyes of Candraśekhar who is lacerated by her charming beauty.[30] In *Indirā*, the entire story is narrated chronologically by Indira, and the characters are seen through the limited and typically feminine sensibility of Indira. In *Rajanī* Bankim uses multiple narrators suggesting multiple point of view.

V

Rajanī deserves some special attention because in his introduction to this novel Bankim acknowledges[31] his debt to two books : *The Woman in White* (1860) by William Wilkie Collins and *The Last Days of Pompeii* (1834) by Edward George Earle Bulwer-Lytton. The first book is mentioned in connection with the narrative method employed in the novel. About his narrative method Collins writes that the story "will be written by more than one pen, as *the story of an offence against the laws* is told in court by more than one witness...."[32] Vincent Gilmore, a character in the novel also later reiterates the plan.[33] The point to remember is that *The Woman in White* is a "story of an offence against the laws" and the main interest of the novel does not lie in the conflicts and complexities of the characters so much as in the unravelling of the story and the final revelation of the secret in Percival's life. But *Rajanī* is not a thriller. Its main interest is not so much in the discovery of Rajani's title to property or the restoration of her rights as in Bankim's profound psychological insight into the unpredictable complexities of the characters. The novel assumes a new dimension when subtle psychological changes come over Rajani as the poor flower girl is touched by love, or when Labanga breaks into a confession of her premarital immaturity in not recognizing her first love. All these go a long way to make *Rajanī* a psychological novel.

The influence of *The Woman in White on Rajanī*, if any, is superficial and pernicious to some extent, because the narrative method adopted by Collins and followed by Bankim leaves an unbridgeable gap between the participating self and the remembering narrator.

Now coming to Bulwer-Lytton's *The Last Days of Pompeii* and the relation between Nydia and Rajani. Bankim says that the character of Rajani is modelled on Nydia. But a careful reading of the two novels shows that the only points of affinity between Nydia and Rajani are that both of them are flower-girls and that both are blind, and there are significant differences between Nydia and Rajani in terms of situation and sensibility. Nydia is painfully conscious of her position as a slave and a "look of resigned sorrow, of tranquil endurance had banished the smile but not the sweetness from her lips."[34] We are also told that "sold early into slavery...the kindlier feelings naturally profuse in the breast of Nydia, were nipped and blighted."[35] Rajani does not indulge in self-pity. She asserts herself and claims to be equal with those who have eyes.[36] She is as much assertive in defying her physical handicap as in declaring her love for Sacindra. Nydia is a taciturn lover, she never speaks out and Gluacus is not perceptive enough to understand her feelings for him. "Glaucus, I am a slave; what business have I with grief or joy?"[37] she says to Glaucus. Unlike Nydia, Rajani constantly asserts herself with unflinching determination, leaves her home, demonstrates her physical strength and capacity for self-defence by breaking a very hard stick and expresses her profound gratitude (not love) to Amarnath.

The Last Days of Pompeii is a historical romance in which Nydia is just a character, instrumental to the development of the plot. In *Rajanī* after whom the title is derived is the most important figure. In the very first section we hear the story directly from her and the narration carries conviction. Like Joyce in *A Portrait of the Artist as a Young Man* or Faulkner in *The Sound and the Fury* Bankim describes the incidents through the sensibility of the speaker. Since *Rajanī* is blind her visual imagination is very weak while her other senses are very strong. Touched by Sacindra she is touched by love, and she describes her experience of sudden wakening to the feelings of love purely in the tactile, olfactory and auditory terms.[38] Nydia, as prototype of Rajanī, is only the starting point for Bankim and that is precisely the point of departure. Nydia simply activates the imagination of Bankim, a born romantic and he creates a character that is far more complex, far more interesting and far more convincing than what it takes its origin from.

VI

In Bankim's novels unforeseen events, astrological predictions, hermits and sages play significant roles in the construction and development of the plot. In *Durgeśnandinī* Abhiram Swami's instruction[39] to ally with the King has a direct bearing on the subsequent development of the story in general and the denouement of the novel in particular. In *Mṛṇālinī* the story is set in motion with Madhabacharya's instruction to Hemchandra. In *Yugalānguřiya* the story is only an enactment of an astrological prediction. In *Candraśekhar* Ramanandaswami plays a crucial role in the restoration of Saibalini and the development of the relation between Candrásekhar and Saibalini. Rajanī regains her vision through the grace of a *sannyasi*. The astrological prediction about Mabarak influences the course of events in *Rājasiṁha*. The cryptic prediction fulfilled in an unexpected way has an important bearing on the plot of *Śitārām*. In *Kapālkundalā* Kapalik is a central figure. The nameless Mahapurus who appears in the concluding section of *Ānandamaṭh* seems to be omniscient.[40] His long speech confirms the impression that he knows everything and can clearly look into the future.

It is evident that sannyasis play an important functional role in the fictive world of Bankim. While the phenomenon may be traced to Bankim's personal belief in the paranormal faculties of a sannyasi, the fact remains nevertheless that sannyasis never appear so crucially in the nineteenth century western fiction. Even in Scott's *The Talisman* the hermit. Theodorick Engaddi dwindles into insignificance as Scott makes history serve his own purposes by inventing characters and situations and blending them with real people and historical events. The predominance of sannyasis in Bankim's novels lends them a local colour and puts them firmly in the Indian tradition.

VII

It remains to be seen how Bankim differs from the eminent British, continental and American novelists of the nineteenth century in plan, policy and practice.

We have already seen the nature of the 'influence' that Scott, Bulwer-Lytton and Collins had on the novel of Bankim. We can now consider a few other Victorian novelists. The 'diffuse positivism of a utilitarian age' that we find in Thackeray (1811-1863) is absent in Bankim. Bankim is superior to Dickens (1812-1870) both as a better artist and a finer psychologist. The novels of Anthony Trollope (1815-1887) deal mainly with a small provincial town and the ecclesiastical world and offer some glimpses of the social life. Bankim has little in common with George Eliot (1819-1880) whose novels are marked by religious doctrines. Bankim is as much free from the eccentricity of George Meredith (1828-1909) as from the utopian vision of Samuel Butler (1835-1902). Bankim does not share the tragic vision of Hardy (1840-1928), nor does he condemn, like Hardy, the whole of modern civilization.

The French literature in the nineteenth century was quite rich in fiction. But a cursory look at some of the important novelists of the century would reveal their differences from Bankim. Stendhal's (1783-1842) *The Red and the Black*, though concerned with psychological realism, is unlike Bankim's novels in that its chief character is a villain. Balzac (1799-1850) was more interested in social realism than psychological realism. The themes of the historical romances of Victor Hugo (1802-1885) are very different from the themes of Bankim's novels. Flaubert (1821-1880), the most influential of the nineteenth century European novelists, is both a romantic and a realist. His novels are marked by excessive romanticism tempered by technical devices including attempts to attain total objectivity. His *Madame Bovary* (1854) is a domestic novel of psychological realism no doubt and the character of Emma may remind one of Rohini of *Kṛṣṇakānter Uil*, but there are vital differences. Emma was a spinster when she fell in love with Charles. Heloise is very different from Bhramar and the ending of Charles is different from the ending of Gobindalal. Alexander Dumas (1822-1870), a writer of historical romance, was a prolific writer. But his characters are flat. Naturalism of Emile Zola (1840-1902) is not to be found in Bankim. Some critics have discovered an affinity between *Le Mariage de Loti* of Pierre Loti (1805-1913) and *Kapālkundalā*. We should only bear in mind that *Le Mariage de Loti*, a romance of sentimental adventure in the langourous setting of Tahiti was published only in 1880 while *Kapālkundalā* was published in 1866.

In Russia great writers like Gogol, Turgenev, Dostoevsky and Tolstoy immensely contributed to the growth of fiction in the nineteenth century. But the world of fiction that they created is essentially different from the world of Bankim. *Dead Souls* of Gogol (1809-1852) is a social satire. Turgenev (1818-1883) was interested in the human details that lie behind the so called history. Dostoevsky (1812-1881), a great writer who paints like 'Rembrandt' is an urban novelist and the world of his novels is the world of overcrowded cities. Tolstoy (1878-1910) puts emphasis on the fact that people are always carried forward by a force which they do not really understand; the characters of Tolstoy are all formed before the novel practically begins. In Bankim a character is evolved from within and is developed through interaction with other characters and often difficult, if not unforeseen circumstances.

When we turn to America we meet three major novelists : Hawthorne (1804-1864), Melville (1819-1891) and James (1843-1916), and their illustrious predecessor James Fennimore Cooper (1789-1851). But Bankim does not share Hawthorne's preoccupation with the problem of evil as evidenced in *The Scarlet Letter* (1850). The symbolic allegory of Melville's *Moby Dick* or the adventure romance of *Omoo* is not Bankim's concern. Henry James was a pioneer in psychological realism and formal architectonics, but his themes are very different from Bankim's. Bankim has only this much in common with Cooper that like him Bankim was also an intensely nationalistic individual who, conscious of the past achievements and potentialities of his country, eagerly looked forward to the development of a great nation. But a sizable number of his novels are concerned with the sea and the navy.

In Italy Manzoni (1785-1873), leading Italian romantic novelist of the nineteenth century, made a heroic attempt to demonstrate that the divine order really does work in reality. Bankim does not evince any such avowed intention.

VIII

Indian fiction was born out of an interaction between the East and the West, and Bankim extremely well-read in Western literature absorbed Western influence, assimilated it into his blood stream and produced novels which are basically Indian. It is evident that in the range of subjects and the depth of feeling, in the depiction of the subtle nuances of human characters, in the grasp of dramatic potentialities of human situations, in the control of his narrative materials and in the understanding of history, society and man Bankim towers above all his Western compeers. It will be no exaggeration to say that Bankim outdistanced the contemporary novelists of the West and anticipated modernism.

It is time the colonial myth that Bankim is the Scott of Bengal was exploded.

SELECTED BIBLIOGRAPHY

(I have indicated by asterisks the items which I have found most helpful.)

*1. Arabindo Poddar, *Bankim Mānas* (Indiana Limited, Calcutta, 1950).

*2. Asit Bandyopadhyay, *History of Modern Bengali Literature* (Modern Book Agency, Calcutta, 1986).

3. Bhabatosh Datta, *Cintānayak Bankimchandra* (Jijnasa, Calcutta, 1973).
4. Bijit Kumar Datta, *Bāṃlāsāhitye Aitihasik Upanyās* (Mitra and Ghosh, Calcutta, 1387 B.S.).
5. Dipak De, *Bankim Mūlyāyan* (Jijnasa, Calcutta, 1381 B.S.).
6. Jiban Kumar Mukherjee, *Bankimchandrer Tragedy Cetanā* (Sahityasri, Calcutta, 1382 B.S.).
*7. Kshetra Gupta, *Bankimchandrer Upanyās* : Śilparīti (Granthanilay, Calcutta, 1974).
*8. Mohitlal Majumdar, *Bankimchandrer Upanyās* (Vidyoday Library, Calcutta, 1979).
9. Moni Bagchi, *Bankimchandra* (Jijnasa, Calcutta, 1965).
10. P.R. Sen, *Western Influence in Bengali Literature* (Academic Publishers Calcutta, 3rd edition, 1965).
11. Sisir Kumar Das, *The Artist in Chains* (New Statesman, New Delhi, 1984).
*12. Srikumar Bandyopadhyay, *Bangasāhitye Upanyāser Dhārā* (Modern Book Agency, Calcutta, 7th edition, 1984).
*13. Subodh Chandra Sen Gupta, *Bankimchandra : A Study of His Craft* (A. Mukherjee, Calcutta-19).
14. Sunil Kumar Banerjee : *Bankimchandra : A Study of His Craft* (Firma KLM, Calcutta, 1968).

NOTES

1. See Gopal Haider's introduction to *Bankim Racana Samgraha* (subsequently referred to as B.R.S.) Swaksharata Prakashan, 1947, p. 17.
2. See Bijit Kumar Datta, *Bangla Sahitye Aitihasik Upanyās* (Calcutta, 1973), p. 69.
3. *Sadhana* 1301 B.S. quoted by P.R. Sen in *Western Influence in Bengali Literature* (Calcutta, 1966), p. 233.
4. P.R. Sen, *Western Influence in Bengali Literature, op. cit.*, p. 107.
5. B.R.S., p. 866.
6. S.C. Sen Gupta, *Bankimchandra* (Calcutta, 1987), p. 50.
7. Moni Bagchi, *Bankimchandra* (Calcutta, 1965), p. 126.
8. Kshetra Gupta, *Bankimchandrer Upanyās : Silpa Riti* (Calcutta, 1974), p. 3.
9. Preface to the Centenary Edition of *Rajmohan's Wife* (Calcutta, 1940), p. ii.
10. See *Durgeśnandinī* Part I, Chapter VI, *Kapālkundalā* Part I, Chapter VIII; *Biṣabṛksha* Chapter XVII; *Rājsiṁha* Part III, Chapter I, for example.
11. Candraśekhar's agony, for example, is amply demonstrated through his burning of the books. The burning episode shows that Candraśekhar who is otherwise so gentle and generous is also capable of very strong feelings. The act of burning serves as a perfect objective correlative for his disturbed state of mind. Similarly, Kapālkundalā's collection of medicinal herbs reveals her solicitude for Śyāma.

12. Srikumar Bandyopadhyay, *Bangasahitye Upanyāser Dhārā* (Calcutta, 1984), p. 115.
13. *Ibid.*, p. 73.
14. Arabindo Poddar, *Bankim Mānas* (*Calcutta*, 1951), p. 87.
15. Bhabatosh Chattopadhyay, "Bankimchandrer Sāhityabhābana : Patanga, Agun O Jal" in *Desh*, 24 February 1990.
16. B.R.S., p. 229.
17. *Ibid.*, pp. 48-54. Bridget's letter in *Tom Jones* might have served as model.
18. B.R.S., pp. 77-78.
19. *Ibid.*
20. *Ibid.*, p. 583.
21. *Ibid.*, p. 127.
22. "We do not know, but Nagendra considered it harmful." B.R.S., p. 210.
23. "Conventionally the marriage should take place at the end; but we have arranged Kundanandini's marriage in the beginning of the novel." *Ibid.*, p. 219.
24. *Ibid.*, p. 220.
25. *Ibid.*, pp. 452-53.
26. *Ibid.*, p. 41.
27. "On account of these Gobindalal found a niche in the mind of Rohini; I do not know the consequences of it, I am just narrating what actually happened." *Ibid.*, p. 499.
28. "Mati asked : 'Any new idea dawning?'

    Pesman : What new idea?

    Mati did not confide it to Pesman; we also won't tell our reader. It will be revealed later." *Ibid.*, p. 113.
29. *Ibid.*, p. 350 and p. 409.
30. *Ibid.*, p. 354.
31. See Bijnapan, *Rajanī*, Bangiya Sahitya Parishad, Asvin 1372 B.S.
32. Wilkie Collins, *The Woman in White* (London, n.d.), p. v. My emphasis.
33. *Ibid.*, p. 109.
34. Lord Lytton, *The Last Days of Pompeii* (London, n.d.), p. 52.
35. *Ibid.*, p. 292.
36. B.R.S. 439.
37. *The Last Days of Pompeii, op. cit., p.* 149.
38. B.R.S., p. 442. See S.C. Sen Gupta, *Bankimchandra, op. cit.*, 79-81.
39. B.R.S., p. 9.
40. "Overwhelmed with grief Satyananda asked, 'Sir if Hindu rule is not established, then, who, I pray, will be the King? Shall we have a Muslim king again?' 'No,' said he, "Now the English will rule." B.R.S., p. 735.

17

Visions of Beauty : Tagore and European Romanticism*

Well read in Western literature, Tagore was quite familiar with the writings of the European romantics. There are many references to English and European poets in his writings. It is interesting to see Tagore's vision of Beauty in the light of the Western notions. Tagore was apparently fascinated by the utterance of Keats ("Beauty is truth, truth beauty") and has referred to it on several occasions. Different poets have touched upon different aspects of Beauty. If Keats spoke of the relation between Beauty and Truth, and again, between Beauty and Joy (*Endymion*), Shelley sang hymns to intellectual beauty and glorified Beauty as something illuminating. Hugo thought of Beauty in terms of harmony or consonance. Balzac held that "the Beautiful can have only one line." Taine believed that Beauty consists in the expression of life. Friedrich Schlegel related Beauty of Nature and the fullness of life. Wilhelm Schlegel held that "the beautiful is a symbolic representation of the infinite." Schiller discovered an affinity between Beauty and divinity. Schelling sought to reconcile nature and mind in the concepts of Beauty. Novalis spoke of the pristine unity, the unity symbolized by the blue flower sought by Novalis's Ofterdingen. Of the later poets and critics with whose writings Tagore was familiar, Baudelaire conceived of Beauty ("Hymne à la Beauté") as including ugliness, terror, cruelty and destruction, and Croce thought of Beauty as expression.

The visions of Beauty that we find in these poets are partial, if not fragmentary. But it is possible to discover a system in Tagore's idea of

* ICLA (International Comparative Literature Association), Tokyo, 1991.

Beauty from various remarks and comments scattered over the entire gamut of his writings, where all the above ideas are woven into an organic whole. There are some essays entirely devoted to Beauty. The essay, "The Sense of Beauty" is one example. While discussing the nature of Beauty, Tagore talks of Good, Truth and Joy, and shows how they form a significant relationship with Beauty. Tagore writes : "Whenever we see the Good and the True, and Beautiful stands revealed. Beauty is Good in its fullness as fullness of Beauty is Good incarnate."[1] Tagore believes that real Good consists in the expression of the self and a transcendental self-knowledge. Ethics is essentially a product of the gregarious spirit. But Good, according to Tagore, is something above need. "Beauty transcends necessity," he says, "wherefore we regard it as opulence or as a power which liberates us into love out of penury of self-seeking." In the essay entitled "Literature" Tagore writes :

> The moralists talk about ethics in view of the needs of the world, but poets express Good in the form of Beauty that defies description.[2]

It may be remembered in this connection that Kant, to whom European romanticism owes a good deal, held that Beauty is the symbol of Good. But the Western philosophers distinguish between Good and Beauty: that is, whatever is Good may not be beautiful. The idea of affinity between Good and Beauty can be traced back to Plato who affirms in *Lysis* that "the good is the beautiful." In the *Republic* Plato also looks upon Beauty as the manifestation of Good. In fact, in the *Republic* the Form of Good appears as an enlightening and creative first principle. For Plato the individual forms of beauty partake in Absolute Beauty which transcends them. Beauty as Idea is a Being by itself, beyond the limitations of space and time and independent of relatives. It reveals the Ideal and the Universal. The notion of symmetry and due proportions, moreover, links Beauty with Good, and inasmuch as Beauty reveals Being, it is related to Truth. In other words, Truth guarantees Beauty or gives Being to Beauty. But Tagore goes one step further and sees Beauty as unity in diversity. "Like the full-blown lotus, or the full moon, they [the beautiful objects] are integrated in themselves and with the rest of the world," he writes. In a short article[3] Tagore appreciatively refers to Hugo's views, and points out how a unity is achieved by distantly placed objects through harmony. Tagore then remarks that although the sun and the lotus and water are separated by huge distance, they are harmonized into a unified existence by Beauty. When mind penetrates matter, it imposes form upon it. Hugo discovers an element of mystery in the nature of

Beauty itself: "Un mystère est au fond de leur grave beauté." In his famous Preface to *Cromwell*, Hugo wrote : "Le beau n'a qu'un type : le laid en a mille." According to Schelling, too, Beauty is the infinite portrayed in finite form. August Wilhelm Schlegel further clarifies :

> Man halte das Unendliche nicht etwa für eine philosophische Fiktion, man suche es nicht jenseits der Welt : es umgibt uns uberall, wir können ihm niemals entgehen; wir leben, weben und sind im Unendlichen.[4]
>
> The infinite is not to be regarded as a philosophic fiction nor to be sought beyond the world : it surrounds us on all sides, we can never escape it, we live, exist and are in the infinite.

And here is Tagore : "The beauty of the world contemplates the beauty of the infinite.... Beauty unites the heaven and earth."[5] And again : "Beauty harmonizes the entire world."[6] In Germany, the theologian Schleiermacher sought to reconcile the outer world and the inner world, while Schelling and Ritter tried to reconcile nature and mind through their philosophy of nature. It was felt that mind and nature were not opposites but aspects of the same force. The Jena group of romantics — Fichte, Schelling, the Schlegel brothers and Novalis, among others — tried to penetrate the mysteries of nature and mind, the separation of which was blamed upon the Enlightenment. The world was at one with itself, they believed, and man's subconscious still knows this pristine unity.

Tagore says : "The job of the soul is to establish communication. This leads to the creation of beauty."[7] He holds that Beauty is created when man establishes a cordial relationship with another man or with Nature. Tagore, in fact, extends Schiller's idea of aesthetic education of man to the unfolding of our feelings of sympathy and social affection. Schiller places the question of Beauty into the perspective of the harmonious development of human nature and the formation of our true humanity. He considers Beauty as an imperative, something which we must achieve. It arises out of the harmonization of the demands of man's sensuous and rational nature, of the two fundamental motive impulses : the material drive (*Stofftrieb*) and the form drive (*Formtrieb*), or, to put it differently, Beauty is neither mere life nor mere form but *living form*. The refinement and the ennoblement of the senses, the connection of the idea of freedom with our aesthetic foundation, and the harmonization of man's faculties, a harmonization which we achieve through our striving for Beauty, have their effect also on ethics and on our relationship with others. Tagore seems to refer to this process when he remarks in the course of his discussion[8] of *Sakuntala*, that in *Sakuntala* love has been elevated from the realm of natural or sensuous beauty to the permanent paradise of aesthetic / moral beauty. Man comes to know himself through the expansion of self which, Tagore feels, is missing in *The Tempest*. But Tagore's nature poetry assumes a harmonious relationship between man and nature. We can find the closest parallel in Wordsworth who, "fostered alike by beauty and by fear," felt that the poet must "bind together by passion and knowledge the vast empire of human society" to produce an "accord of sublimated humanity." Tagore considers Beauty as an instrument of unification. He writes :

> When our sense of beauty speaking out of every conflict of the pleasurable and the painful, the good and the bad, finally bursts into flame — all the contrast of separateness becomes consumed in it. What happens then? Then Truth and Beauty become one. Then we perceive that in the realization of Truth there is joy and the quintessence of beauty.[9]

This identification of Beauty with Truth reminds one of Keats and his famous utterance in "Ode on a Grecian Urn" : "Beauty is truth, truth beauty." Tagore refers to this line in his letter to Amiya Chakrabarty and comments : "It means that only the Truth realized by the heart, intellect and the mind is beautiful." In other words, felt truth is the real truth. Scientific truth and philosophical truth serve our mundane purposes; it can never satisfy the soul. Tagore discovers an affinity between Keats's idea of Beauty and the sayings of Yajnabalkya. He writes : "This is what Yajnabalkya has said : I truly realize myself in whatever is dear to me. That it why it is dear, that is why it is beautiful."[10] Tagore refers to Keats in the concluding section of his essay, "The Poet's Reply," and glorfies the dictum, "Beauty is truth, truth beauty." Keats again comes up in Tagore's essay, "Information and Truth," where Tagore refers to the Grecian urn to show how Beauty acts as a unifying agent. He writes : "Keats in his poem has suggested the unification of the Greek urn and the entire world. He has said : 'Thou silent form dost tease us out of thought / As doth eternity'... because the finite, whatever may be its form, reveals the infinite. That is why it defies description."[11] Tagore sounds Aristotelian when referring to Keats in his essay, "Modern Poetry," he remarks : "The poetry of Keats is concerned with contemplation and creation of Beauty of Form."

In his letter to Bailey dated 22 November 1817, Keats remarked : "I am certain of nothing but of the holiness of the Heart's affections and the truth of the Imagination. What Imagination seizes as Beauty must be Truth." This Beauty is Truth, because it is achieved through intuitive perception. As in Keats, so in Tagore the idea of Beauty is not just aestheticism but a noble human and spiritual idea. Victor Hugo had also remarked :

> Sous le monde réel, il existe un monde idéal qui se montre resplendissant à l oeil de ceux que des méditations graves ont accoutumes a voir dans les choses plus que les choses.[12]
>
> Beneath the real world there is an ideal world which reveals itself in all its brilliance to the eye of those accustomed by serious meditation to see in things more than just things.

In *Endymion* Keats makes the emphatic declaration : "A thing of beauty is a joy for ever," and thus associates Beauty with Joy. The association of Beauty and Joy can be traced back to Plato. Plato contends in the *Symposium* that we are attracted to the real in the guise of the beautiful and the response to this attraction brings joy. To overcome egoism in its protean forms of fantasy and illusion (*per tanti rami cercando*) is automatically to become more moral, and the proper apprehension of beauty is joy in reality through the transfiguring of desire. Thus, as we respond, we experience the transcendence of the real, and the personal ego fades as we "escape from the mean petty slavery of the particular case and turn towards the open sea of beauty." Tagore also says that with the intuitive perception of Beauty, "Truth and Beauty become one. Then we perceive that in the realization of Truth there is joy and the quintessence of Beauty." And again : "Art and Literature bring home to us that what is True is Joy, what is True is Eternal. They annotate over and again the truth propounded by the Upanishads : *Raso vai sah. Rasam hi evāyam lavdvanadī bhavati....* He is Truth in all its Beauty and to realize Him is to taste joy everlasting."[13]

By ascribing to Beauty the highest value, a kind of divinity, in fact, Tagore shares the nineteenth-century attitude to Beauty in general, as in the nineteenth century the Romantic and Victorian poets, the Transcendentalists and those who cultivated art for art's sake never failed in ascribing to Beauty the highest value, a kind of divinity. Even much earlier St. Augustine held that God as the Absolute Beauty is the principle and source of all that is beautiful in this world. St. Augustine follows Plato in adopting the dialectical method of ascent; he differs however in the conception of the stages : the mind rises from the sensuous appearance of Beauty, an appearance to which St. Augustine gives full significance, to the contemplation of the soul; from there to measure and proportion, to the idea, and ultimately to God.

It is evident from the above discussion that Tagore's vision of Beauty appropriates Plato and Plotinus, St. Augustine and Yajnabalkya, British, German and French romantics and many contemporary critical ideas. All these influences are absorbed into a unified sensibility in Tagore's vision of Beauty.

NOTES

1. "The Sense of Beauty" (translated by Kshitis Roy from the Bengali essay "Saundaryabodh") in *Rabindranath Tagore on Art and Aesthetics* (Calcutta : Orient Longmans, 1961), p. 5. Subsequently referred to as *Art and Aesthetics*.
2. *Rabindra Rachanavali* (Government of West Bengal, 1961), vol. 13, p. 756. My translation.
3. "The Distant Beauty" ("Sudur Aikya") in *Rabindranath Rachanavali*, vol. 14, p. 606.
4. August Wilhelm Schlegel, "Vorlesungen uber schone Kunst and Literatur," *Kritische Schriften*, vol. VI, pp. 81-82.
5. *Rabindra Rachanavali, vol.* 14, p. 624.
6. *Ibid.*, p. 605.
7. *Ibid.*, p. 637.
8. "Sakuntala," in *Rabindra Rachanavali*, vol. 13, p. 661. My translation.
9. *Art and Aesthetics*, p. 8.
10. *Rabindra Rachanavali*, vol. 14, p. 292. My translation.
11. *Ibid.*, pp. 313-14.
12. Preface to "Odes" (1822), *Oeuvres poetiques*, vol. I, p. 265.
13. *Art and Aesthetics*, p. 10.

18

Monologues of Tagore : A Generic Approach*

The monologues of Tagore, like his endeavours in other art-forms — music and painting — run into thousands, and offer a rich aesthetic experience in infinite variety of texture and structure, in length and in tonal variation. The range of possible audience to whom these monologues are addressed is equally wide, leaving practically nothing *en route*.

It is neither possible nor necessary to discuss all the monologues. I should like to make just a sample survey to illustrate the versatility of Tagore in his use of monology as a literary form.

Take, for example, the poem "Flute Music" (*Bā̃śī*). It is a dramatic monologue in which the audience is neither present nor implied. It is more in the form of loud thinking addressed *ad vacuuo*. But the monologue is dramatically contextualized in time, place and action. The speaker is sharply individualized. We know what he is, where he is, and, in the course of the poem we are offered a glimpse into the unfulfilled aspirations of him and the kind of fulfilment that he realizes through the music of Kantobabu when he transcends his mundane existence and is transported to the world of art where he equals Akbar, the Emperor of India. Other characters that figure in the poem — the girl in Dacca sari and Kantobabu are also presented through the unifying consciousness of the speaker. But while the girl is presented through powerful visual image ("dressed in a Dacca Sari, vermillion on her forehead") in the case of Kantobabu the description starts with physical features ("Long hair carefully parted/large eyes...") but reaches

* INCLA (Indian National Comparative Literature Association), Jamia Milia (Delhi), 1987.

out to the auditory. Like most of the Browningian heroes the speaker is a failure in love, and possibly also in life, and like a Browningian hero again, he refuses to accept failure and the poem moves on to a transcendental plane where "torn umbrella and royal parasol merge / Rise on the sad music of a flute / towards one heaven." Structurally, however, the poem begins in the form of a narrative. As the first seven lines describe the setting in cinematic montages we are inclined to take it as a descriptive poem. But the seventh line ("Another creature apart from me lives in my room / For the same rent / A lizard") introduces the speaker. And, immediately, the poem takes on the form of a monologue.

A very different structure is worked out in "A Half-acre of Land" (*Dui Bighā Jami*). The speaker in this monologue narrates how a half-acre land that he tried to keep after selling off all his lands was fraudulently grabbed by a greedy landlord ("Everything was sold, debt claimed through a fraudulent deed"), and how he was branded as a "Pukka robber" when he returned home after fifteen years of roaming about the world. There are a number of other characters — the rich, hypocritical, greedy landlord, the gardener, a top-knotted Oriya looking like "a messenger of death," and the sycophants of the rich zamindar. All these characters are realistically delineated as instruments of social exploitation. "The sweethearted women returning home with water" partly offset the bitterness with a touch of perennial pleasure, *joie de vivre* and suggest the possibility of redemption. In this monologue, as in many others, Tagore makes use of the dramatic device of conflict, both internal and external, and conversation between characters. The first stanza actually records the conversation that had taken place between the landlord and the speaker more than fifteen years ago. The last stanza also records, in direct narration, the utterances of various characters, during the furore over the mangoes. The scene also changes from the garden to the tank where "the landlord, rod in hand, was fishing with his retainers." There is a significant tonal variation, as within the framework of the monologue, the speaker, on his return to homeland, pays an encomium to the motherland. The form of this stanza beginning "I bow, I bow to my beautiful Motherland Bengal!" is that of a religious rite, an obeisance. It describes the luscious greenery of the landscape, the villages "that are nests of shade and peace" and the "sweethearted women." As the speaker trudges on to his home, his native village comes to life with its pottery, temple, market place and granary. In keeping with the tone of obeisance an emotional bond, the bond that binds a mother and a child ("I call you Mother") is established. In the next stanza the bond is snapped as the speaker, looking around, notices that "all the signs of the past have gone completely." The "Mother" of the previous stanza, "a goddess," degenerates into "a servant" in the eyes of the speaker by the end of this stanza. But, in the next stanza, as "two ripe mangoes fall to the ground" beside the speaker, he muses : "My mother still knows her son, may be." The speaker takes that "gift of love" and the child is reconciled to the mother. These three stanzas presenting the dramatic cycle of order-disorder-order affect the poem both structurally and texturally.

The form of obeisance is elaborately developed in luxuriating details in the monologue "Earth" (*Pṛthibī*). A dramatic setting is suggested as the speaker stands before Earth "bowed at the altar of the setting sun." In the manner of a Vedic hymn the speaker enumerates various aspects and points out how the opposites are reconciled in the nature of Earth. Earth is both "gentle and fierce" and unrelentingly ruthless. This, incidentally, is quite in keeping with the nature of religious hymns. Dakshina Kali, for example, is described both as frightening (*Karālabadanāṃ ghorām*) and pleasantly attractive ("*sukhaprasannabadanām*"). It is different matter, however, that the "homage" that the speaker pays to the Earth is a personal homage of Tagore as "the setting sun" metaphorically stands for the poet in his seventies (16 October 1935) who sees the spectre of death from a measurable distance.

In an earlier monologue (1915), "Offerings" (*Anjali*) the speaker who is the poet himself, makes a profound obeisance in elaborate religious ritual, in the evening. The lexical items are all drawn from the register of worship. The peculiarity of this monologue is that it begins in the form of loud thinking and we are not aware of the presence of an audience until we come to line 7 when the speaker directly addresses an audience (Oh my guests..."). But as we move on to line 10 ("As you left...") we realize that the guests have already left and the monologue is actually meant for the departed guests.

Some of these introspective monologues are marked by an element of uncertainty about the presence of a listener. Take, for example, the monologue "Late" (*Bilambita*). The speaker, possibly the poet himself, is a tired traveller who has still miles to go. At the metaphorical level, the seasonal change refers to the change in literary taste over the passage of time, and when the speaker says, "Now is the time for different kinds of songs, different tunes/now make a garland with different flowers in different fashion" it is not certain whether the speaker is addressing himself or giving tips to his successor. The uncertainty arises out of the ambiguity inhering the imperative mood in which the line is written.

Another monologue of the same period, "Indifferent" (*Udāsīn*) is interesting for its texture. The monologue begins in a carefree, nonchalant mood. The tone is light, almost chatty. But towards the end of the second stanza we suddenly get a glimpse, in a lightning flash, of the abysmal depth of the psyche. The speaker says : "I don't stir, even by mistake, the memories that are lying at the bottom of my mind." The superficial placidity is seriously threatened by tragic potentialities. As a result the monologue approximates the texture of a dark comedy.

In most of the monologues in the collection of poems entitled The Child (*Śiśu*) there is a listener. The speaker is generally a child and the supposed listener is the mother. In "The Hero" (*Bīr Puruṣ*) the speaker, a child, daydreams a hazardous journey in which he accompanies his mother, is attacked by a band of robbers, fights with them and returns victorious only to be gathered and caressed by his mother. The monologue packed with intense dramatic action anticipates, at every stage, the emotional and behavioural reaction of the mother. The dramatic nature of the monologue is evident as much in the progress of action as in the pitched battle in which the child fights unaided and singlehanded with a band of dangerous dacoits. All the characters — the mother, the palanquin-bearers, the dacoits and even the elder brother of the child — are briefly and sharply sketched. There is, however, one minor problem about the first two lines. The lines, "Suppose, after roaming far and wide, I am escorting my mother to a far off place" (*mane karo yeno bideś ghure / māke niye yacchi anek dūre*) would imply a listener other than the mother. But in the third line it is directly addressed to the mother and then on the mother continues to be the listener, either real or imaginary, up to the end of the poem. Incidentally, in his translation of this poem Radice circumvents the problem by making the child directly address the mother from the very beginning ("Say we made a journey, mother / Roaming far and wide together").

The same kind of emotional bond marks the tender sentiment expressed in another monologue in the same collection of poems. The title of the poem is "Hide and Seek" (*Lukocuri*). The playful mood of the mischievous child is developed through an imaginary conversation with the mother. In fact, the responses of the mother are all anticipated by the child who voices the expected reactions of the mother. The loving, affectionate nature of the mother as well as her daily routine are revealed through this monologue. The peculiarity of this monologue is that the listener is actually silent but she is made eloquent through utterances attributed to her.

But there are monologues where the listener is not only definitely present but the actual reactions of the listener are also faithfully recorded in the manner we have it, for example, in Browning's "My Last Duchess."

The monologue "Auspicious Moment" (*Śubhakṣhan*) is an instance. The two sections of the poem are, in fact, two monologues by the same speaker, presumably an adolescent girl. There is a time gap. The first monologue is made before the prince passes by the road overlooked by the window of the girl's house. The second monologue is made after the departure of the royal procession. Both the monologues are addressed to the mother. The first monologue records the romantic expectations of the girl; the second, her distressed disillusionment. The reactions of the mother are evident in the line, "Mother, what's the matter? Why are you looking so strangely at my face?" The sentence placed in the middle in both the monologues highlights the contrast between a mature mother and her immature daughter.

A silent but very busy listener engaged in toilet is implied in "Ever-Coming" (*Cirāyamānā*). The speaker anxiously waiting outside for his sweetheart to join him becomes increasingly impatient and tries to impress upon her that she should hurry and not so much bother about her ornamentation. The listener is obviously in the audible range of the speaker.

In terms of the listener or addressee "The Picture" (*Chabi*) is a remarkable monologue. The monologue is first addressed to a picture, a portrait, in fact. But as the speaker becomes engrossed in the profoundly philosophical question of the truth-value of a picture, the portrait assumes life, as it were. In the imagination of the speaker the portrait becomes fleshed and it throbs with life as the speaker reminisces his long, intimate association with the person portrayed. The monologue ends on a transcendental plane where all the differences between the static and the dynamic, between the living and the lifeless, vanish in the unifying consciousness of the speaker.

The later monologues of Tagore can be broadly divided into two categories : the narrative and the autobiographical.

To take some of the narrative monologues first where the story element predominates. In "Camellia" the speaker, a robust young man, a footballer is bent upon establishing communication with a girl named Kamala, a frequent co-traveller in a tram, and looks for an opportunity to demonstrate his 'chivalry'. Eventually he quarrels with an anglicized youngman sitting beside the girl, smoking a cigar, hoping that the girl would immediately fall for him. But the girl who can take care of herself gets off midway and goes away in a taxi. The speaker goes to Darjeeling in summer where he expects her. But the girl does not show up. Instead he meets his admirer Mohanlal and his sickly sister Tanuka. Before the speaker gets down to the plains Tanuka presents him a potted plant of camellia. After a few months the speaker goes to Santal Pargana where Kamala is also expected to spend the vacation with her maternal uncle. Kamala comes but completely disregards the speaker. Meanwhile the plant flowers and the speaker decides to send this first blossom to Kamala through a Santal girl, a maid-servant. But as the Santal girl comes, and at her call the speaker comes out, he notices that the girl had already plucked the flower and had decked herself with it. The speaker sees the girl and the flower and sees how it has enhanced the beauty of the girl; and when the girl asks, "Why have you called me?" He simply replies "Just for this," and soon afterwards the speaker returns to Calcutta. This brief outline does little justice to the poem, but it would be clear even from this bare outline that what we have actually is a short story in free verse. The episodes build up a tension which is suddenly released in the sharp, unexpected turn of the ending. The speaker is a much wiser man at the end of the poem than he was at the beginning. The monologue spanning a period of a few months thus also registers the growth of the speaker as a character. The vainglorious, boorish, braggart mellows into an admirer of aesthetic beauty. All the characters— Kamala, the youngman with a cigar, Mohanlal, Tanuka and the Santal girl — are brought to life in a few powerful strokes. It is worth remembering that the poem was composed at a time when Tagore had already started exploring another art-form *i.e.* painting.

"An Ordinary Girl" (*Sādhāran Meye*), written around the same time, is another monologue in which the speaker, an unrequited young girl, talks about her first experience of awakening to love and daydreams of vindicating herself by rising higher than her truant and possibly faithless lover, through her academic achievements. The monologue is meant for Saratbabu, a writer whom the speaker is giving a story outline.

"Unexpected Meeting" (*Hathāt Dekhā*), written a few years later is a monologue in which the speaker narrates the unexpected meeting he had with his erstwhile sweetheart, in a train compartment. When asked what remains of their love — "The days that we had / Are they forever gone?" — the speaker remains silent for a while and then says : "All the stars of the night only lie hidden / in the dazzle of the day." The structure of the monologue is episodic.

The other group of monologues — these in fact far outnumber the former — is autobiographical. In these one can distinctly hear the poet reminiscing his literary career, reviewing the path his poetic career has taken and stoically recognizing and accepting its insignificance in the face of eternity. Just a few examples. In "It's time for the bird to go" (*yābār samay holo bihanger*) the speaker, obviously the poet himself, expresses his gratitude for the warm hospitality he has received from Earth. He also recalls, how, at times, the blasts of Vaisakh have disabled his wings. Yet the poet considers himself blessed and duly honoured.

The same note of stoical passivity marks the monologue "Remembrance" (*Smaran*). In "Birthday" (*Janmadin*) the speaker describes the nature of his bond with the earth and realizes that he will be lost to oblivion. He says : "With the end of the day my silenced Veena will fall fainted at the feet." In "Concert" (*Aikatān*) the poet admits his shortcomings as a poet of the earth because he has not been able to treat realistically the sorrows and sufferings of the downtrodden, and eagerly awaits the coming poet who will voice the feelings of the speechless sufferers. He says : "Come, O Poet and please take care to allay the pain of the Mute multitude." In "Earthly dust sweet as honey" (*madhumay pṛthibīr dhūli*) the poet again pays a glowing tribute to Earth, considers the dust as joyous manifestation of Truth and wants to mark his forehead with it before his final departure. It partly echoes the sentiment expressed in an earlier monologue, "Earth." In another monologue written in the year of his death (1941), "On the banks of the Rupnarayan" (*Rupnārāner kūle*) the poet confronts and recognizes his real self, and says : "I have come to know myself through ordeals of trials and tribulations." The only way to realize Truth is to be true to oneself: "He discovers Truth in the core of his heart lit up by his own Being."

It should be evident from the above discussion of what constitutes only a small fraction of Tagore's monologues that here is simply "God's plenty." The monologues vary in length and character, in texture and structure, in the role of the listeners, and in the range of addressees that include Death, Rudra, God, earth, picture and innumerable persons of different categories. The characters that appear in these monologues are no less varied. It is really difficult to define the nature of Tagore's monologues which outshine and far outnumber the monologues of Browing and Tennyson.

Geordano Bruno, the great Renaissance philosopher-critic who had strong contempt for all Aristotelian rules, seriously maintained that there are as many kinds of poetry as there are poets. Taking cue from Bruno we can also say about the monologues of Tagore that there are as many subgenres of Monologue as there are monologues.*

---

* English renderings of the excerpts are based on William Radice's *Rabindranath Tagore: Selected Poems* (Penguin, 1985). Passages left out by Radice are translated by the present author.

19

Thomas Mann and the Legacy of Schopenhauer*

Thomas Mann's admiration for Schopenhauer amounting to almost adulation is evident in the following statement of Tonio Kroger:

> "And would you still laugh today even after I have become something like a famous man? Yes, that you would, and you would be right to laugh. Even if I in my own person had written the nine symphonies and *The World as Will and Idea* and painted the last judgement, you would still be eternally right to laugh."[1]

Arthur Schopenhauer died at Frankfurt only fifteen years before Thomas Mann's birth. In his young days Mann was strongly attracted by the philosophy of Schopenhauer, particularly because in him he found a formal confirmation of his youthful belief that the high elements of Germany's burgher culture had certain built-in features which led to pessimism and estrangement of the individual. Tonio's doctrine that knowledge unmans, that art is at best a melancholy business is very German.

> "And then, with knowledge, its torment and its arrogance, came solitude; because he could not endure the blithe and innocent with their darkened understanding, while they in turn were troubled by the sign on his brow. But his love of the word kept growing sweeter and sweeter, and his love of form; for he used to say (and had already said it in writing) that knowledge of the

---

* 1976.

soul would unfailingly make us melancholy if the pleasure of expression did not keep us alert and of good cheer."[2]

As in Schopenhauer so in Mann, the reading type is, in a profound sense, excommunicated.

"There was always something queer about him, and he was alone."[3]

And Mann hastens to assure us that this loneliness (of Tonio Kroger) was not due to any rootlessness, for he had a sound family background; he was no "gypsy in a green wagon."[4] Knowledge is, therefore, according to Mann a veritable curse that leads to "an unresolved conflict between icy intellect and scorching sense,"[5] and the man remains unhappy both in life and in love.

"There is something I call being sick of knowledge, Lisabeta : when it is enough for you to see through a theory in order to be sick to death of it, and not in the least in a forgiving mood. Such was the case of Hamlet the Dane, the typical literary man. He knew what it meant to be called to knowledge without being born to it. To see things clear, if even through your tears, to recognize, notice, observe — and have to put it all down with a smile, at the very moment when hands are clinging, and lips meeting, and the human gaze is blinded with feeling — it is infamous Lisabeta, it is indecent, outrageous — but what good does it do to be outraged?"[6]

Literary men, on account of their knowledge, are estranged from the mainstream of life. They are "daemons, kabalds, impious monsters, and spectres dumb with knowledge."[7] In contrast, Herr Krank is ordinary.

"His eyes did not plumb the depth of things to the place where life becomes complex and melancholy."[8]

And there comes cynical realization :

"to be able to walk like that, one must be stupid; then one was loved, then one was lovable."[9]

Tonio Kroger's spying, towards the end of the story, on Hans Hansen and Ingeborg Holm assumes a deep aesthetic significance in the light of Mann's attitude to knowledge. Inside the hall Hansen, and Inge, Kroger's sweetheart were engaged in an orgy of dance and mirth. Just outside, behind the glass panel of the entrance stood Kroger consumed by his jealousy and remorse and helplessness. Crestfallen he came back to his room and then :

> "He looked back on the years that had passed. He thought of the dreamy adventures of the senses, nerves and mind in which he had been involved; saw himself eaten up with intellect and introspection, ravaged and paralysed by insight, half worn out by the fevers and frosts of creation, helpless and in anguish of conscience between two extremes, flung to and fro between, austerity and lust; *raffiné*, impoverished, exhausted by frigid and artificially heightened ecstasies erring forsaken, martyred and ill."[10]

And all this is inevitable, for, after all, he is a "bourgeois manque." Hence his sense of isolation, an estrangement from society that at times brings him close to the solitude of a criminal, without being one. Apart from its Byronism Mann's Tonio philosophy — the portrait of the artist as a youngman — found confirmation in Schopenhauer's belief that the presence of genius has an oppressive effect on others.

Parallel to Mann's Schopenhauerian treatment of knowledge runs his treatment of love. According to Schopenhauer there are two grounds for pessimism in the fact that the blind striving will is the inner reality of nature and the essence of life. The will is doomed to privation; it is striving because it is unfulfilled. Secondly where it does find fulfilment, that fulfilment turns out to be illusory.[11] Mann seems to subscribe fully to these views of Schopenhauer. The stranger in "Disillusionment" makes a caustic remark :

> "What is man? asks young Werther — man the glorious half-god? Do not his powers fail him just where he needs them most? Whether he soars upwards in joy or sinks down in anguish, is he not always brought back to bald, cold consciousness precisely at the point where he seeks to love himself in the fullness of the infinite?"[12]

In *The Transposed Heads* Sita appeals to the goddess :

> "Desire did not become my noble husband Shridaman, it became neither his head nor his body, which after all, you will agree is the important factor. His body lying there, so piteously severed from his head, did not know how to shape the rights of love so that my whole heart would hang upon them. He did indeed awake me to desire but could not still it. Have mercy, Goddess ! The lust of thy awakened creature was greater than its satisfaction, its craving greater than its joy."[13]

In an unconscious bid to make amends Sita transposes the heads of Shridaman and Nanda[14] and then retains Shridaman with the body of Nanda. She feels that she has won, because now she has combined the right head and the right body. But in course of the story it turns out to be an illusion. Mann remarks :

> "Nowhere does the magic of Maya, the preserver, life's fundamental law of illusion, deception, inauguration which holds all creatures in thrall — nowhere does it more show its deluding power than in love, in that tender craving of one single creature for another, who is so precisely the pattern and prime content of all the attachment, all the involvement and entanglement, all the delusions on which life feeds and by which it is lured to perpetuate itself."[15]

"The Transposed Heads" is a brilliant illustration of Schopenhauerian concept of the polarity between the will and the idea. "This tale of ours," remarks Thomas Mann, "is but an illustration of the failures and false starts attending the effort to reach the goal."[16] The conflict between flesh and spirit inevitably leads to a kind of psychic departmentalization where physical love is only a function of frustration. It offers a momentary escape into the world of illusion:

> "He had no friends, never had one but this, his exquisitely groomed darkly beautiful counterpart, whose moist and slender hand he held while the richly gilded, empty-eyed hours slipped past. They took fresh flowers with them on their walks, a bunch of violettes or lilies of the valley, smelling them in turn or sometimes both together, with languid yet voluptuous abandon."[17]

It sounds almost Lawrencian. One would think that Mann is an eloquent advocate of the pleasure of the senses, but then comes the sweeping, disastrous comment :

> "They were like self-centred individuals who absorb themselves in trifles as narcotics to console them for the loss of hope. With an inward gesture of renunciation they doffed aside the evil smelling world and loved each other alone smelling world and loved each other alone for the priceless sake of their uselessness."[18]

"Death in Venice" registers a further advance. Nature of the mind is such that it gives birth to an infinite number of desires utterly disproportionate to any possiblity of their being realized."[19] Art, at its best can offer only a temporary escape.[20] When that is not acceptable death is preferred to life. The key concept is Schopenhauerian and the story can be seen as a fable of the revenge of Will upon Idea.

Gustave Aschenbach, the distinguished author of Maia (an unmistakable legacy of Schopenhauerian philosophy) has been a rigorous votary of art.

> "Bearing the burden of his genius, then upon such slender shoulders and resolved to go far, he had the more need of discipline."[21]

But suddenly he experiences *it*. He sees beauty glistening in the body of the Polish boy Tadzio. And

> "...his frenzy left him capacity for nothing else but to pursue his flame; to dream of him absent, to lavish, loverlike endearing terms on his mere shadow."[22]

He is in "illicit adventure,"[23] seized of the "exotic excesses of feeling."[24] Maddened, ultimately, he dies of his love.[26] But before his death he ruminates on the Platonic teaching that of all the intelligible Forms upon which the world is fashioned, only beauty is visible to the senses. He even fancies himself as a dissolute Socrates trying to establish a relationship at once erotic and pedagogic.

The Idea-Will dualism is also found in *The Magic Mountain*. Here the dualism is made concrete in the first half by Settembrini-Clavdia polarity. In the second part Naphta and Peeperkorn strengthen the sides of Idea and Will respectively.

A man of contradictions Naphta is an ideological centaur. He is a militant Catholic and an ardent Marxist. The contradictions are carried out in the decor as well — his humble room and silken hangings. Such contradictions are unnatural and it is not surprising to learn, therefore, that shortly before his suicide he suffers psychotic spells, and more significantly, the bullet destroys his brain — the seat of Idea.

Peeperkorn, on the other hand, represents Will. He constantly overpowers the 'cerebral' Naphta and Settembrini by the strength of his inarticulate presence. A Dionysian disciple of feeling he is in a state of constant drunkenness. Metaphorically he is always intoxicated by feeling. And his death has both ideological and naturalistic explanation. In view of his sexual impotence, his inability to reach his beloved through the senses, his melodramatic suicide is a bowing out and a renunciation. And, significantly again, Peeperkorn's strychnine convulses the entire nervous system. Both Naphta and Peeperkorn are impossible men. One is Idea without Will : the other is Will without Idea. Peeperkorn is life without mind racing itself to pieces collapsing in hysteria.

After showing the two extremes, Mann contends through the vision of Hans Castrop that Art is the only mediator between Will and Idea. Man himself, though a delicate child of the cosmos, is the only bridge between Nature and Spirit. And the pride and the glory of man consist in his determination to defy death, to let death have no power over his life and thoughts.

It can be seen in the light of the foregoing discussion that every Mann performance is an elaborate illustration of the philosophy of Schopenhauer — the world as Will and Idea, and how Will gets the better of Idea. But what is important to note is that although the influence of Schopenhauer runs through the entire gamut of Mann's writings, it does not in any way affect the greatness of Thomas Mann as a literary artist: the vision, the order and the direction he gives to his artistic perception are entirely his own. Judged by the literary or aesthetic criteria Mann is a great writer in his own right. But when a work of art satisfies the cognitive criteria as well, its claim to greatness becomes unquestionable.

REFERENCES

1. Thomas Mann, *Stories of a Lifetime*, Mercury Books, London, 1961, Vol. 1, p. 206.
2. *Ibid.*, p. 172.
3. *Ibid.*, p. 164. It is, perhaps, possible to work out a correspondence between Schopenhauer's belief and his distressing experience at Hamburg University where in his pedantic arrogance and pride he kept the timings of his class identical with those of Hegel and, in consequence, had to lecture in an empty class.
4. *Ibid.*
5. *Ibid.*, p. 173.
6. *Ibid.*, pp. 180-181.
7. *Ibid.*, p. 182.
8. *Ibid.*, p. 167.
9. *Ibid.*, p. 187.
10. *Ibid.*, p. 207.
11. cf. Tagore, "yāhā pāi tāhā chāinā, yāhā cai tāhā bhul kore cai" (We do not want what we get, and what we want, we want wrongly).
12. *Ibid.*, Vol. I, p. 33.
13. 'The Transposed Heads.' *Ibid.* Vol. 2, p. 252.

14. cf. *Ibid.*, p. 256.
15. *Ibid.*, p. 273.
16. *Ibid.*, p. 276.
17. *Ibid.*, p. 344.
18. *Ibid.*
19. cf. Abode of Morpheus in *The Odyssey*.
20. cf. "Ode to A Nightingale."
21. *The Stories...*, *op. cit.*, Vol. 2, p. 13.
22. *Ibid.*, p. 54.
23. *Ibid.*
24. *Ibid.*
25. One remembers the Tristan sonnet which Mann was never tired of quoting : "Wer die Schouheit angeschant met Augen/1st dem Tode schou auheimgegeben"

    or, "He who has once looked on Beauty is already given over to Death."

20

Camus's Existentialism as a Strategy of Revolt*

Revolt is a metaphysical concept and philosophical attitude. As a radical thinker in his own right Camus used the idea of the existential absurd in order to probe the meaning/lessness of conventions, traditional notions, and so-called allegiances. He found that men themselves created or foisted meanings in this life which was a form of self-deceit. But ultimately the honest man, like Meursault of *The Outsider*, could stoically refuse to surrender to any form of self-deceit. This constituted, according to Camus, his heroism and revolt. Meursault's steady refusal to compromise with hypocrisy and compromise his own austerity of perception, that leads to the tightening of the noose around his neck, springs from this revolt that also simultaneously liberates him as an honest, solitary individual.

One may be reminded of Ihab Hasan's observation on existentialism in this context :

"Existentialism, we know, plumbs the solitude of man. It follows through the nihilism of Neitzsche, denies all essences, all *a prioris* in the human condition, and achieves a transvaluation of values despite itself" (143).

It is this philosophy that finds expression in Meursault's attitude of revolt to life and death as well as in his approach to the conventional assumptions regarding god, love, human relationship, human behaviour. It is also because of this perception that Meursault remains an outsider.

The position of revolt that Meursault represents may be examined with reference to his response to the questions : god, love and the event

* International Colloquium on Albert Camus, Poitiers, France, 1999.

of parental death. That Meursault loved his mother is evident.[1] But he refuses to conform to the set customs of a sentimental show. It is a reticent, silent, very private feeling which he is not eager to explain or expose before others. Again, it is also precious to him; that's why he cannot bank on it during the trial; it seems indecent. So he rejects the suggestion of the defence-lawyer that he shot the Arab because he had still been under the trauma of 'Mother's' death. Yet it is evident from the text that with the death of 'Mother' the young son's only familial bondage is snapped, and she continues to reappear as a persistently remembered presence in the conscience of her son. At night, coming back home, he suddenly remembers mother; and again in his solitary cell, and finally on the eve of his death. But he does not believe that mother's death should make him put up a mourner's appearance — the grave look and long face —, withdraw from normal life, and other such shows as the society expects of him. Immediately after he comes back from the funeral he is after pleasure and happiness. He knows deep within himself that pleasure and happiness were not inappropriate as far as his 'mother' was concerned. "With death so near his mother must have felt like someone on the brink of freedom, ready to start life over again. No one, no one in the world had any right to weep for her" (120). So he realises with great clarity on the eve of his own death. But he knew it instinctively from the very beginning. He refused to pretend what he did not feel, and what the society commanded him to feel and show. As a result the trial and the verdict go against him, — not because of homicide but precisely because he did not weep at his mother's funeral.

Meursault proclaims his revolt by quietly refusing to conform to traditional standards and attitudes of the society. This refusal shocks people. Considered in this light of revolt, Meursault's attitude to love seems to be an extension of his attitude to filial emotions. He does not sentimentalise love; nor does he consent to pretend what he does not feel about 'love' as it is regarded by others. Here also a bare honesty shines out through the apparent callousness. In *The Myth of Sisyphus* Camus explains his stand regarding the idea of love. "It is only on the basis of a collective way of seeing, for which books and legends are responsible, that we give the name *love* to what binds us to certain human beings." One finds an echo of this in *The Outsider* : "So she wanted to know whether I loved her. I answered...that it didn't mean anything, but that probably I didn't love her" (48). Sartre cites this as proof of an unfeeling nature with "no desire to know these noble, continuous...feelings." But it is also possible that when Meursault admits — "probably I didn't love her" — he may have meant that he did not feel about her the way books and legends dictated one to feel; that word 'love,' profaned by too much insincere use, had ceased to carry any genuine meaning for him : "it didn't mean anything." His is an honest stand *vis-à-vis* the girl-friend : he won't comfort her by false pretensions that convention may require of him, if he does not feel that way. This honesty is rooted in his existentialism. As Sartre notes, "he lives in the present and the concrete." Meursault's relations to his mother and Marie are determined by this philosophy of living and thus underscore his revolt against the basic absurdity of so-called sentiments and ideas regarding filial duty and romantic love. But that should not be taken to mean there is no place for love in his world; only it is felt in a different way, as an honest unprofaned feeling. Camus provides his own definition of love in *The Myth* which helps us to understand Meursault's stance : "All I know of love is that mixture of desire, tenderness and intelligence that binds me to someone."

Camus's attitude to god and faith was also befitting with his revolt. He rejected the idea of transcendence and viewed the Christ-figure as an emblem of human suffering. In Christ he found god sharing man's conditions :

"The Christ came to solve two principal problems, evil and death, which are essentially the problems of rebels. His solution consisted first of all in taking on their condition. The God-man suffers also — with patience. Evil and death are no longer imputable to him in as much as he suffers and dies. The night on Golgotha has so great an importance in the history of men only because the divinity, ostensibly abandoning its traditional privileges, lived through to the end the anguish of death and despair.... That God might be man it is necessary that he give up hope" (*The Rebel*).

Elsewhere Camus had defined "Faith" as being "not so much a peace as a tragic hope" (*Actuelles*). To this logically followed what Camus had said in a debate with Mauriac in 1945 : "We consent to be deprived of God and of hope, but not to do so easily without man" (*Actuelles*). [Quoted by T.L. Hanna, "Albert Camus and the Christian Faith" in *Camus* (ed. Germain Breer)]

But this is a position which itself denotes revolt, and is not generally understood or accepted. In *The Outsider* the magistrate cannot believe that his prisoner, or anybody for that matter, did not believe in God. He gives Meursault the chance to repent for his sin; meanwhile he brandishes the crucifix before the prisoner's eyes. And in the ensuing conversation Meursault would again be confronting the absurd. "Do you wish my life to have no meaning?" Though Meursault sees no point in this challenge, the magistrate, mouthing conventional sentiments, tries to mount an emotional pressure on him. "How can you not believe that he suffered for your sake?" And, "all the criminals... wept when they saw this symbol of our Lord's sufferings" (73). Meursault, however, fails to be convinced by histrionics, though he listens to his passionate logic of surrender in a half-amused half-indifferent manner. But he gets really furious when the chaplain visits him on the eve of his execution. His outpourings to the priest (118-19) seem to offer an impassioned argument on the subject. It is a complete rejection of the chaplain's complacent but shallow assumptions about God, sin, after-life, in which he represented the general social attitude. Face to face with death Meursault realizes the vacuity of all this with perfect clarity. "Nothing, nothing had the least importance for me" (118). This sequence, introduced right at the end but for the last paragraph, sums up Meursault's revolt against the imposition of a coherent faith on him who has seen the incoherence of life.

As one examines Meursault's attitudes one is reminded of Camus's assertion : "There is only one thing left for us to try, and that is honesty without illusion, a wise loyalty..." (Quoted by Serge Doubrovsky). Meursault's revolt is a protest against the human destiny. Amid the indifference of a world devoid of God, nothing has any importance or value except the pure act of living in the moment. Meursault and his author reached this truth through revolt.

In the trajectory of revolt encompassed in the literature of our times Camus occupies a special position. This revolt involves an amount of courage. "The wine of the absurd and the bread of indifference" which, Camus hoped, would nourish man's greatness, can indeed nourish only great minds. His perception of the situation could be summed up by the hero of Gide's *Oedipe* : "I am sprung from the unknown, without a past, without a model, without anything on which to rely... Oh Creon... not to know one's parents is a call to valour (quoted by Cruickshank 7). There is no a *priori* meaning for this hero. Meaning is to be created by the individual out of his own experience of revolt.

As a writer of revolt Camus could not accept traditional abstractions which had become "sterile myths" for him. As he observed in *Notes* in 1938 : "The most repellent form of materialism is not what is usually thought of as such but the kind that wants to make dead ideas masquerade as living realities and to divert towards sterile myths that obstinate and lurid concern which we have with what is mortal in ourselves" (Quoted and translated by Cruickshank).

But this also means insistence on human responsibility. The individual is now devoid of all metaphysical or inherited values. So he has to face his life alone. This act of facing leads to the positive side of the revolt, because this act also means a freedom. The vision of the open sea at the end of *The Outsider* is symbolic of this freedom, this journey beyond negation to affirmation.

What Paul West considers an "almost Christian" message in the theme of Camus's writings actually sum up his lonely but positive revolutionary position: "In tribulation, in this century of fear, we should seek neither solitude nor solidarity; we should be neither maenads nor ascetics, neither men of stone nor mock-gods, but simply 'present' to another and responsible to ourselves" (Paul West 174).

Camus's hero represents an attitude of metaphysical rebellion. By revolting against the absurd he rediscovers himself, a part of himself which he finds important and essential. It is with this self-knowledge that he confronts the absurdity of existence. Though apparently negative, the revolt is positive in the sense that it reveals to him those elements within him which should be defended. There is no comforting complacency, but an adherence to his own truth, however difficult it may be.

As Cruickshank rightly claims : "He leads his readers away from the relaxing climate of intellectual complacency towards the more bracing air of hope being rebuilt on the ruins of many traditionally held beliefs. In all this it is the idea of revolt, not consent, which provides him with a means of penetrating beyond the menacing to the promising" (4-5).

One may conclude with Tolstoy's message in *Happy Ever After* : "All of us...must discover all the futilities of life in order to come back to life itself" (Quoted by Paul West 66).

NOTE

1. Camus's notebooks, posthumously published, also bear evidence to his sad deep love for his mother. "I loved my mother with depair," he writes.

REFERENCES

Camus, A., *The Outsider*, Penguin, 1961.

——, *The Myth of Sisyphus.*

——, *Actuelles* (Translated in *Resistance, Rebellion, and Death* (Alfred A. Knopf, Inc., 1961).

Cruickshank, J., *Albert Camus*, N.Y. : O.U.P., 1960.

Doubrovsky, S., "The Ethics of Albert Camus," *Camus* (Ed. Germain Breer) N.J. : Prentice-Hall, Inc., 1962.

Hasan, Ihab, *Dismemberment of Orpheus.*

Sartre, J.P., "An Explication of *The Stranger*." *Camus* (Ed. Germain Breer). West, Paul, *The Modern Novel*, London : Hutchinson, 1963.

21

Northrop Frye and Contemporary Indian Literary Criticism*
— A Question of Possible Influence —

Contemporary Indian Literary Criticism is born out of the vital interaction between the East and the West in a colonial situation. Following Macaulay's Minutes on Education (1835) and the introduction of English Education in India, English became a compulsory subject in the academic curriculum and by 1859 when Isvar Gupta, the great Bengali poet-critic, died, English education had already spread from cities to distant villages. Students were attending colleges and the University of Calcutta had been established. Literary Criticism formed an important component of the syllabus of English at undergraduate and post graduate levels. Now in this vast country of 700 million people there are nearly two hundred universities and English is taught everywhere. The intellectual milieu and the academics are constantly exposed to the trends in literary criticism in the West and the Indian critics naturally apply the insights to their examination of literary works in Indian languages. Before we proceed further we must bear in mind that India is a multilingual country and each regional language has a rich literature of its own. But it is believed, at the same time, that Indian literature is one literature written in many languages. This fact is very important in understanding the possible influence of Frye on Indian literary criticism. The 'unity in diversity' situation is found to be most conducive to the application of the critical insights of Frye.

* International Conference on The Legacy of Northrop Frye, Toronto (Canada), 1992.

Even a cursory look at the history of Indian literary criticism, in any language for that matter, would make it abundantly clear that it has always tried to absorb the western influence and has changed with the changing modes of literary criticism. During the heyday of New Criticism there could be seen a concomitant rise of new critical approaches in Indian literary criticism, and just when the Indian critics were looking for some newer direction Northrop Frye appeared on the scene. It will not be wrong to say that in India Frye's popularity started with *Fearful Symmetry*, published in 1947, the year India became independent. The popularity was not only due to the fact that it is a seminal book on Blake who figures in every English syllabus, but more importantly, because of the connections Frye had suggested between Blake and the *Bhagavadgita*. *Fearful Symmetry* immediately found a place in all university libraries and gave a new direction to Indian literay criticism in regional languages. By the time Indian critics, mostly with a sound background of English education, became familiar with Frye as a critic *Anatomy of Criticism* (1957) appeared. The book more than fulfilled the expectations roused by *Fearful Summetry*. Since literary criticism is part of the M.A. syllabus in English in almost all the Indian universities *Anatomy of Criticism*, soon after its publication, was recommended as a standard reference book in most universities. In some universities, as in Burdwan, for example, the book is recommended even for the Honours course in undergraduate classes. The third essay, "Archetypal Criticism : Theory of Myth" made the position of Frye as a myth critic abundantly clear. The position was further clarified with the publication of *Fables of Identity : Studies in Poetic Mythology* (1963). The first two essays, "The Archetypes of Literature" and "Myth, Fiction and Displacement" are included in many critical anthologies the most popular of which is *Twentieth Century Criticism : The Major Statements* edited by William J. Handy and Max Westbrook. The first Indian edition — and a very cheap one — came out in 1976. This book is prescribed in the post graduate syllabus of many universities in India. Mention also must be made of the fourth essay in *Anatomy of Criticism* : "Rhetorical Criticism : Theory of Genres" which also seems to have a great impact on Indian literary criticism.

While all the books of Frye have been well received in India, the interest in most of them — in books like *T.S. Eliot* or *A Study of English Romanticism* — has remained more or less confined to the specialized readers or the academics. But *Anatomy of Criticism* is a brilliant exception. It suddenly opened up new horizons and led to a very enthusiastic critical activity in new areas since the 60s. India with its rich cultural heritage and multilingual situation proved most amenable to myth criticism and archetypal criticism. Indian literary critics took no time in discovering a fertile field of myth criticism. The theory of Genre also provided the Indian literary critics with a new critical method of approaching a literary work.

II

There are so many regional languages and literatures, and corresponding literary criticism that it is well-nigh impossible to cover all of them in the time and space allotted to me. I shall, therefore try to give an overview and I shall take up these regional literatures in alphabetical order, more for convenience than for any other reason, and call attention to the particular writers and/or particular works possibly influenced directly or indirectly by the critical writings of Frye.

Since Independence (1947) — thanks to the rapid development of higher education and the incentives to literary research given by established literary and publishing concerns — a number of treatises have appeared in Assamese. Of these mention may be made of *Sahitya Alocana, Sahityakala aru Tar Bichar* (1971) by T.N. Goswami. The book has helped a lot in disseminating the ideas of Frye, among others, and has given rise to myth criticism and archetypal criticism in Assamese literary criticism. A retired teacher of English T.N. Goswami shows familiarity with the critical methods of Frye and has apparently applied them to some extent in his *Adhunik Asamiya Galpa Sahitya* (Modern Assamese Stories 1965). Satyendranath Sarma (b. 1917) has presented a comprehensive account of the epic and narrative poetry in Assamese, and has analysed them generically. If Satyendranath follows the Fryesque method of genre criticism, Profulla Chandra Goswami brings into focus the value of studying folk literature and culture determining the social ethos of the Assamese community. The figure of Frye looms large in the background.

Bengal has always been intellectually alert and sensitive to what is happening around. The leading critics of Bengal — Buddhadev Bose, S.C. Sen Gupta, Amalendu Bose, *et al.*— incidentally have been teachers of English. They seem to have used the critical insights of Frye in their examination of Bengali literary works. The possible influence of Frye is evident in the large body of myth criticism, archetypal criticism and genre criticism that we have in Bengali literary criticism.

In Dogri literary criticism, the possible influence can be traced back to the historical event of the first Dogri Writers' Conference held in 1967. The papers were published in book form in 1969. About the same time came out *Dogri Sahitya Charcha* (1969) by Laxmi Narayan who possibly under the influence of *Anatomy of Criticism* made an attempt to present in Dogri the definitions and characteristics of different literary genres. The book had a salutary effect so that in 1975 *Seeraz*, a literary journal brought out a special issue, *Alochana Ank* devoted to literary criticism and it made a critical survey of different genres of Dogri literature.

English being an official language of India, literary criticism in English must also be considered as part of Indian literary criticism and this is really a vast, almost intractable area. There are a large number of journals devoted to criticism and here one comes across a sizable number of essays dealing with Frye or applying his methods to Indian literary works. V.S. Seturaman's two books, *New Bearings in English Literary Criticism* (1977) and *Contemporary Criticism : An Anthology* (1989) deserve special mention. The first essay in the anthology is Frye's "The Drunken Boat : The Revolutionary Elements in Romanticism" from *Romanticism Reconsidered.*

In Gujarati literary criticism Suresh Joshi has brought about an interest in Western Criticism and in recent times Radheshyam Sharma, Sitanshu Yashachandra, Suman Shah and Chandrakant Topiwala have applied the Fryesque critical insights to their literary criticism dealing with Gujarati literary works.

Serious literary criticism in Hindi which is the national language of India, started soon after the establishment of Hindi department at the post graduate level at Benares in 1920. In contemporary Hindi literary criticism Nanddulal Vajpayi, Hazari Prasad Dwivedi, Nagendra, Ramesh Kuntalmegh and Kumar Vimal have done some signigicant work in the field of myth criticism. Archetypal criticism also has not lagged behind. The great Indian epics — *The Ramayana* and *The Mahabharata* are storeshouses of myth and archetypes. Saraswati Ramnath writes in his Foreword to *Kamba-Ramayana* (1977) that inspite of the diversity of languages there is an unmistakable unity in India, and this unity is provided by the archetype of Rama. In 1981 *Sarika*, a Hindi literary journal, brought out a special number : "Mythical Stories : Modern Criticism." Attempts were made by Amrita Pritam, among others, to reinterpret a myth in the light of the present and to bring out the contemporary significance of an ancient myth. Full length studies in myth criticism are also available in contemporary Hindi literary criticism. *Mithakiya Kalpana aur Adhunik Kavya* (Mythic Imagination and Modern Poetry 1985) by Jagdish Prasad Srivastava is a brilliant example of the salutary influence of Frye. In his introduction to the book Srivastava writes: "During the last three or four decades new horizons have been opened up in literary criticism. This may be called myth criticism," and reaffirms the stand of Frye regarding the importance of the study of myth, their universality and their relevance in understanding a literary work. In 1987 came out *Bharatiya Sahitya Me Ramkathā* (The Story of Rama in Indian Literature) edited by Kumar Vimal who refers to different versions of the story of Rama in the *Ramayanas* of different regional languages, and does fine archetypal criticism. Hazari Prasad Dwivedi and Nagendra, have emphasized, like Frye, the need for evaluating all trends and writers in the broader cultural context of their time. In their works they have attached great importance to the deep, inherent cultural traditions and have recommended the study of a literary work through motifs and myths, because they represent the cultural consciousness of the race.

In Kannada literary criticism the writings of Masti Venkatesa Srinivas Iyenger, P.T. Narasimhachar and G.S. Shivarudrappa evince the possible influence of Frye in their critical approaches. In modern Kashmiri literary criticism some special issues of the Research bi-annual of the P.G. Department of English, Kashmir University viz. *Kashmiri Abduk Fikri Post Manzur* (the Philosophical Background of Kashmiri Literature) and *Adbi Tanquid* (to Literary Criticism) bear visible marks of *Anatomy of Criticism*. In Maithili literary criticism Jayadhari Singh, Durjanath Jha and Jaykant Misra, among others, have made some significant studies in archetypal criticism. In Malayalam literary criticism Ayyappa Paniker, Narayana Pillai and Thomas Matthew have made some experiment in myth criticism in their discussion of Malayalam poetry. Similarly in the studies of Malayalam fiction P.K. Balakrishnan, M. Achutan and V.P. Saratchandran have applied Fryesque insights in genre criticism. In Marathi literary criticism B.S. Mardhekar, R.B Patankar and Prabhakar Padhyc, all of whom should be quite familiar with the writings of Frye, have put into practice his theories of myth/archetypal criticism and, not infrequently, genre criticism. In Oriya, journals like *Dangaroo*, *Jhankar* and *Diganta* familiarized the Oriya critics with the critical concepts of Frye, and, in consequence, influenced their literary criticism. The writings of Sarala Das, Upendra Bhanja and Jagannath Das, among others, bear testimony to the influence of Frye. In Punjabi literary criticism Tarlok Singh and Atamjit Singh have done some work in myth criticism and archetypal criticism. Gurbhakat Singh and Gurcharan Singh and many others Punjabi critics seem to have applied the formulations and assumptions of Frye to original Punjabi writings quite fruitfully. In Sindhi literary criticism that came of age only in the sixth decade of the present century the influence of Frye can be discerned in *Sahitya Saar* (Essence of Literature 1961) in which Tirth Basant, an eminent writer in Sindhi, discusses the elements of various genres of literature. In Tamil literary criticism T.P. Minakshisundaram who is regarded as one of the makers of modern Tamil literary criticism makes archetypal criticism in his *Kutimakkal Kappiyam* (The Epic of the People 1961). In more recent times S. Sankararaju has tried to explore the archetypes in his *Comparative Study of Kamba Ramayana and Tulsi Ramayana* (1979). Telegu literary criticism also employs various types of literary criticism including, of course, archetypal criticism. Even Urdu literary criticism is not free from the possible influence of Frye. Since 1960, following the publication of *Anatomy of Criticism* (1957) Gian Chand, Sandar Ali Jafri and Taracharan Rastogi, to mention a few, have opened up new horizons in Urdu literary criticism.

III

Historically speaking, the study of myth began with the new developments in the fields of anthropology and psychology following the publication of Frazer's *The Golden Baough* and Jung's concept of the collective unconscious — and its corollary — his notion of archetypes as images that draw their power from their long history of the collective unconscious. Ernest Cassirer's *Philosophy of Symbolic Form*, published between 1923 and 1929 was one of the early studies in myth criticism. Maud Bodkin's *Archetypal Patterns of Poetry* (1934) investigated some of the ways, in which myth and archetypal patterns operate in literary work. Suzanne K. Langer in her *Philosophy in a New Key* (1942) tried to explore myth as a way of knowing. In The *Quest for Myth* (1949) Richard Chase suggested that all genuine poetry is a form of myth. In 1955 the American Folklore Society published a symposium on myth which tried to make a critical review of the works relating the anthropological and psychological studies of myth to literary criticism. All these studies were either partial or fragmentary in nature although they evinced, not infrequently, quite powerful critical insight. But it was Frye who in *Anatomy of Criticism* (1957) developed myth criticism into an elaborate critical system in which anthropological, psychological, semantic and critical ideas were brought into an organic relationship. The Indian critics are now more or less convinced that 'every poet has his private mythology, his own spectroscopic band or peculiar formation of symbols' and that the critic is a kind of cultural anthropologist exploring the presence of mythic patterns in their seriously displaced and fragmented forms. I have a growing conviction that the sudden spurt of Fryesque criticism in India since the 60s is not just a coincidence. It is the possible influence of Frye, however imperceptible, subterranean and unacknowledged it may be.

22

Do You Mean What You Say?*

The problem of meaning has engaged the attention of masterminds for ages. Philosophers like Socrates, Plato[1] and Aristotle have spent a great deal of effort in defining the meanings of various words. Analytical philosophers have become involved in persistent disputes over what a given word means or whether two expressions can have the same meaning. In the East, the serious concern of the Sanskrit linguists about the relation between 'Vāk' (word) and 'Artha' (meaning) finds a crystallized expression in Kalidasa.[2] And one wonders if the 'organs of speech' were primarily meant for speech. The tongue, the most important organ of speech, for example, has functions more vital than merely enabling us to talk.

We start here with the notion that language, as a human activity, is a means of communication of an idea, and the purpose of the present paper is to examine the nature of meaning in the light of this notion and in relation to speech. We are not concerned, therefore, with historical or lexicographical semantics but mainly with some aspects of what is called expository semantics.

Before we proceed to the main subject, it will be worthwhile spending some time in reviewing briefly the present position in semantics. To begin with, there are a large number of theories in the field, which can be broadly grouped under three categories *i.e.* the Referential theory, the Ideational theory and the Behavioural theory. According to the referential theory[3] the meaning of an expression is that to which it refers. The ideational theory[4] identifies the meaning of an expression with the

---

* All India Philosophical Congress, Pune, 1970.

idea with it is associated. And, the behavioural theory[5] with the stimuli that evoke it and the responses that they in turn effect.

The referential theory has been under expert fire in recent times and people have drawn our attention to cases where two expressions have different meanings but the same referent. Russell's classic example is that of 'the morning star' and the 'evening star'. These two linguistic expressions, refer to the same star, but they have different meanings. Furthermore, there are syncategorematic terms, like conjunctions which do not refer to anything. If you try to explain a conjunction in terms of its conjunctive function, you have not demonstrated any extra-linguistic reference.[6]

The ideational and behavioural theories, on the other hand, endeavour to ascertain those features of the *use* of language that give linguistic units the meaning they have. For, according to these theories, words have meaning because of what people do when they use language. What makes a linguistic expression meaningful is the fact that it is regularly used in communication as the mark of an idea. The ideas with which we do our thinking have an existence and a function which is independent of language. In other words, we could do away with language if none of us had any idea to put across. It is largely because we feel a need to convey our thoughts to others, we have to decide upon a code. This code is language. The hearer has to decode what the speaker encodes, in order to receive the message.

This theory has an important bearing on the problem of communication, but the theory as such seems to suffer from certain serious deficiencies. If we go by this theory, every expression would presuppose an idea and as long as the communication is successful, the expression would have to call up the same idea in the mind of the hearer. This condition is, in fact, not satisfied. Again, we do not look for ideas in the minds of speakers and listeners in order to settle questions about what a word means in language or about the particular sense in which a speaker has used a term. For instance, if I have some confusion about the exact sense in which you have used the word 'order' in something you have just said, it would be absurd on my part to try to find it out by asking you to carefully introspect and make sure to me what imagery accompanied your utterance of that word. Moreover, if meaning were an image, then it should not form part of language, and the very fact that there is a broad concensus regarding what various words mean indicates that meaning is a function of the aspects of communication situation that are open to public inspection.

II

There are two aspects of meaning : one is temporal, and the other timeless. Any linguistic expression can have both a temporal and a timeless meaning. The historical linguists and lexicographers examine various factors before giving their verdict on the meaning of a word. They take into account the social and dialectal structure prevalent at a time, foreign influences, standards of style, popular associations etc., in order to believe in what Trier[7] calls 'linguistic fields,' (wortfeld) and hold that if the meaning of any word in a speech community has undergone some change, then the meanings of all the others must have changed, since its relevance to each of them is now different. The analogy is that of a game of chess. At each stage of the game the values of the pieces depend on their position with respect to one another. And with every fresh move the entire pattern changes.

But the case is entirely different with expository semantics. Here, what you say is either forever true or forever false. No subsequent change in the language or change of meaning of different linguistic expressions can alter your meaning. This is borne out by the fact that the questions about the meaning of what a man says, always try to remove the ambiguities and find out the intended meaning. We ask for the less familiar to be interpreted in terms of the familiar. Hence a theory like Frege's[8] misses the whole spirit of expository semantics when he conceives of meanings as external denizens of a third realm.

III

We must bear in mind that in a conversation, in an actual communication situation, the listener is more interested in the intended meaning of a speaker than in the actual meaning of what he says. More so, when a remark is vague or ambiguous. And the intended meaning is no less a fact than the actual meaning, for his intended meaning is just the actual meaning of any remark that would have made his intention clear. That is why when communication seems to have broken down and when we feel that what we have encoded is not being correctly decoded we try to expound the meaning in either of the two main ways. The first is to explain the given utterance-sentence. Take, for example, a remark like this : 'Cheating shopkeepers can ruin business.' In case of any confusion regarding the intended meaning we explain whether 'cheating' is a gerund or a participle and indicate whether by the expression 'cheating shopkeepers' we mean 'cheating of shopkeepers' or 'shopkeepers who cheat.' Or take the following two sentences :

John is eager to please ....(1)

John is easy to please.................................. (2)

When somebody has some confusion about the meaning of sentence no. (2), because of its apparent syntactic similarity with sentence no. (1), we go about explaining that in the second sentence 'to please' is a passive infinitive, and the sentence, therefore, means that it is easy for others to please John. If this method fails, we go on to the second method in which we fill in the details by more familiar words. Let us take an example. When the bus-conductor only says 'tickets, please' and a villager who has boarded the bus for the first time is confused by the remark, we explain it by saying, 'he wants you to buy tickets from him for your journey.' We have not actually amplified the idea contained in the actual text of the remark. We have only clarified the conductor's supposed intention. In other words, we have substituted a report on the conductor's state of mind for the actual text of the original remark in order to drive home the intended meaning. So, we have to go, occasionally, outside the said sentence to one or more other sentences. Sometimes we may have to take resort to a translation or a paraphrase. We must hasten to add, however, that there is a certain level of achievement in translation as well as in paraphrase, beyond which they fail to communicate.

IV

When Berlo[9] contends that 'meanings are found in people, not in words,' he is actually thinking in terms of the intended meaning of the speaker. The words used in a speech must have meanings of their own, howsoever different they may be from the meanings that are actually intended by the speaker. But the extreme contextualists who deny that the meaning of a word has a nucleus which is independent of environment, often miss this point. They tend to overlook the fact that if we use words according to their meaning, then the meaning of the word precedes the use of the word, just as the use of a language presupposes knowledge of that language. And since meaning comes before usage, meaning obviously exists before the incidental context and is independent of all contexts. But the case is very different in expository semantics. In conversation — and language is primarily speech — context plays a very important role in determining the meaning. The remark 'Look at the table' which apparently is ambiguous might be quite unequivocal to one who knows the context. Suppose I was trying to draw the attention of a workman to some of the manufacturing defects in the dining table he has made. Then the inherent ambiguity of the word 'table' is automatically resolved. We should not lose sight of the fact that language is used in a situation and not in vacuum.

Next to context, stress and intonation largely indicate the intended meaning of an utterance. A simple utterance like 'I didn't request you to go to the pictures' will have a wide range of meanings in cold print wherein stresses and intonation are not indicated. With varying stresses on different words the sentence can be read in many ways and may be made to yield different meanings. If the stress is on '*I*' for example, it would mean that 'not I but somebody else requested you to go to the pictures.' Similarly, if the stress is on *the pictures*, then it would mean that 'I didn't request you to go the pictures but to school' etc. Even in an apparently unambiguous expression like *do ya tin bacce, bas*! (two or three children, that's all!) the note of exclamation can be misconstructed, whereby the intended meaning would be totally lost.

Then there is punctuation and juncture. Take, for example, the following sentences :

'The boy' said the teacher, 'was an idiot'.... (3)

The boy said, the teacher was an idiot.... (4)

A juncture is of course a function of punctuation. And not the least contributing factor is the accompanying behaviour. When someone utters the word 'fire' his behaviour goes a long way in telling us whether he is ordering someone to shoot or he wants to draw our attention to a fire that is ablaze.

V

In the foregoing sections we have tried to distinguish between different theories of meaning and have shown their inefficacy so far as the problems of communication are concerned. We have also distinguished between historical and lexicographical semantics on the one hand and expository semantics on the other. We have also shown that the contentions of lexicographical semantics, though valid elsewhere are irrelevant to our purpose. We only agree with them in that there can be an infinite number of meanings of a word in space-time continuum, but we hold that the meaning of a word or even an utterance is limited by space and time, and is, consequently, final and timeless. The factors that contribute to the intended meaning have been examined and we conclude that, in conversation, if we want to avoid confusion and misunderstanding, we must find out a suitable objective correlative in order to effectively put across our ideas.

NOTES

1. *Great Dialogues of Plato*. New York, 1956, pp. 25, 34, 63.
2. Kalidasa : Vāgarthāviva sampriktau vāgartha pratipattaye
   Jagatha pitarau vandye Pārvati parameshwaraū
   Raghuvamśam. Canto. I. Verse I.

   One also remembers the age-old dispute amongst the Sanskrit grammarians over the status of 'genitive' and its anomalous relation to 'case ending'.
3. Frege, Gottlob, 'On Sense and Reference' in *Philosophical Writing* edited by Peter Geach and Max Black, Oxford, 1952.
4. Stevenson, C.L., *Ethics and Language*, New Haven, Conn., 1944.
5. Ogden C.K. & Richards, I. A., *The Meaning of Meaning*, 5th edition. New York, 1938.
6. Chomsky, N., *Syntactic Structures*, 1957. Chomsky contends that even the dummy carrier 'did' in 'Did he come', has no meaning.
7. Trier, Jost, *Der Deutsche Wortshatz in Sinnbezirk des Verstandes*, Vol. I, 1931.
8. Frege, G., Über Sinn and Bedeutung in *Zeitschrift für Philosphie and Philosophische Kritik*, 1892.
9. Berlo, David K., *The Process of Communication*, London, 1963.

REFERENCES

Alston, William P. 1964. *Philosophy of Language*, Englewood Cliff, N.J.

Ayer, A.J. 1954. 'Can there be a private language?' *Proceedings of the Aristotelian Society Supplement*, Vol. xxviii.

Antal, Laszlo. 1963. *Question of Meaning*, The Hague.

Berlo, David K. 1963. The Process of Communication, New York.

Carnap, R. 1955. 'Meaning and Synonumy in natural languages' *Philosophical Studies*, vi.

Catford, J.C. 1965. *A Linguistic Theory of Translation*, London.

Cohen, L.J. 1962. *The Diversity of Meaning*, London.

——. 1955. 'Can there be artificial minds?' *Analysis xvi.*

Flirth, J.R. 1957. *Papers in Linguistics*, 1934-51.

Gardiner, A.H. 1932. *The Theory of Speech and Language*, Oxford.

Harvey, H. 1957. 'The private language problem', *Philosophical Quarterly* vii.

Kemeny, J.E. 1956. 'A new approach to semantics,' *Journal of Symbolic Logic*, xxi.

Laird, Charlton. 1961. *Thinking about Language*, New York.

Morris, C.W. 1947. 'Foundations of the theory of signs.' *International Encyclopaedia of Classified Science*, Vol. I, No. 2, Chicago.

Ogden, C.K. and Richards, I.A. 1938. *The Meaning of Meaning*, 5th Edition, New York.

Popper, Karl. 1953. 'Language and the body-mind problem.' *Proceedings of the 11th International Congress of Philosophy.*

Rhees, R. 1954. 'Can there be a private language,' *Proceedings of the Aristotelian Society Supplement*, Vol. xxviii.

Russell Bertrand. 1940. *Enquiry into Meaning and Truth*, New York.

Strawson, P.F. 1950. 'On referring', *Mind xix.*

Ullman, S. 1957. *The Principles of Semantics*, New York.

23

Derrida and the Indian Theory of Language*

It was in October 1966 during the symposium on "The Language of Criticism and Sciences of Man" held in Johns Hopkins University that Derrida presented his now famous paper "Structure, Sign and Play in the Discourse of Human Science" and initiated something like a Copernican revolution in the fields of Philosophy, Linguistics and Literary Criticism. His critique of Western metaphysics struck at the very root of all Western philosophical discourses which attempt to establish the signifier as offering an unobstructed view of an autonomous signified whether it is truth or reality or being. In the process he questioned the primacy of speech and put forward a theory of writing — *écriture* or archewriting that prefigures both speech and writing. Furthermore, it contains within it the potentials of everything that may be written or spoken. It is only what is contained in the *écriture* that can be either verbalized or orthographed.

Writing, for Derrida, is not just the inscription of words on paper but includes the neuronal traces in the brain which Freud identifies as memory. In "Freud and the Scene of Writing" Derrida writes :

> Freud does not simply use the metaphor of non-phonetic writing : he does not deem it expedient to manipulate scriptural metaphors for didactic ends. If such metaphors are indispensable it is perhaps because they illuminate, inversely, the meaning of a trace in general, and eventually, in articulation with this meaning, may illuminate the meaning of writing in the

* World Sanskrit Conference, Melbourne (Australia), 1994.

> popular sense ... the gesture sketched out by Freud ... opens up a new kind of question about metaphor, writing, and spacing in general. (Derrida 1978 : 199)

And again :

> Finally, what must be the relationship between psyche, writing and spacing for such a metaphoric transition to be possible, not only, nor primarily, within theoretical discourse, but within the history of psyche, text, and technology? (Ibid).

Derrida refers to Freud's insight into language by calling attention to Freud's example.

> Assume, for example, says Freud, that I have dreamed of a letter (*Brief / epistola*), then a burial. Open a *Traumbuch*, a book in which the keys to the dreams are recorded, an encyclopaedia of dream signs, the dream dictionary which Freud will soon reject. It teaches us that letter must be translated (*ubersetzen*) by spite, and burial by engagement to be married. Thus a letter (*epistola*) written with letters (*litterae*), a document composed of phonetic signs, the transcription of verbal discourse may be translated by nonverbal signifier which, inasmuch as it is a determined affect, belongs to the overall syntax of dream writing. The verbal is cathected, and its phonetic transcription is bound, far from the center, in a web of silent script (Ibid 207).

For Derrida writing is nothing but dynamic expressive difference. It does not depend on sound and writing, but is the condition for such sound and writing. Although it does not phenomenally exist its possibility is anterior to all experiences.

For Bhartṛhari, Brahman, as the Word-Principle, is an intrinsically dynamic and expressive reality, and the language is its manifestation through the process of temporal beginning. In the very opening verse of his *Vākyapadīya* Bhartṛhari, possibly the greatest exponent of the Grammarian School has given a brilliant exposition to the unique nature of the Eternal Verbum. Bhartṛhari does not use Derridean words like trace or archewriting but uses the word *śabdatattva* or Word-Principle. In Bhartṛhari the Eternal Verbum is conceived as an eternal principle having neither production, nor annihilation, nor any sequence of things and this objective world, according to him, is nothing but its illusory modification :

> *Anādinidhanam Brahma śabdatattam yadaksara*
>
> *Vivartate 'rthabhāvena prakriyā jagato yatah*
>
> (*Vākyapadīya* 1 : 1)

In order to drive home his point Bhartṛhari conceives of certain eternal powers (*Saktis*) residing in the Eternal Verbum, of which Time-power (Kāla-Śakti) is the chief one inasmuch as it regulates all the other powers. In order to disarm criticism, that is how the unitary character of the Eternal Verbum can be postulated if the myriad objects of the world be its manifestations, he argues that its unitary character can never be denied outright since, though it is really one and undifferentiated, it appears to be manifold and different owing to the superimposition of differentiation belonging to the eternal powers creating diverse objects :

Ekameva yadāmnātam bhinnam śaktivyapāsrayāt
Aprthaktvepi Śktibhyah prthaktveneva vartate
(*Vākyapadīya* 1 : 2)

He continues further that though the powers are eternal, the possibility of successive occurrence of the six states of things, namely production, existence, modification, growth, dimension and destruction, cannot be objected, for it is the apparent sequence in its Time-power which is solely responsible for the occurrence of these transformations in succession :

Adhyāhitakalām yasya kālaśaktimupāśritāh
Janmādayo vikārāh sad bhāvabhedasya yonayah
(*Vākyapadīya* 1 : 3)

It is language that allows every form of knowledge to be manifested. In other words, had our knowledge lost linguistic form it would not have been manifested at all :

Vāgrūpatā cenniskrāmedavabodhasya śāsvatī
Na prakāśah prakāśeta sā hi pratyavamarśinī
(*Vākyapadīya* 1 : 124)

Language, according to Bhartṛhari, is consciousness in the form of external and internal experience, since consciousness in all creatures is never devoid of comprehension of words :

Saisā samsārinām sajñā bahirantaśca vartate
Tanmāt rāmanatikrāntam caitanyam sarvajantusu
(*Vākyapadīya* 1 : 120)

This is evident also in the fact that all the persons are impelled to react through language and that they become devoid of consciousness like a piece of wood or wall when language ceases :

Arthakriyāsu vāk sarvān samīhayati dehinah
Tadutkrantau visamjño yam drśyate kāsthakudyavat
(*Vākyapadīya* 1 : 127)

Bhartṛhari contends that just as one cannot conceive of an object entirely independent of knowledge, in a similar manner one cannot have any knowledge from language which is the only medium of its expression:

Na so sti pratyayo loke yah śabdanugamādrte
Anuviddhamiva jñānam śarvam śabdena bhāsate
(*Vākyapadīya* 1 : 123)

So, the fundamental principle must be knowledge or knowledge *par excellence* imbibed with linguistic principle. Thus knowledge is revelation, revelation is expression and expression is communication. It is thus that consciousness and language are combined into one principle the Eternal Verbum or *Śabdabrahman*.

Like Derrida, Bhartṛhari also sees the inherent trace consciousness of language as conditioning all psychic experience from deep sleep to dreams, to ordinary awareness and even to the mystical, the states in which direct supersensuous perception of the meaning is obtained. In the dream state the only difference is that the seeds or traces of language function in a more subtle manner. For Bhartṛhari, as for Derrida the experience of self is the unobstructed experience of *śabdatattva* or archewriting manifested in the temporal dynamics of language.

Before we proceed further it would be worthwhile to have some idea of Bhartṛhari's theory of *Sphoṭa* in order to appreciate the points of affinity between Bhartṛhari and Derrida regarding their theory of language. *Sphoṭa* or more precisely the theory of *Sphoṭa* in its rudimentary form maintains that a word or a sentence is not just a collection of sound units or phonemes arranged in a particular order, but a single whole. The audible sounds, the 'noisy realities' are regarded in this theory as the means by which the whole, the relevant *Sphoṭa* is made public. The implication is that language is what is revealed finally and not the phonemes themselves. Early Indologists like Keith, for example, described *Sphoṭa* as a mysterious or mystical entity. But it was established by later scholars, by Brough and Kunjunni Raja, for example, the *Sphoṭa* was not a mystical entity.

Bhartṛhari, in fact, begins his discussion of *Sphoṭa* by reference to the two distinctions made by his predecessors. In 1 : 44 he says that the linguists comprehend two types of *śabda* among the *upādāna śabda*, linguistic sound. One is the causal root of its manifestations and the other is applied, being manifested, to convey meaning. In other words, in the sequenceless nature of the speech (*vāk*) both powers to be articulated in sound or audible from the power to convey meaning are intermixed.

Sound is the linguistic unit properly understood. It is the real language while the first is what manifests or expresses it. This may be seen as *sphoṭanāda* distinction. *Nāda* manifests *sphoṭa* and *sphoṭa* conveys meaning. The *sphoṭa* is an indivisible unit, a partless, sequenceless whole, and it is connected with the verbal dispositional ability of the speaker or the listener. For the sake of communication between language-users *sphoṭa* must necessarily be made explicit. The potentiality must be realized so that the listener may receive it. But this cannot be done without *nāda* the sequential utterances of the phonemes. This is how the *nāda* becomes the causal factor for making *sphoṭa* explicit. *Sphoṭa* is also shared by the listener, and as a result the listener's *sphoṭa* is awakened by the utterance of the speaker. This awakening of the listener's *sphoṭa* is what is called the comprehension by the listener. This is what is meant by the claim that the sentence uttered must already be present in the listener. From the point of view of the speaker, however, the *sphoṭa* already present in him will be the causal condition of the *nāda* or the sequential word utterance. In verse 1 : 46 Bhartṛhari says that as fire resides in the *arani* stick and being manifested becomes the cause for manifesting other objects, *śabda* resides likewise in the mind (*buddhi*) and, being manifested becomes separately the cause for manifesting the meaning as well as itself. In 1 : 48 Bhartṛhari tries to account for the general wrong notion that *sphoṭa* is sequential. He says that since *nāda* or sound arises in sequence, *sphoṭa* which has neither a former nor a later stage and which is sequenceless or *akrama* appears to be having a sequence of parts because it is apprehended through *nāda*. Thus the properties of *nāda* are transferred to the *sphoṭa*. He tries to clarify the situation with a simile. The moon resides in a separate location, say, in the sky. But the reflected image of the moon shares the operations of objects in a separate location. If the image is reflected in waves in water it assumes the movement of the waves. Similarly, *sphoṭa* being manifested in *nāda* shares the properties of *nāda*. Like Derrida, Bhartṛhari believes that the temporal transformation of the originating source of language through speech and writing is continuous. Derrida uses the technical term "sign" to refer to the whole, and this is Bhartṛhari's *sphoṭa*. And what is "signified" for Derrida is *artha* for Bhartṛhari. For both Derrida and Bhartṛhari the linguistic whole — the sign or *sphoṭa* — has an inherent force of differentiation that produces the double manifestation in inner meaning (signified / *artha*) and spoken sound (signifier / *dhvani*). Although sign and *sphoṭa* are irreducible, neither can be experienced in pure presence. The pregnant push towards sequencing, spacing, punctuation or differentiation in space and time is rooted within language even in its most holistic form. In *Vākyapadīya* (1 : 99 and 1 : 5) Bhartṛhari asserts that *śabdatattva* symbolized by AUM is sequenced by the power of time into the various recitations of the Veda and all spoken words. For Derrida the image is one of sign as the linguistic whole being differentiated by spacing on the page and pause in speaking into articulated meaning and sound-image. According to Derrida, since a sign which is supposed to indicate the unity of the signifier and the signified cannot be produced within the plenitude of absolute presence, there is therefore no full speech, no absolute truth or full meaning. For both Derrida and Bhartṛhari the *sphoṭa* and the sign are manifested, and in the dynamic tension of that manifestation lies truth. Both see truth contained in the dynamics of the language rather than arriving at a scepticism of language that it is devoid of any truth.

Bhartṛhari contends that even before the utterance the language along with whatever it conveys or means is like the yolk of a peahen's egg. In that state all the variegated colours of a full grown peacock lie dormant in potential form. Later these colours are actualized. Similarly in the self of the speaker or listener all the variety and differentiation of linguistic items and their meanings exist as potentialities. Language and thought are identical at this stage. Bhartṛhari even believes that the nature of the self is nothing but identical with the nature of language-thought. This state of complete identity of language and thought is called the *paśyanti* stage of language. Before the proper articulation of the sound-sequence or utterance there is another intermediate stage (*mādhyamik vāk*) where the language and the thought it conveys are still one and undifferentiated, but at this pre-verbal stage the speaker sees them as differentiable. In other words, he recognizes the verbal part, which he is about to verbalize either to himself or to another, as distinct and separable from the *artha*, meaning or thought. This perception impels him to speech which results in *nāda-sphoṭa* differentiation.

Derrida's critique of the Western metaphysics focuses on the privileging of the spoken over the written word. Barbara Johnson summarizes Derrida's position in the following words :

> The spoken word is given a higher value because the speaker and listener are both present to the utterance simultaneously. There is no temporal or spatial distance between speaker, speech, and listener, since the speaker hears himself speak at the same moment as the listener does. This immediacy seems to guarantee the notion that in the spoken word we know what

we mean, mean what we say, say what we mean, and know what we have said. Whether or not perfect understanding always occurs *in fact*, this image of perfectly self-present meaning is, according to Derrida, the underlying ideal of Western culture (Derrida 1981 : ix).

Derrida calls this belief in the self-presentation of meaning "logocentrism," from the Greek logos. Writing, from the logo-centric perspective, is seen as a secondary representation of speech to be used when speaking is impossible. As the writer reduces thought to writing he distances it from the immediacy of speech and enables it to be read by someone far away, even after the writer's death. All of this is seen as a corruption of the self-presence of meaning, an opening of meanings to forms of corruption which the presence of speech would have prevented. It should be noted here that Derrida's critique is not aimed at reversing the value system, and showing writing to be superior to speech. What he actually tries to do is to dissect the whole system of metaphysical opposition upon which the speech versus writing debate is grounded. Derrida shows that both speech and writing are beginninglessly structured by difference and distance. The very experience of meaning is itself an experience of difference, and Derrida shows that this difference inhabits in the very heart of what appears to be immediate and present. In his commentary on Freud's mystic writing pad Derrida has shown that difference is present even in the structures of the unconscious. The apparent experience of a unitary self-presence of meaning and consciousness actually arises from the repression of the differential structures from which they spring.

Derrida finds support in a passage in Plato's *Phaedrus* in *The Dialogues of Plato*. The relevant passage runs as follows :

Socrates Is there another kind of word or speech far better than this, and having far greater power — a son of the same family, but lawfully begotten?

Phaedrus What do you mean, and what is the origin?

Socrates I mean an intelligent word graven in the soul of the learner, which can defend itself and knows with whom to speak and with whom to be silent.

Phaedrus You mean the living word of knowledge which has a soul, and of which the written word is properly no more than an image?

Socrates Yes, of course that is what I mean.

(Plato 1953 : 185-186)

This other kind of writing, 'graven in the soul of the learner' is arche-writing for Derrida and this is the preverbal stage in Bhartṛhari's theory of *sphoṭa*.

If all knowledge comes through language, is there a source or ground of language which lies outside of or beyond language? Can we say that language depends on something else — God or Brahman? Both Bhartṛhari and Derrida would hold that there is no such extralinguistic source of language. For Bhartṛhari as is clearly enunciated in *Vākyapadīya* the absolute is the *śabdatattva*, the Word-Principle, and therefore is not something outside or beyond language. Derrida deconstructs the Western metaphysics and the notion of any extralinguistic source of language through his understanding of writing as *différance* containing all of spoken language and inscribed language.

It should be evident from the above discussion that there are many striking affinities between Bhartṛhari and Derrida in their notions of language. Both believe that speech and writing are beginninglessly structured by difference and distance. Both break down the barriers between literary criticism and philosophy. Both believe in the wholeness of the preverbal stage which precedes both speech and writing, and none of them believes in any extralinguistic source of language.

It would not be possibly wrong to say that Bhartṛhari as an exponent of the Indian theory of language prefigured much of Derrida's critique of Western metaphysics.

WORKS CITED

Bhartṛhari. 1976. *Vākyapadīya*, Varanasi, Benaras Sanskrit University.

Derrida, J. *Writing and Difference*, London, Routledge and Kegan Paul, 1978.

Derrida, J. 1981, *Discrimination* Trans. By Barbara Johnson, Chicago : Chicago UP.

Plato. 1953, *The Dialogues of Plato*, Trans, by B. Jowett, Oxford : Clarendon Press.

24

The Ramayana, The Red Oleander and *Surfacing* : An Eco-Feminist Perspective[*]

Margaret Atwood's *Surfacing* (1972) and Rabindranth's *Raktakarabī* (1924) translated as *The Red Oleander*, separated as they are by half-a-century and thousands of nautical miles, may seem to have nothing in common. But considered from an eco-feminist perspective the Canadian novel and the Indian play appear to highlight certain interesting points of affinity in perspective.

Tagore's play, *Raktakarabī* (*The Red Oleander*) was written towards the end of 1923. The title, then, was not *Raktakarabī* but *Yakshapurī* or *The City of Yaksha* (the demon-king). Tagore further revised the manuscript and retitled it as *Nandini* after the name of the female protagonist of the story. In the final version published in *Pravasi* in 1924 the title was further revised to *Raktakarabī*, the red oleander. The shift in emphasis, it can be noticed, is from the city (Yakshapuri) through a character (Nandini) to a flower (*Raktakarabī*) and makes *Raktakarabī* essentially a symbolic drama.

Raktakarabī has been and is still widely staged in Bengal by various theatre groups because of its continuing relevance to modern times. The play weaves round one Yaksha-King Makarraj who has an insatiable lust for gold. This anonymous demon king remains inaccessible behind the hard metal walls of his Yakshapuri. But he exercises complete control over his people, ruthlessly exploits them for more and more of gold, and

* International Conference of Indian Association of Canadian Studies, Jammu, 1996.

grossly outrages nature in the process. As a result the society is vitiated by pervasive greed, mistrust and fear, and the harmony of life which was originally agriculture-oriented and, therefore, responsive to the rhythms of nature, also gets disrupted.

In the Preface to the play Tagore calls our attention to *The Ramayana* and offers a new perspective to this great epic of ancient India. He writes :

> In the *tretāyuga* Ravana the powerful king with enormous ambition and greed used to capture many gods and goddesses, and make them work for his pleasure. But in midst of his anti-god prosperity suddenly appeared a woman and the epic with the triumph of virtue (Preface).

If Ravana is an epitome of material power and prosperity and evinces the evils of materialism, Sita, actually, a daughter of the earth, a *bhūmikanyā* represents the benevolent aspects of nature. She shows a remarkable spirit of defiance against Ravana, the king of Swarnalanka. For Tagore it implies the triumph of the values of an agricultural society over those of an industrial system through a lone woman's integrity and moral protest. Using Swarnalanka, a city of gold, as a metaphor Tagore further comments :

> The Swarnalanka may, indeed, be traced in various places of the world, and at various levels. That the great poet (Valmiki) knew about that undefined and yet definite existence of Swarnalanka is beyond doubt (and) it was Kabiguru (the first poet Valmiki) who had stolen my story beforehand by means of his intuitive imagination, because...there are thousands of evidences that Swarnalanka is a thing precisely of our times (Preface).

Indeed, Tagore noted with deep concern the assault of the industry-oriented materialistic life upon the agriculture-oriented rural ways which had taught men to live in harmony with nature. He was also worried over the exploitative materialistic society's insatiable accumulative instinct which enjoyed wielding enormous power. The extra heads and hands of Ravana whose kingdom is made of gold *i.e.* glittering "metal" civilization, signified, according to Tagore, the vulgar excess of concentrated wealth and callous power.

Again, like Valmiki's epic, Tagore's play, too, has a woman at the centre, who manifests the spirit of defiance against the dictates of this powerful killer. Sita's spirited defiance started the process of and ultimately brought about Ravana's downfall. In Tagore's play it is just a frail girl, the daughter of this earth symbolically suggested through the ripe corn-ears colour of her dress, who refuses to comply with the dictates of the Yaksha regime. There is a hint towards the end that this refusal of Nandini will finally snowball into a revolution that will shatter the walls of this demonic palace. Nandini represents the negation of all the values that the yaksha kingdom stands for, as Sita rejects the norms (greed-luxury-voluptuousness) of Swarnalanka.

In is interesting how similar points of comparison may be drawn between Tagore's play and Atwood's novel. True, the socio-cultural scenario of the times, the vision-consciousness-techniques of the authors are only too obviously different to encourage any comparison. Yet an affinity is there. What Tagore defines as Swarnalanka and Ravana-culture is the same as termed "the American" by Atwood's narrator. The nameless protagonist in *Surfacing* remarks :

> It does not matter what country they are from,...they're still Americans, they're what's in store for us, what we are turning into. They spread themselves like a virus, they get into the brain and take over the cells and the cells change from inside and the ones that have the disease can't tell the difference (129).

In *The Red Oleander* Nandini, the lone woman fighting against the king of the dark chamber is presented, in Tagore's own words, as the embodiment of the benevolent aspects of Nature. Tagore remarks :

> The entire play is an elaborate portrait of Nandini, a woman. She represents the joy of life, the simple beauty and pristine purity of Nature (Preface).

The king, like the 'Americans' is an epitome of consumerism, muscle power and man's insatiable greed. Through Nandini Tagore tries to impress upon us how consumerism, an effect of industrialization, has robbed man of his soul. Degenerated into a monster he is running after money and materialism. In the process happiness has been the first casualty; and, how he is frantically trying to divert himself with physical comforts and consumerism. As a result Nature is ruthlessly exploited. The womb of the earth is ripped open to collect gold, a symbol of material wealth.

When they stab the bass and begin to cut it the protagonist in *Surfacing* muses :

> We were committing this act of violation, for sport or amusement or pleasure, recreation they call it these were no longer the right reasons. That's an explanation but no excuse (117).

False notions of strength arise out of man's vanity and a bland ignorance about the perennial values of life. She says :

> That was the armour, bland ignorance, heads empty as weather balloons straight power they maintained it (127).

In *The Red Oleander* Nandini warns us :

> Man's basic needs are limited. Physical appetite has a limit. But there is no end to man's desire (662).

In *Surfacing* while exploring the island the team came upon a dead bird, a heron. The bird was strung up "like a lynch victim" (116), and the nameless narrator wondered :

> Why didn't they just throw it away like trash? To prove they could do it, they had the power to kill (116).

And again in course of travelling through the forest she notices gigantic stumps, level and saw out and she deplores :

> The trees will never be allowed to grow that tall again, they are killed as soon as they are valuable...the trees they cut on have grown swollen edges around the wounds, scar tissues (46).

In *The Red Oleander* Nandini deplores in a similar vein :

> They cannot construct. They can only destroy. They break everything to pieces (653).

Both the girls — Nandini in *The Red Oleander* and the nameless narrator in *Surfacing* try to make us aware of man's suicidal violence against Nature and strike a strong note of protest. The nameless narrator clarifies :

> ...it wasn't the men I hated, it was the Americans, the human beings, men and women both. They'd their chances but they turned against the gods (154).

And here Nandini :

> The Earth gives away her treasures happily through Nature. But when man in his pride and arrogance exploits Nature by doing violence to her a curse falls on him (656).

As Nandini represents the innocence and opulence of Nature the call of Pauș, the harvesting season is a call of Nature in her pristine purity and limitless bounty. In this harvesting song which may be regarded as the theme song of the play Nandini refers to the cosmic harmony of Nature. The song of Nature is a song of selfless love. In the course of the play Tagore repeatedly tells us that Nandini is the embodiment of Nature. She epitomizes the beauty and splendour of the earth. In midst of materialistic din she is always serene, "a finely tuned musical instrument" (675). Sometimes her simple presence becomes a menace to materialism because of the moral force that she carries about with her. Nandini knows that she is a woman but the fact that she is a woman should not be underestimated. She is fully conscious of her potential strength. She is like a lightning that contains the potential thunder :

> "I have brought the thunder. I shall strike the golden citadel," she says (681).

In *Surfacing* the protagonist identifies herself with Nature :

> I lean against a tree, I am a tree leaning...
>
> I am a place (181).

And again :

> I am part of the landscape. I could be anything, a tree, a deer skeleton, a rock (187).

To demonstrate her reaction against the violence on Nature she would also like to destroy the Americans :

> I wanted there to be a machine that could make them vanish, a button I could press that would evaporate them without disturbing anything else, the way there would be more rooms for animals, they would be rescued" (154).

And she remembers nostalgically and approvingly that her father "admired what he called the eighteenth century rationalists, he thought of them as men who avoided the corruption of the Industrial Revolution..." (38). The industry-oriented society is a demonic system governed by insensitive lust and aggression, bent upon destroying environmental balance and peace. The female protagonist of *Surfacing* had been caught in the trap of this system once, and as a result she was "amputated" with death implanted within her. But she did not end up there. True, she has no army of follower. But alone she registers her protest by withdrawing from the society and returning to primeval Nature for spiritual regeneration. After her complete rejection of everything that is associated with the "metal killers" (186) and her plunge in the ancient glacial lake she "resurfaces" with the power "to refuse to be a victim" (191).

By the end of *The Red Oleander* we find the King moved by the spirit of Nandini and there is a clear hint that ultimately the order will be restored and the human values will triumph. In *Surfacing* when Joe returns to the island in search of the protagonist after David and Anna have left he is actually prompted by love. The nameless narrator says :

> ...he isn't an American, I can see that now, he isn't anything, he is only half-formed and for that reason I can trust him (192).

Thus seen from the eco-feminist perspective both the works lay bare the damage done to Nature on account of man's insatiable thirst for power and greed. In both the works the women who identify themselves with the benevolent aspect of Nature renounce materialism and strike back. Both the works end on a note of hope for the restoration of ecological balance and consequently possible redemption of man. Although the literary forms are different...one is a play and the other is a novel...there is a fundamental similarity in the fabric of the vision projected in these two works — one by Rabindranath Tagore and the other by Margaret Atwood. Through her rejection of the values and ways of a violence-ridden society and through her search for the secret of spiritual regeneration in Nature Atwood corresponds to a fibre of an age-old Indian thought so powerfully verbalized by Valmiki and dramatized by Tagore.

NOTES

I have used the original Bengali play, *Raktakarabī* for my discussion. All the incidental translations are by the present author.

REFERENCES

Atwood, Margaret. 1972. *Surfacing*, London.

Tagore, Rabindranath. 1961. *Raktakarabī, Rabindra Rachanabali.*

25

America in the Twentieth Century: From the Melting Pot to the Mosaic*

[Until the end of the nineteenth century they came; they came from every corner of the globe to shape the perfect society. Not only the white, English-speaking Anglo-Saxons, but Europeans from every corner of the continent; South Americans who were white, native Indians and mulatto; Asians including the Chinese, Japanese, Filipinos, Koreans and Indians; and Africans, mostly as slaves. They differed vastly in religion, colour of the skin, language, to say nothing of their customs and clothes, food and nourishment, habits, private and public behaviour, rites and rituals and the way they were used to being governed! They met the seas (most of them), then the Ellis Island and, at last, the Promised Land, the realization of a Utopian dream. At first at least, compelled by circumstance and charmed by the new land and its seemingly infinite opportunities, 'melting' came easily. Learning the new ways was tantamount not so much to conforming as to expressing one's thankfulness to the new blessing destiny had conferred on them. However, as the decades rolled by and there was no more a frontier (in every sense) to explore, the large human vista began to exhibit smaller, narrower human islands; contradictions, too, rooted in this vast enterprise, came to the fore. As this essay states, the French savant Crevecoeur's ecstatic dream as well as his

---

* Indian Association of American Studies, Mysore, 1996.

wise, cautionary words have been vindicated. While the outer fabric (political, institutional, financial, social etc.) of the U.S. held firmly, more and more the melting pot began to resemble a variegated mosaic. As the new millennium dawns, its new dynamism may have a new reality to unfold — *Editor*]

The idea of America as the great melting pot where immigrants of different nationalities and creeds abandon their individual identities and get happily assimilated into the grand stew of American culture can be traced back to the writings of J.H. St. Jean de Crevecoeur (1735-1813). A man of French origin, he had a stint in England, arrived in Canada about 1754 as a lieutenant in the French army, fought at the battle of Quebec in 1759 and then came to the American colonies and adopted New York citizenship in 1765. His twelve essays published as *Letters from an American Farmer* (London, 1782) became an immediate success in London and on the continent. In one of these essays, Letter III, in fact, entitled 'What is an American?' he writes :

> He is an American, who leaving behind him all his ancient prejudices and manners, receives new ones from the new mode of life he has embraced, the new government he obeys, and the new rank he holds. He becomes an American by being received in the broad lap of our great *Alma Mater*. Here individuals of all nations are melted into a new race of men, whose labours and posterity will one day cause great changes in the world (p. 233).

He becomes ecstatic in describing the American life and manners, and almost in a Rousseauistic vein declares that in America 'man is as free as he ought to be...the most perfect society in the world.' But a close look at the literary situation prevailing in America today would compel us to reconsider the validity of Crevecoeur's metaphor of the melting pot. Different religions and ethnic groups, regionalists and immigrants of different nationalities are all engaged in a search for identity, and insist on a recognition of their independent entity. They refuse to be merged into the grand stew or be lost into the melting pot. Consequently, society is fragmented and each group mainly addresses its own audience. Thus the African-American writers write mainly for the African-American readers and try to inspire in them a sense of solidarity. Women writers in their female quest for identity are engaged in taking stock of their situation and wage war against male domination and gender discrimination. Jewish writers talk about their special problems and feel that, though culturally they are superior, they are victimized in a predominantly Christian world. Every group feels that it is marginalized, and tries to come to the centre.

Let us start with the southern literature. For many years the South's conviction in its superiority did not allow the southern literary mind to develop a sense of belonging to the American culture. It is true that a few writers like William Faulkner created in the southern novel a compelling drama of self and history, But the distinction between the writings of the southern novelist and a non-southern novelist persists. The writings of Faulkner, Robert Penn Warren and Eudora Welty have carefully retained their regional autonomy within American literature. While, on the one hand, the southern writers have fought long and hard to nationalize the most complex experience of their community, on the other hand, they have never surrendered their southern identity. Again, the southern Roman Catholics such as Flannery O'Connor, Walker Percy and John William Corrington have tried to move out of history toward the absolute. They try to show an interest in the ultimate things, in the nature of the soul, for example. O'Connor feels that it is the sense of existential reality rather than of historical liberalism that characterizes the southern biblical mode. She, therefore, focusses on situations in which an individual faces the apocalyptic intensity of the existing moment. Unlike O'Connor's characters, Walker Percy's characters have a societal context and awareness, although like O'Connor's, Percy's characters are also somewhat grotesque as their motives are developed from within for a quest for salvation. But what is supremely important is that Percy's imagination as storyteller is deeply rooted in the memory of the southern community and the consequences of its interaction with the modern world. William Barrett in Walker Percy's *The Last Gentleman* shows the loneliness arising out of a sense of loss of community. Aunt Emily in Percy's *The Moviegoer* is a conscious keeper of southern culture of memory. Percy might not have meant them as southern novels, but the characters, just mentioned, reveal his regional roots and his concern for the southern values. Another interesting case is that of — Shelby Foote. After writing five remarkable novels and the three-volume *The Civil War : A Narrative*, sometime described as the 'American Iliad' she takes up in *September* (1977) the school desegregation crisis in the South. This shows how deep the roots are — the roots that clutch. There are, of course, some southern writers who started as chroniclers of the South but soon passed on to other areas. Elizabeth Spencer, for example, turned to Italian settings. Yet departure from the southern settings has never been an established trend on the part of the southern writers. Madison Jones, Jesse Hill Ford, Ellen Douglas are some of the southern writers who have been consistently faithful to their homeland. Anne Tyler lives in Baltimore and her novels are mostly set in Baltimore, Maryland, and her focus is on the cultural heritage of the South. In brief, the southern writers starting with Faulkner through Percy to Tyler have tried to focus on the southern culture which they consider to be of higher quality than what may be called the essentially American culture.

Apart from the large group of southern writers there are novelists who also may be called regionalists in the sense that they use a particular city as the locale of their novels. Herman Wouk, Larry McMurty, Ward Just, Jim Lehrer, Susan Richards Shreve and Marita Golden have mainly used Washington, D.C. as their locale while New York city figures dominantly in the writings of E.L. Doctorow, Richard Prices, Avery Corman, Paul Auster, David Leavitt and Tama Janowitz, among others.

Another important cluster comprises the Jewish writers in a country which is predominantly Christian. Jewish writers like Norman Mailer, Bernard Malamud, Joseph Heller, Philip Roth, Saul Bellow and Jerry Kozinski have made significant contribution to American literature. But they evince a keen awareness of the rich tradition that the Jewish immigrants had brought with them to America. It is generally believed that Jewish fiction arose out of an interaction between the experience of the Old World and the New. Naturally the values of this fiction are neither traditionally Jewish nor comfortably American. A close scrutiny of the writings often reveals Jewish writer's faith in what is known as Jewish gnosticism, in which it is not the individual but the community that is given primary importance. Jewish gnosticism, when seen in the light of Talmud and Torah, becomes evident in the writings of Bellow, Malamud, Roth and Kozinski. One also notices a feeling of Jewish diaspora in most Jewish fiction. Son of immigrant Russian parents Malamud, for example depicts in *The Assistant* (1957) the miserable condition of family of New York Jews. In fact, wherever Malamud's hero finds himself — Rome or Vermont — he is always in the ghetto psychologically bound to whatever he tried to run away from Malamud's novels are mostly stories of unfulfilled love, disappointment and loss. And, at bottom, his novels show conflicting cultural perspectives and the emphasis is unmistakably on Jewish gnosticism by combining Hasidism and Spinozism in that, while according to Hasidism God is in heaven and the human welfare depends on His benign blessings, to the Spinozists God and the world are one. Bellow seems to be conscious of the cultural predicament of a Jew. *Dangling Man* and *The Victim* are depressing books. If *The Adventures of Augie March* (1953) gives the impression of expansiveness, it is immediately undercut by *Seize the Day* (1956). Even in *Augie March* the depression is turned inside out and Augie March, the young Chicago Jew, who out-Hucks Huck in sheer adventurousness, recognizes that 'everyone got bitterness in his chosen thing' but retains his optimism and decides to discard his Jewish, foreign habits of thought. But the over-adventurousness and loud proclamations only reveal the hollow within, the impossibility of getting over the Jewish diaspora. Bellow also seems to advocate Jewish gnosticism as a way out or as a means of reconciling with a different culture. Bellow's ability to create great art out of conflicting feelings and his humanist vision can also be seen as a function of his faith in Jewish gnosticism that recommends healthy, interpersonal relationships. Philip Roth depicts the lives of young Jewish intellectuals at the University of Chicago, New York and other places in *Letting Go* (1962). *Portnoy's Complaint* depicts the middle class New York Jewish world. The Professor in *The Professor of Desire* is Jewish. Explicitly Jewish is his *My Life as a Man* (1974) in which Peter Tarnapol's failures at love become a community problem and calls for a commentary like a Talmudic text. Roth comes out in the open in *Reading Myself and Others*, a collection of essays, in which he tries to interpret the intricate emotional dynamics of modern lives and Jewish novels. The Jewish writers have focussed directly or indirectly on the problems arising out of the complex feelings of Jewish diaspora. They seek their roots in the Jewish cultural tradition and suffer from a strange sense of alienation. It would be a travesty of truth to say that they are really assimilated into American culture.

Small immigrant groups like the Chinese-Americans, the Indian-Americans, the Spanish-Americans, the Caribbeans, etc., have also been trying to assert their identity and address their writings primarily to their respective communities.

But the most formidable threat to the idea of the melting pot has come from the large body of African-American writers who have gone to the extent of searching their roots in Africa and have tried to effect a cultural nationalism by using African folklore and oral tradition in their writings. In order to understand their quest for cultural identity it should be borne in mind that since the African-American writers originally came from different cultural cosmologies they developed a double consciousness. Anyway, as a writer of African origin, an African-American writer is painfully conscious of the widely prevalent notion that the blacks are intellectually and culturally inferior to the whites. But as an American he has faith in the American ideal of freedom and democracy. In *The Outsider* Richard Wright explores the metaphor of alienation on account of being black in a predominantly white world. The idea of the social protest that we notice in *The Outsider* can also be discerned in Wright's *Native Son.* James Baldwin's *Go, Tell It on the Mountain* (1953) shows the vital force that religion plays in the life of the blacks. His intense personal essays, *Notes of a Native Son* (1955), considers the situation of the northern black intellectuals *Blues for Charlie* records the antagonism between the black and the white. *The Third Generation* (1954) of Chester Himes shows how the third generation becomes the victims of the cultural clashes of the parents. In this novel, Charles, the son of a pure black father and a mulatto mother is used as a metaphor for America. The classic African-American fiction is of course Ellison's *Invisible Man* (1952) which focuses on the incompatibility between two cultures through a powerful account of the black experience. In spite of his recognized qualities the nameless protagonist is not properly accepted by the white world. Since nobody offers him a way into the prevailing culture he remains alienated and he chooses to become an underground man. In 1968 Julius Lester said: 'I'm an Afro-American. This implies that I'm an amalgam. It is my responsibility to reflect the *Afro*-side of the hyphen. The other side has been too much reflected' (229). Such tendencies were always there, but in the 'sixties the idea surfaced clearly so that an old commitment was elaborated into a separatist ethnicism and a programme was gradually worked out in such magazines as *Freedomways, Negro Digest, The Black Scholar* and in scores of conferences. An attempt was made in favour of a radical reordering of western cultural aesthetic. In 1955 Baldwin had explained in *Notes of a Native Son* how he had been grafted onto the west and how distant from the roots of African experience he considered the world of western literature and aesthetic. Mention must be made in this connection of Alex Haley's *The Roots* published in 1976. A great cultural event in the history of African-American literature, the book gives a vivid account of the author's search for his antecedents. The book is a product of years' of research in libraries and archives in three continents and an extensive reading of history and anthropology. The author carries conviction when he says : 'To the best of my knowledge... every lineage statement within *Roots* is from either my African or American families' carefully preserved oral history, much of which I have been able conventionally to corroborate with documents' (p. 728).

The quest for identity takes on a new dimension in the writings of African-American women on account of their being women in a male dominated society. So their writings often become a mirror image of sexism and racism. The African-American women suffer on two counts : first as African and then as woman. Therefore, they place emphasis on reflecting the process of self-definition and understanding both in terms of a woman and an African-American. Gwendolyn Brook's *Annie Allen* (1949), a verse narrative tells about a black girl's perception of her race's isolation as both spiritual and racial. Her verse militantly treats the lives and problems of the blacks. Particularly noticeable is her volume of poems, *Aloneness* (1971). Her *Maud Martha* is important for other reasons. It gives us the portrait of a black woman, first as daughter, then as mother. The importance of the book, in the present context, lies in the way Maud Martha sees the contradiction between her real value as a black woman and how she is valued by those around her and realizes the limits set on her by her family, her husband, her race, her class and the American society. Alice Walker's *The Third Life of Grange Copeland* which is much concerned with racism and sexism was published in 1970. The same year saw the publication of Toni Morrison's *The Bluest Eye*. Through the central character Pecola, Morrison shows the devastating effect of the standardized western ideas of physical beauty and romantic love on the black community's perception of its worth. Paule Marshall's *Browngirl, Brownstones* (1951) emphasizes how the black community, its customs and mores affect the process of black woman's exploration of self. As a corollary to the quest for identity there is a visible tendency among the African-American writers to use African motives, African folklore etc. in the narratives. Ntozake Shange, for example, uses African motifs in *Sassafras* (1982). She also links African rhythms, dance and style to a uniquely Afro-American woman culture. Alice Walker uses the functional art of African quilt making, by making use of diaries, letters and various other tropes in *The Colour Purple* (1982). In *The Women of Brewster Street* (1980) Gloria Naylor derives her language mainly from the metaphors of endurance in African-American folk-speech.

The nature of the African-American writings whether by male or by female authors clearly indicates that the writers would not like to glorify their own culture, assert its values and identities, challenge and compete with the Western standard of aesthetics. They want to have a space of their own.

The other small but strong voices heard are those of Asian-Americans, Chinese-Americans, Vietnamese-Americans, etc. There are differences between the native-born and the immigrants. Each group is clamouring for its identity in such a way that what we get is a multicultural perspective. Since the country is culturally and ethnically fragmented, each fragment is trying to maintain its distinction from the other subtly alerting the readers to cultural differences and ethnic and sexist discriminations.

It should be evident from the preceding that the metaphor of America as a melting pot '*where individuals of all nations are melted into a new race of men*' (233, emphasis added) has lost its significance. The facts explode the romantic myth. Different religious, ethnic, cultural groups and immigrants of different nationalities search their roots in the respective ancient prejudices and manners, rites and rituals and cultural traditions, and incorporate them into their writings and claim a mark of recognition. The result is that America which is increasingly less English-speaking and less white is turning into a colourful mosaic of an infinitely varied pattern. Incidentally, at one point of his essay Crevecoeur made a remark which has assumed an enormous significance now. He said : 'Whoever traverse the continent must easily observe those strong differences which will grow more evident in time' (235).

Crevecoeur was wise. In the course of a little more than two hundred years the great melting pot has cooled and frozen only to reveal a beautiful mosaic of complex pattern.

REFERENCES

Crevecoeur, J.H. St. Jean de. 'Letters from an American Farmer.' *The Literature of the United States. Rev.* ed. Vol. I. Eds. Blauir, Hornberger, Stewart. Chicago : Foreman and Co., 1953, pp. 229-243.

Haley, Alex. *The Roots*, New York : Dell Publishing Co., Inc., 1977.

Lester, Julius. 'The Arts and Black Revolution,' *Arts in Society* 5 no. 2 (Summer-Fall), 1968.

Index

Q

R